THE MIRACLE

THE
MIRACLE

THE FOOTBALL TEAM THAT
SHOCKED THE WORLD

VASILIS SAMBRAKOS

First published by Pitch Publishing, 2021

Pitch Publishing
A2 Yeoman Gate
Yeoman Way
Worthing
Sussex
BN13 3QZ
www.pitchpublishing.co.uk
info@pitchpublishing.co.uk

A CIP catalogue record is available for this book
from the British Library.

ISBN 978-1-78531-783-5

Typesetting and origination by Pitch Publishing
Printed and bound in India by Replika Press Pvt. Ltd.

Contents

Foreword
By Michael Calvin

OLD TRAFFORD had emptied. An hour earlier it had been raucous, incredulous, ablaze with colour and alive with noise. Now, only the gentle hum of the groundstaff's choreographed lawnmowers competed with the urgent tapping of computer keyboards in the tight, narrow press box. That is the sound of football writers in their element, chasing a succession of deadlines.

Last-minute goals instil terror and exhilaration in our business. The adrenaline rush of reacting to the moment is addictive. David Beckham's free kick against Greece had secured qualification for the 2002 World Cup finals and demanded an instant rewrite on the whistle for first editions; we crashed through the gears because the storyline had shifted, from abject failure to national celebration.

I was just about to send what I prayed was my definitive column when my attention was drawn to an instantly recognisable figure, shuffling between the seats. As ever, he was shadowed by security guards. It was Beckham, going to join his family in the hospitality boxes behind us, at the back of the main stand. Neither he, nor we, were prepared for what happened next.

Hardened hacks rose as one, pausing frantic thoughts and finely judged phrases, and began to applaud. Beckham slowed, smiled shyly, and was transformed from burgeoning brand to bashful boy. He could barely bring himself to mouth the words 'thank you'. He knew the significance of the spontaneous act of respect. In later years, when his evolution from Galactico to global citizen was complete, he would cite the moment as one of the most memorable of a celebrated career.

Little did we know, as we settled back down to file our copy that we would be telling only half of the story. This book seeks to redress the balance by giving an insight into one of international football's most unlikely successes. We didn't realise it at the time, but, in little more than two years, that Greek team would develop into European champions.

They were 150-1 outsiders, going into the 2004 finals in Portugal. Greece had not qualified for the European Championship since 1980, and their previous experience of a major tournament, losing all three group games without scoring a goal in the 1994 World Cup in the US, was seared into the national consciousness.

Vasilis Sambrakos, a renowned Athens-based journalist who combines television analysis of the international game with his work as executive editor of a leading website, covered the tournament for Greek readers and viewers. Constantine Gonticas watched it from the UK as an increasingly awestruck fan before he, too, headed for Lisbon, and the manifestation of the miracle, a 1-0 win over the hosts, Portugal, in the final at Estádio da Luz.

Football, for all its faults and foibles, can form powerful bonds of friendship. This book is the product of just such a shared passion. Vasilis and Constantine, introduced by a mutual friend, were determined to give depth and clarity to the achievement of an under-appreciated Greek team by challenging the assumption it represented no more than a masterclass in defensive rigour.

Vasilis, a senior writer for the newspaper *To Vima* at the time, had daily contact with a core group of up to a dozen players during the tournament. He revisited them to reinforce his research for this book, which began to take shape in his head as early as 2002, when he sensed the significance of the change in collective mentality instilled by Otto Rehhagel. Under him, Greece climbed from 66th in the world rankings to eighth.

Vasilis was from the same generation as the players on whom he reported. I can identify with the strange sense of emotional osmosis that can occur in such circumstances. Despite the broader picture of collective suspicion and antagonism towards the media in the modern game, the individual relationship between writer and footballer often straddles the line between professional and personal.

Players become friends, rather than subject matter. Over time, trust and respect becomes mutual. No wonder Vasilis admits to crying with happiness for the first time at a football match when the final whistle blew in Lisbon. He did not stop until Theo Zagorakis lifted the trophy, with both hands, above his head in a blizzard of blue and white confetti.

I got to know Constantine a decade ago, during a season embedded at Millwall, the club of which he has been a director for 15 years, for my book *Family: Life,*

Death and Football. The game, for him, is an extension of a love story that began in his grandmother's house when he was aged seven, and entranced by week-old, black and white transmissions of English Football League matches on Greek TV.

A globally focused financier, he has retained that childhood wonder at football's sense of freedom and opportunity. We occasionally have lunch when he finds himself in London, and I have become accustomed to his entreaties to come to my own conclusion, by watching extended videos of that 2004 team. He sees beauty where others see functionality.

I'm taken by the parallel he draws between Millwall, his adopted club, and the Greek team that became a manifestation of national pride. Each has an underdog mentality and an underpinning sense of defiance, reflected by a fiercely committed fanbase. If you do not like them, they do care, deep down.

Just as the Millwall team I chronicled was shaped by the solidity and authenticity of the Guvnors, my term for the core group of senior players who set personal and professional standards in the dressing room, the Greek team was pivoted by strong characters and infectious personalities, like Giorgos Karagounis, Theodoros Zagorakis, Antonis Nikopolidis and Traianos Dellas.

The book features insights from manager Otto Rehhagel, his assistant Giannis Topalidis, and experts, ranging from psychologists to neurologists and data analysts. It contains tactical summaries that give another dimension to one of football's greatest upsets. Enjoy: you have nothing to change but your mind.

Chapter One

Curtain Up

DUTCH REFEREE Dick Jol blew the final whistle. The Greek journalists who were at Old Trafford on the afternoon of 6 October 2001 to watch Greece's match against England hugged each other with the passion of fans whose team had just achieved a historic victory.

We shared that joy with David Beckham, who was on a victory lap with his team-mates. They were celebrating with 65,000 singing English fans. The other thousand spectators, cheering just as loudly, were Greek students. The 2-2 draw was historic, not only for sending England to the 2002 World Cup finals in Japan and South Korea, but also because it was the most positive result achieved by a Greek national team against the Three Lions in a competitive match. The previous high water mark had been a 0-0 draw in a friendly at Wembley in 1983.

Beckham's 93rd-minute goal deprived Greece of a seminal victory. It did not, however, overshadow the Greek team's outstanding performance. In this, his second game in charge, Otto Rehhagel went from 'dark' – the 5-1 defeat against Finland on his managerial debut in

Helsinki a month earlier – to 'light'. The German coach had just provided an early indication of what he would be trying to achieve with the team he had taken over. He had used Old Trafford as a screen on which to show a trailer of the show he was planning to stage at Euro 2004.

That tournament would not only turn into the most extraordinary event in Greek football, but would also constitute one of the biggest surprises in the history of the international game. That Saturday afternoon at Old Trafford was the first hint of a dream, the unveiling of the future European champions. Rio Ferdinand, at the heart of the England defence in that 2-2 draw, was suitably impressed.

'Of course I remember the match,' he said, with the hindsight of many years' experience. 'Greece were a difficult team to play against. Tough, disciplined, with good players. Very stable. I certainly didn't expect them to win the Euros, but it was a tough team to beat. Its greatest advantage? Tactically, it was very stable and solid. A very tough opponent. I followed them and noticed that they were improving, I realised they would present other teams with difficulties, but back then I certainly couldn't say they would become champions.'

What had happened on the pitch at Old Trafford? How could a team that had already been eliminated and was still recovering from an embarrassing 5-1 friendly defeat against Finland, lead until the last minute against a team that had just come from a 5-1 win against Germany in Munich and had produced five consecutive wins during the qualifying stage – one of which had been a 2-0 defeat of Greece in Athens?

Once we had overcome the initial shock of what we had just witnessed, the Greek journalists headed towards the press room to interview Rehhagel. We felt joy at the performance and the result at Old Trafford, a stadium we knew as the Theatre of Dreams, but we had all feared would turn into a lions' den for the Greeks. It was time to make amends.

We felt guilty about the severe criticism we had levelled against the seemingly unapproachable Rehhagel, following the heavy defeat against Finland. We wanted to shake his hand in order to congratulate him and wish him more days like this. Our surprise at the team's performance was matched by the surprise provoked by the German manager's attitude. It was not just the glint of satisfaction that one could see in his eyes. Irritation was clearly visible too, and his wrinkled forehead betrayed the anger he felt at Beckham's goal, or rather at the foul given by referee Jol for Konstantinidis' challenge on Sheringham.

Rehhagel was furious. He wanted to publicly castigate the referee, particularly for his performance during the final stages of the match and for the 'non-existent' foul. Giannis Topalidis, his assistant, and some other members of the the Greek Football Federation, the EPO, managed to calm him down and persuade him not to vent his anger during the press conference.

At the time, many thought that Rehhagel was upset because the 2-2 result was not enough for his beloved Germany to confirm qualification. Their goalless draw against Finland, which took place at the same time in Gelsenkirchen, kept them in second place in the group, below England. Time has shown however, that Rehhagel's frustration was based on the knowledge that the magnitude of a victory against England would have provided him with a short cut in his attempt to assert himself in Greece. It would have afforded him the time that he needed to build the team he envisioned, with fewer difficulties.

When I asked Rehhagel to reminisce about the start of his, and the team's journey, he answered: 'I always knew what I wanted, and I always tried to impose what I wanted on both the team and the EPO. I tried to get my way. Sure enough, success was the crucial factor. That made everything easier.' To his mind, 'the result is everything. Those results were our way of achieving the creation of this team.'

During the 31 days from the evening of 5 September in Helsinki to that afternoon in Manchester, the 63-year-old manager had been to hell and back. Heavily criticised for the poor performance and subsequent heavy defeat during his first match as Greece's coach, he found himself being enthusiastically praised. That result against England had an impact on both the Greeks, who had now seen fit to give him their approval, and on the German media. He had always followed the German press closely since his playing career, and was counting on their positivity. His plan was to create enough of a good impression in Greece to allow him to move back to Germany, and manage another big Bundesliga club, or the national team.

Those 31 days provided Rehhagel with an extremely accurate indication of what his work would be like over the next 24 months. This initiation period lasted until 11 October 2003. On that night he was on the pitch at the Leoforos Alexandras Stadium in Athens, a short distance from his beloved Acropolis, celebrating his first Greek miracle. Greece had just qualified for the final stages of the European Championship for the first time in 24 years.

In Manchester the team that he was trying to put together had given him the first convincing sign that not only could he succeed as a national team manager, but that he could also be successful outside Germany. He quickly understood the nature of the challenge he faced in attempting to impose his methods on the Greeks. It would be an exhausting struggle. For at least two years, he lived from game to game, aware that his position and his plan were precarious to the extent that they depended solely on each result. He feared that he needed to be ready to relocate to his home in Essen at a moment's notice.

The EPO had announced they would offer Rehhagel a contract on 9 August 2001, his 63rd birthday. 'Time will tell if this is such a wonderful present. It is a difficult and very interesting job,' was his first public statement to the *Frankfurter Allgemeine Zeitung* newspaper. The German manager did his best to conceal his enormous satisfaction at being offered the chance to manage a foreign national team after ten months of unemployment and a lifetime in German football.

Rehhagel was ready to work abroad for the first time, but his initial ambition was to manage the national team of neighbouring Austria. He reasoned this would allow him to move to Vienna, a city he and his wife Beate loved. They planned to combine work with frequent visits to the opera. It took almost three years and the achievement of a historic victory over France at Euro 2004, before the German manager publicly revealed his original plan. In an interview with the Austrian daily *Kronen Zeitung* he stated that 'Austria could have been as successful if they had chosen me'.

Beate Rehhagel had been the one who opened the door to Greece. A childhood sweetheart, she had been his wife since 1963. Otto referred to her as 'my best friend', but she was also his closest advisor throughout his coaching career. Willi Lemke, his boss during his golden 14-year stint with Werder Bremen and one his few close friends, understood the dynamics of their marriage. He marked his 80th birthday in August 2018 by writing an open letter to Otto: '… you should be incredibly pleased at what you have achieved with the support of a wonderful woman'.

Beate had been informed that the EPO had advertised for the position of manager on its website. She located secretary-general Giannis Ekonomidis' telephone number in FIFA's yearly official communications guide, and called him to state her husband's intention to interview for the position. The opposition was strong. Terry Venables, Javier Clemente, Marco Tardelli and Nevio Scala had done the same via their agents.

Vasilis Gagatsis, the then president of the EPO, remembers: 'As far as the committee I had formed was concerned, it came down to two candidates, Scala and Rehhagel. The significant difference in their financial demands [Scala was asking for one million euros after tax per year, Rehhagel for around 400,000 euros] led us to the German manager. I had respected him greatly since the time he had won the Bundesliga with FC Kaiserslautern.'

When his wife aired the possibility of working in Greece, Rehhagel recalled the only time he had seen the national team play live, at the Olympic Stadium, (OAKA), in Athens. Four months earlier, on 28 March 2001, he had been invited by the German FA to watch Greece play

Germany. The Greeks lost 4-2, but the result did not reflect what Rehhagel had seen at the half-full stadium. Greece had been competitive until the final 10 minutes, when they conceded a third and then a fourth goal to a ten-man Germany. Defeat cost them qualification for the 2002 World Cup.

'Greece weren't bad,' Rehhagel told his assistant, Giannis Topalidis, in October 2001, during talks regarding the possibility of their working together. 'I realised that the quality of the players was interesting. That was my initial thought when they approached me.' This explains the fact that, of the 14 players he first saw that night, he took six to the European Championship three years later. Four of them (Zagorakis, Basinas, Karagounis and Charisteas) formed the nucleus of the team he went on to put together. The remaining two were Goumas and Georgiadis.

Five days after shaking hands with Vasilis Gagatsis in Athens, without having signed a contract, Rehhagel boarded a plane to Moscow, where Greece were playing a friendly against Russia on 15 August. He told Gagatsis that he wanted to sit on the bench, but was convinced otherwise by the president. 'You don't even know the names of the players, why take the responsibility for the result?' Gagatsis told him, 'You will sit in the stands with me.'

'The plane was full of EPO executives that wanted to go to Moscow. I remember him talking to us before the match and watching from the stands,' recalls Stelios Venetidis, one of his future players. Theo Zagorakis, who would become captain under Rehhagel, also had a powerful initial impression: 'We wanted to appear serious for his first trip, because he was travelling with us,' he remembers. 'But he still thought it was a circus. Go figure ...'

As a manager with 29 years of experience in ten different coaching jobs, Rehhagel spent the trip observing everything with a view to preparing future changes. Over 48 hours in Moscow, he would experience the essence of the previous two and a half years of Greek football at international level. From October 1997 – when the team came close to qualifying before elimination from the 1998 World Cup – until the day Rehhagel arrived in Athens, the Greek national team had been in persistent decline.

Antonis Nikopolidis, the goalkeeper who had been a member of the national team since 1999, admits: 'The team had been completely discredited. The players weren't showing any interest. They came, they went and all they cared about was boasting that they played for the national team. Lacking clear goals and motivation, they didn't themselves believe that they could achieve anything. They picked which games to play. They would be there for one match, gone the next, and this resulted in ongoing infighting among the players. Some of us would show up for friendly matches, in order to get the team into shape supposedly, and were dropped for official qualifiers for the sake of other players. This did not contribute to a feeling of unity. Why kill yourself doing that when you know someone else is going to play in the end? There was a lot of preferential treatment which ruined the atmosphere. You didn't believe that the coach was getting the squad he wanted. There was also tension between players from the big clubs. At Panathinaikos there were voices urging the players not to join "Gagatsis' national team". In 1999, we had reached the lowest point ever. There was open conflict between the EPO, Panathinaikos and AEK, two of the biggest clubs, with AEK players stating they would leave the national team due to the state of the Greek league.

'The national team was not held in high regard, not by players, not by fans, not by the press … no one. It was a shambles in terms of organisation and priorities. It would adjust to the needs and demands of the clubs. And that was the root of all evil, that it wasn't above them. What bothered me the most was that there was no real desire to wear the colours of your country. Rather, the priority was to become established in your club and get a good contract. And that attitude was obvious and it was perpetuated. We very rarely played in full stadiums, with the exception of the match against Denmark in 1997 in front of nearly 65,000 fans – when we missed the chance to qualify for the 1998 World Cup. The national team was held in extremely low regard in world football.'

Nikos Dabizas, who made his international debut in October 1994, immediately after Greece's first appearance in the final stages of the World Cup, was equally scathing: 'The Romanian coach Anghel Iordanescu tried to change things but failed, due to the special relationship he developed with AEK. To everyone's mind each previous coach had had a preference: Polychroniou favoured Olympiakos, Iordanescu AEK and Daniel Panathinaikos. It was a vicious cycle of colours changing but the situation staying the same. Iordanescu made a serious attempt to change things but he didn't receive any support, so we remained victims of the same situation.'

Giorgos Karagounis, who would go on to win a record 139 caps, agrees with his team-mate: 'We would train in Vironas one time, Nikaia the next … anywhere there was a pitch going … it was all very slipshod. My first manager with the national team, Vasilis Daniel, tried to balance it all out, have three players from each of the big clubs so that he didn't have to face any front-page criticism the next day. That was no way to do things. Things wouldn't change with a Greek manager. We had to find someone indifferent to all that, who wouldn't be affected by it.'

Angelos Charisteas' first impression of the national team was discouraging, to say the least: 'We barely had kits back then. I remember my first training session in Crete, for a friendly against Russia in 2001; the vests were torn, the shorts falling apart. It was tragic compared to what you were expecting to find in the national team. As far as the make-up of the team, it was very cliquey, let me put it that way. They didn't all hang out together. You had Olympiakos players there, Panathinaikos there, AEK there, "foreign" players (players who played abroad) there. It wasn't a team. At the end of that friendly, Niniadis, who was very good, complained to the coach, Vasilis Daniel, because he replaced him with Zagorakis after 19 minutes, so that Zagorakis wouldn't make a fuss. So he went and asked why he had been taken off. "You will be in the starting line-up for the next competitive match," said the coach … They explained things to the players back then.'

Takis Fyssas continues the theme: 'My first time, February 1999 with Anghel Iordanescu at the helm, I entered the conference room, it was about midday. I am a quarter of an hour early and I take a seat at the very back thinking that the senior players would go to the front, to hear the coach. Also, I was very green. So here comes this guy behind me, taps on my shoulder and says, "Kid, move, this is my seat." I get up like I've been caught red-handed,

I apologise, say that I didn't know and go sit somewhere else. It made a really bad impression on me. It was like being in the army the way he spoke to me so abruptly. That's how the more senior players behaved and it made me never want to act like that. I reminded that particular player of the incident years later and he laughed, he didn't even remember it; that's how commonplace it was.'

Demis Nikolaidis remembers: 'The image I have in my mind of the national team I first joined in April 1995 is that of an amateurish team. It was also a public relations situation. This many players from Olympiakos, this many from Panathinaikos, this many from AEK. Internally, without being on bad terms, we each hung out in our corner with our team-mates from the club. We didn't mix.'

The EPO's first attempt to upgrade the national team and extricate it from power plays, conflicts of interest and corruption took place in 1998. Sotiris Alimisis' administration, as a result of the infamous Alexandroupolis elections – which had been the object of an inquiry by the prosecuting authorities, led to questions being asked in parliament, and had gone down in Greek football history as one of its biggest scandals – decided in February 1998 to offer around 400,000 euros per year to Anghel Iordanescu for a two-year contract.

The Romanian, who led his home national team to the round of 16 during the 1998 World Cup, made his Greek debut on 6 September 1998, in the first qualifying game for the 2000 Euros, a 2-2 draw against Slovenia in the Athens Olympic Stadium. To this day, it remains a mystery how an administration that was in thrall to various controlling interests decided to hire a foreign manager who would not give in to pressure and would not be controlled.

'Iordanescu's stint was an oasis,' says Demis Nikolaidis. 'He was a very serious and strict manager, who gave the impression that he would do good work. However, we didn't get to work with him much ...' Six months after his first appearance, the Romanian manager quit on the night of 27 March 1999, after a 2-0 home defeat against Norway, which drove Greece further away from the goal of qualifying for the finals.

Giorgos Papalanis worked for the EPO for 43 years before his retirement. He was responsible for providing the Romanian manager with administrative support, and went on to be team manager of the squad which won Euro 2004, but admits: 'The EPO didn't have any money. It failed to even cover the players' travel costs. It was also remiss in its stated obligations towards Iordanescu. We had found a 500 square metre house for him in the Dionisos area, which only had beds in it. No furniture, no electrical appliances, no other household goods. I can still recall very clearly the moment I brought him, after some time, a small fridge to store milk for his one-year-old child. He was horrified. He couldn't bear that the house we gave him didn't even have a fridge.'

Iordanescu tried to convince the EPO to take the national team seriously. He asked for a training facility to be created, and insisted on finding a better hotel for the players. Until then, they had been staying at one of those cheap short-term hotels for illicit couples. He also asked for upgraded services and care for the players, so that they started to see their participation as a privilege and not as a chore. He kept pressing, and began to be seen as an irritant by an administration that had looked askance at his decision to make Demis Nikolaidis captain.

'He was a great guy and a very serious manager, but as soon as he made me captain, that was it,' recalls the former AEK and Atletico Madrid forward. This, however, wasn't the only reason that caused the federation to put the pressure on Iordanescu. He was damaged by a rumoured meeting with a representative from AEK, which had been arranged by an EPO executive in order to discuss the possibility of him working for the national team and AEK in tandem.

Gagatsis, who, at the time, served as secretary-general of the EPO, admits: 'It was the administration's fault at the time that we didn't provide him with the right people. We did not show him the necessary trust. We were not able to convince him regarding the upgrade attempts we were making. As he was innately rather insecure, he quit.' Theo Zagorakis offers additional insight: 'When Iordanescu arrived, the conflict between Olympiakos and AEK had reached extreme proportions, so the internal issues of the Greek league carried over to the national team. That was one of our biggest problems.'

Before Iordanescu made his escape, he managed to convey his ideas regarding the steps they had to take in order to upgrade the national team to EPO president-to-be Gagatsis. One of the more intelligent executives in the federation, he could not help but pay attention to the ideas of a manager that had led Romania to the quarter-finals of the 1994 World Cup. They spent many an evening discussing the most efficient model of running an international programme.

During the next 30 months or so, until Rehhagel's arrival, the team was in freefall. Iordanescu was succeeded by Vasilis Daniel. Takis Fyssas recalls: 'With Daniel, I experienced something for the first time. With Iordanescu, you saw players from different clubs sitting close, mingling at the hotel. When I joined Daniel's national team, there was the Olympiakos table, the Panathinaikos table, the AEK table, all separate. That's how we ate. One time I didn't have anywhere to sit and there was an empty seat at the Olympiakos table. I remember Georgatos saying, "Come, sit with us, we're not eating." That's what was going on then. There was this "we are the best, we are the national team" thing. But it was the manager and the EPO who allowed that. It wasn't the players making the rules. Maybe they didn't know there was another way. They couldn't think of that.'

Stelios Venetidis adds: 'Back then, in 1999, when I was called up for the first time, the FA had signed a contract – in order to make money – for the national team to play three friendlies in a row, on Sunday, Tuesday and Thursday, like a touring company, in nearby cities like Kavala, Trikala and Larissa. The team was like a free-for-all. We would be invited to join just like that. It was difficult for a Greek manager to solve those issues under so much pressure. The Greek status quo demanded that he take three of each colour, green, red and yellow, one black and white and whatever else. The national team had been discredited.

'You had the feeling that you came from your club to rest, unwind, with everything that entails. You didn't have a sense of responsibility for being on the national team. The mentality and climate created a sense that you're on a team that rated lower than the club you played for. Our club managers would say, "Careful there, take it easy, don't overdo it." The players were more lax in the hotel. There was not a bond between them. The primary motive of those players that played abroad was to get a taste of Greece again, to let off some steam. I still remember managers and agents showing up at the hotel to talk. It was like a free-for-all.'

Zagorakis builds up the picture: 'In those days, the manager would receive a lot of pressure and interventions regarding who he wanted to call up to the squad and the final line-up. These came from the administration. I don't know if they dictated which players he should use, but I knew that they would ask that a certain player be excused so that he wasn't injured. The club would say, for instance, "We have a major match on Sunday. Don't let them take so and so, he'll be tired." I experienced things like that. I remember being accused by people at my club, PAOK, that I was being too serious about the national team. "You play well, you give it your all, why?" they would ask, as if I was doing something wrong. I was proud of wearing the colours.'

After signing a preliminary contract on 9 August in Athens, in the presence of his lawyer, Robert Wiesman, who had been on the board of FC Kaiserslautern during Rehhagel's stint with the club, the German manager started looking for an assistant. The EPO suggested that Nikos Christidis, the veteran international goalkeeper would stay on, as he had been on Daniel's technical staff and had also undertaken goalkeeper coaching duties for the friendly against Russia in Moscow. Rehhagel refused and did not give in to Gagatsis' insistence to retain Christidis as goalkeeping coach. The president of the EPO then recommended former international goalkeeper Nikos Sarganis, whom he also rejected. 'He was put under a lot of pressure, but he didn't want anyone connected to the world of Greek football so he persevered,' Giorgos Papalanis remembers.

Not being in any particular hurry to find an assistant, Rehhagel, who had done his homework, travelled to Helsinki without an assistant or an interpreter for his first match against Finland. He had an interpreter for the media, journalist Ferry Batzoglou, who had been sent to the EPO by the German consulate. He also chose to use one of the players he had called up, Kostas Kostantinidis, a defender who had been born in Germany and was playing for Hertha Berlin, to interpret for him during training and the match itself.

On the flight to Helsinki, Rehhagel was reacquainted with the 'charter flight of joy', as we journalists had christened the flights of the national team. The plane was full of executives from the country's 53 local football unions and a myriad of hangers-on from all divisions and leagues in Greek football. Gagatsis admits: 'In Finland we made a mistake. We had even taken our wives with us. That's when I said, no more ...'

Chapter Two

The 24th Man

DURING THE final training session, on the eve of the match at the Helsingin Olympiastadion, Rehhagel picked Gregoris Georgatos as his left-winger. Georgatos was considered the leading Greek left-back at the time. It was his preferred position and he had just re-joined Inter Milan, playing alongside the Brazilian Ronaldo. He had travelled to Finland with the confidence of a starting player in a leading Serie A team.

Leonidas Vokolos sets the scene: 'As a way of expressing his displeasure at his manager's decision, Georgatos kicked the ball off the pitch during training, causing Rehhagel to pause the session and ask what had happened. Georgatos told Konstantinidis: "Tell him to go f*** himself, I won't play in that position." Rehhagel understood the point from Georgatos' body language, but still asked for a translation. Konstantinidis tried to explain that Georgatos says he cannot play in that position. The next day, when Rehhagel announced the starting line-up, Georgatos is at left-back and Fyssas, who had been told he would be starting in that position, is on the bench.'

Vokolos was an unused substitute as a Greek team lacking cohesion, and seemingly confused by all the positional changes, lost 5-1. The performance was listless and bland. 'I may have been at the helm for a short period of time, but I still would like to assume part of the responsibility for the defeat,' Rehhagel insisted. 'My players were not at all dynamic and were ineffective on the pitch.'

His starting line-up, in a 4-3-3 formation, featured three forwards – Charisteas, Vrizas, and Machlas. It had been characterised as offensive, but the German, when asked to explain his decision, only said that he 'wanted to press for a win'. This was the last time he would publicly defend his choices. His demeanour in public was initially that of a man who did not feel the pressure to deliver immediate results. During interviews, however, it became clear that such an impression was deceptive: 'I have not received a continuance,' he stressed during the pre-match press conference. 'I am the manager of the Greek national team. There are no continuances in football. That only happens in the case of criminal acts, where the defendant requests time to prepare his defence.'

That night, after that heavy loss, Nikos Dabizas started to realise that Rehhagel was not some kind of diva, who had come to Greece to retire and relax. 'The manager and those of us who played for teams outside Greece remained in Helsinki for one more day. That's when I saw a man who was torn apart emotionally. A man who came from Germany, from a really advanced league, who had won many titles, and who felt his image had been tarnished because of a team which no one thought constituted the biggest bet of his career and that therefore he could take things easier.

'I said, "Mister, this is not us, it's early days yet. We will be able to perform much better. We are talented, you will get to know us, and we will get to know you ...". He shook his head and I saw a man who had been hurt. He didn't even feel like speaking. "Mister, shall we go have dinner together?" I asked him. He didn't even come down, he disappeared. That's when I realised that he wasn't there just for the sake of it. I thought, he is driven, he has an ego. He wants to succeed. I also saw that he had something special about him.'

Takis Fyssas remembers: 'Rehhagel's toughest moment until 2004 had been Finland – his first match. After that he was composed, he felt secure, he felt trust and confidence. Even when the whole place was on fire, he remained calm.'

After the game, Gagatsis, who was really worked up, asked the manager to explain why he chose to use Georgatos, who lacked discipline: 'I expected him to explode during that episode with Georgatos but he didn't react at all. After the match I said, "Coach, I expected you, perhaps erroneously, to call me at the first instance of indiscipline and tell me that so and so is out of the squad. Instead, you let him play and things got worse." He replied that I shouldn't be in such a rush.'

Rehhagel had already been confronted by Fyssas, the player he had left out of the final line-up: 'Before the match started, I asked to speak to him and I said, "Mister Otto, I was in the team yesterday but not today. I know that you spoke to Georgatos. Know this, I will sit on the bench because I honour the colours I wear, but I don't have any respect for what you did. I know what's going on, I am a smart man. I just want to tell you, I will sit on the bench, and I will be at your disposal even if for only a second."

I meant it. I had no respect for him because of what he did. But his subsequent course showed what his strategy had been. I thought I had been the one to pay the price at the time, but I later realised that this had been when I registered in Rehhagel's conscience as someone with a personality.'

During the 31 days that followed until the match at Old Trafford, Rehhagel spent little time in Greece. He already had a rough plan of what the team he wanted to play in England would look like. Fyssas expands: 'He was following Panathinaikos in the Champions League. He saw us beat Schalke 2-0 in Gelsenkirchen, Mallorca also 2-0, and Arsenal 1-0 in Athens. He thought of "copying" our defensive style, as well as any other tactic that suited him in order to design the national team he wanted to put together.'

Rehhagel did the same with AEK and Olympiakos. He would watch European matches, either in person or on TV, searching for the missing pieces for his first team. At the same time, he would travel in order to watch players that were playing for clubs overseas. Giannis Topalidis, his assistant, explains: 'This had been the initial action plan he had concocted after the heavy defeat in Finland.

'We would base the team on Panathinaikos and add players from AEK, Olympiakos and abroad. He was convinced about the Panathinaikos players due to their performances in Europe. "Giannis, anywhere I went to see them, they faced the opponent head on," he would tell me, right from the beginning. He was pragmatic. He went straight to the point. He didn't care for players from smaller clubs creating a sensation, because he believed that national team level matches demand players that had been battle hardened at the top European level.'

The matter of his assistant, who would also assume the responsibility of being his voice to the players, had been his second concern in the period between the matches against Finland and England. 'Language is a big problem, which I had initially underestimated,' Rehhagel said in an interview with the German magazine *Kicker*. He explained he was not really looking for an assistant. He believed that it would be enough to find 'a translator who knows football'.

Luck, which he would often cite, sent him Giannis Topalidis. A son of Greek immigrants to Germany, he had been born and schooled in Greece and had graduated from the Cologne football coaching school in Germany. At the time, after a short playing career in the German amateur divisions, the 39-year-old Topalidis worked for Hertha Berlin as a talent scout. He had lived in Greece but did not have connections to the Greek football community. He loved football, admired Rehhagel and was desperate for an opportunity to return to his homeland.

'I was going through some personal problems in Germany and wanted to return to Greece. My dream was to work in football in Greece, live it up in the sun. I had spoken to Kostas Konstantinidis, whom I knew because he played at Hertha, but he had said, "Leave it. It's been a mess after the match with Finland." A friend had suggested I get in touch with Wolfgang Fege, who had had Rehhagel as a coach at Borussia Dortmund, and was still good friends with him. I called him and he asked me to send him my CV.' On Fege's company's website, Rehhagel still holds the highest place in the 'hall of fame' section.

Topalidis concedes that his timing was impeccable: 'It was my good fortune to have been at the match against Finland, in order to check out this Finnish player on behalf of Hertha, so I had an impression of what had happened during Rehhagel's first match. After a few days, my phone rang: "I am Otto Rehhagel. I want to schedule an appointment." I thought that someone was playing a practical joke, but we arranged to meet at a central hotel in Berlin the next day.

'He was very direct: "I can't promise anything, I will take you with me for the match in England and we shall see." At the time, I thought he wanted to scare me, show me that I was being screened. Later, however, I realised that he did that because he hadn't been at all certain whether he would be staying on after the game in Manchester. He hadn't even signed a contract. For me, though, even one game would have been enough. I would have been living my dream, an immigrant on the bench of the national team. "I'm coming, even if it is for one game," I answered.'

Rehhagel's next concern had been to convince Demis Nikolaidis and Michalis Kasapis to return to the team. The two of them, along with Ilias Atmatsidis, had walked out in protest two years earlier, as a way of denouncing the state of the Greek league. They did so after an away game between their team, AEK, and Olympiakos, in November 1999. That particular match had become a reference point for the so-called era of the 'Shack', as the nerve centre of the behind-the-scenes manipulation and fixing of Greek football had come to be known.

Olympiakos had won 2-0 in a match held behind closed doors. At the risk of being flippant, it had still been quite eventful. One of the few spectators died of heart failure. The bodyguard of the then president of the Football Limited Companies Association, Victor Mitropoulos, fired shots in the air and Kasapis attacked the referee, for which he was suspended for 24 weeks.

Demis Nikolaidis felt wanted. 'Rehhagel asked me to meet him, so we got together at a hotel on Syggrou Avenue. He asked me to separate the national team from the state of Greek football, from everything that was going on in the domestic league. He didn't have to go on for long, though. I had been part of national teams since I had been 15 years old. I missed it. I had never been away from the national team until I was 26. When we met, it had been two years since I had left. During my absence no one had called me back. No one else had showed any interest. I wanted to make sure that something was changing before I went back. He didn't have to insist or exaggerate and, of course, he never said I would be treated any differently.'

Antonis Nikopolidis understood the significance: 'His move to bring Demis and Kasapis back was important for us. I don't know how he managed to persuade them. I believe that Demis realised that this manager is untouchable and has nothing to do with the rest of the football world in Greece. "I am independent, no one controls me, the team is my only priority," that's what he must have told him to persuade him. That's the impression we had back then.'

Things began to change. 'Demis helped Rehhagel,' confirms Giorgos Papalanis. 'He took it upon himself, with some of the older players, to remedy the situation in the dressing rooms. Rehhagel trusted him.' Giannis Topalidis notes: 'The manager held him in very high regard. When Nikolaidis was on top form, he couldn't be held back. That's what he always told Demis.'

Players, manager and federation officials were tense on the eve of the England game. The players expressed their anger that they had not met as often as they had expected with Rehhagel, to the press. The manager had rejected the EPO's proposal to call up the squad two days earlier than normal in order to secure additional training sessions. This apparent reluctance to take any opportunity to get to know his players troubled officials.

Rehhagel did not feel confident about the potential quality of his team's performance at Old Trafford. Despite promising his former player and friend Rudi Voller, manager of the German national team, that he would do everything to deprive England of points in order to help his countrymen qualify for the 2002 World Cup, Rehhagel did not dare imagine what he would witness in Manchester. 'He was very cautious at first,' remembers Topalidis. 'He was telling me that this could be his last game. He was considering the possibility of not staying. In the event of a 3-0 or 4-0 defeat in England, he would leave.'

'I have good players at my disposal, but there is a serious attitude problem and I don't think I will be able to change that in time for the game against England,' Rehhagel stated to a *Guardian* reporter three days before the game. 'I am not yet well acquainted with the team and its capabilities, but they certainly aren't as bad as they seemed in the match against Finland.'

Rehhagel had set his first plan in motion and waited to see if it would work as impatiently as the Greeks did. He had chosen to base his team on Panathinaikos, as seen in the Champions League. He had reinstated Nikolaidis, the best forward in Greece, and Kasapis, and had found an assistant who ensured a better level of communication with the squad. In addition, he had been able to shake up his players, perhaps even more than he himself expected, with his decision to exclude the highly rated Georgatos for his indiscipline.

The manager also dropped goalkeeper Dimitris Eleftheropoulos, but the example, of effectively making Georgatos the 24th man, was of key importance in the formation of the 2004 European champions. His exclusion shocked the players and convinced them that they were obliged to play by Rehhagel's rules. Angelos Charisteas, one of the new breed, sensed the significance of the moment:

'In Finland, as he was revealing the line-up on the board, he was watching the players one by one, in order to read their reactions, their expressions, everything. He wanted to know us from our reactions. You could see that he could tell what was happening within the team and what its weaknesses were. Then we get to England. I saw a squad of very professional players, with an exceptional attitude. Vokolos, Kasapis, Patsatzoglou, players who were dedicated to football and their careers. And he also had Demis, who was back with a vengeance. The mood changed from the get-go, straight from training. Bodies fell left and right. As soon as they saw that the manager had dropped the best and most expensive Greek player at the time, Inter's Georgatos with the magic left foot, everyone got the message. "If this manager stabilises the team, there's no more kidding around." That was the message and as soon as the senior players realised it, the entire team absorbed it. We younger players didn't need much prompting, Rehhagel wanted to change things around and he showed it from the start.'

Before the team's departure for Manchester, and the defining game of his bedding-in process as coach, Rehhagel played his last card, by publicly relating to the players' sense of patriotism. 'The national team is a matter of heart,' he announced. 'I have realised that the national team does not rate as high as the clubs in the eyes of the Greeks. This has to change and I hope that we will move towards this direction immediately. Anyone who plays or works for the national team has to do so with passion.'

He also responded openly to Georgatos, who had made a statement after leaving the national team: 'I have learned how a footballer must behave before, during and after a game. Footballers need to show good character not only professionally, but also as people. Those who do not do so, on or off the pitch, will not play in the team.'

Rehhagel had strategically chosen to press the patriotism button on the emotional keyboard of his players. It was his primary motivating tool, and he rammed home his central point in his last press conference in England: 'The key point is for them to show me that their heart beats for their country as well as their team. We have to fight well and, regardless of the result, leave the pitch with our heads high. If we die, we must die like heroes.'

Giannis Topalidis, his assistant, reflects that, 'If you asked me what the motivation was in the early days, I would name only one, patriotism.' But what of Rehhagel's tactical plan for that pivotal game? 'The fundamental part of our tactics was to block England's right side in order to restrict Beckham. For that reason, he placed two defenders on our left side, Fyssas as a full-back and Kasapis as left-midfielder.

'Rehhagel would tell me "I've done such things in the past, play a full-back as a wide midfielder in order to block the opponent's full-back as well. It works, you'll see." He told the players that we needed to block England's right side and that we wanted to play defensively, with counter-attacks. So he placed Charisteas on our right side, in front of Patsatzoglou, to press Ashley Cole and not allow him to develop the game.'

Gary Lineker was one of several prominent figures in English football to praise the strategy. 'We have to give credit to Otto Rehhagel,' he wrote in the *Daily Telegraph* the day after the match. 'He recognised that England's best avenue between defence and attack is through Ashley Cole so he blocked it.' England manager Sven-Goran Eriksson was also impressed: 'Greece were better throughout the match,' he acknowledged. 'We didn't play well. Even in the second half the Greeks could have scored more goals. Nigel Martyn made some wonderful saves.'

The performance and result was a major confidence boost for Rehhagel. The German media and his country's football community applauded him as an intelligent and insightful manager. He had the first convincing evidence that further successes with Greece could polish his brand name enough for him to re-enter the German and international football market. The power of his personality was making itself felt.

The Greeks were ready to capitulate, to give in to his pressure for them to do things his way. Also, and perhaps more importantly, the players started to recognise their potential, if they faithfully followed his methods. Nikos Dabizas describes the impact: 'It was with the performance at Old Trafford that we entered the mind-set of success. We realised that, with new faces, with a certain logic and a specific plan, we could achieve many things. It was the first powerful stimulus that made us understand what we could expect to achieve if we filled that empty shell of a team.'

'The game against England was a landmark,' agrees Stelios Venetidis. 'It was like "a team is born, something new is being created". It came at a moment when the manager had already been pressuring the EPO and was taking a lot of flak because he demanded that the team plane be emptied of all executives and hangers-on. He insisted that we be made to feel important, not have executives and journalists under our feet. He cared, he was protective. That was his attitude. Gradually the administration started trying to implement his wishes.'

Antonis Nikopolidis recalls: 'The manager hadn't had the time to do much with us before the match. He had made some changes and had deployed three defenders. The security fostered by three centre-halves helped, compared with the match against Finland. The feeling of fear also helped. It puts you in a state of vigilance. The arrogance of the English also played a role. They came on to the field with a sense that they would beat us easily with the crowd on their side.

'It wasn't a great plan; it came together on the pitch during the game. We were leading, the English found it hard to enter the spirit of the game. They started to feel danger, while we didn't have anything to lose. We were starting to feel good. I don't remember seeing them pressing us until the start of the second half. There was so much pressure then that I turned to look at the time thinking we had been playing for 25 minutes and we'd only been playing for eight. We were locked in. We couldn't leave the penalty area. If they had started like that, they would've killed us.'

Topalidis edged closer to fulfilment of his dream: 'After our game in England, we were ecstatic because there was such a great reaction in Greece. That result benefited Rehhagel, so he thought he could operate effectively in Greece. It was the beginning of the bond that developed between us, with a person who did not form attachments easily. When he called me he said, "We have two friendlies, with Estonia and Cyprus, and I told them I want you to come as my assistant." I had already decided I would go, even when he clarified that he couldn't promise 100% that we would continue.'

The trip to England also marked the start of a collaboration with another important member of the team, Giorgos Papalanis, who would operate as team manager up to, and including, the 2004 Championships: 'After the game with Finland, while I was away with the Mediterranean Games team, my phone rings. It was Vasilis Gagatsis: "You're joining the senior men's national team." After the game in Manchester I had three meetings with the manager and his assistant. I told them of my career with the EPO, my seven years in the United States, the state of Greek football, and answered all their questions. I realised that, most of all, he was intrigued by the fact that I had lived and worked in America. Two more meetings followed, at which I was asked to bring my wife. We were also joined by Beate Rehhagel for those meetings.'

Rehhagel always followed this procedure before putting his trust in a new colleague or signing a new player. Klaus Alofs described the way Beate operated during Rehhagel's time with Werder Bremen to Norbert Kuntze, author of a biography of Rehhagel: 'After the initial contact, they would invite the footballers with their girlfriends or wives to Bremen, where Mrs Rehhagel would act as hostess. I am certain that they talked about these issues like every manager does with his assistant. She knows a lot about football.'

Papalanis, who had started working for the EPO as a messenger boy in 1967, when he was 14, eventually retired as executive director of the department of National Teams and Refereeing. He had his enemies. 'Rehhagel didn't just happen to take me on,' he explained. 'I went through five interviews. When I got to know Topalidis better, he revealed that when he informed the EPO that Rehhagel wanted me to join as team manager, they told him to be wary because I was a scumbag ...'

The German had only been in Greece for two months and had hired a colleague from the local football community recommended by the president of the EPO, only to be warned off by other officials. Rehhagel ignored the comments and fortune smiled at him for the second time. Thanks to Gagatsis' clever decision to suggest Papalanis, Rehhagel acquired a colleague with expert knowledge of Greek football, both on the surface as well as behind the scenes. He was also familiar with different generations of footballers, having worked with them in the junior national teams.

What's more, Papalanis had been part of the Greek delegation to the 1994 World Cup, Greece's only previous appearance in the finals. He had direct experience of the mistakes made by the EPO, which suddenly acquired 11 sponsors. The federation was seduced by the influx of money and sent the team to the US four weeks before the start of the tournament, parading them around events for Greek expatriates who had paid for tickets to meet them. They eventually returned to Greece having suffered three defeats, without scoring a goal.

Papalanis recalls, pensively: 'The first thing I saw when I arrived at the hotel at which the team was staying in 1994, just outside Boston, is etched into my mind. The manager, angry, sitting with his daughter and son in one corner. Five players in the opposite corner, three in another, journalists and fans milling around the lobby. That's the kind of scene that brings anything but a team to mind. "Look, if you ever join the national team, don't perpetuate this ..." Giorgos Dedes, the vice-president of the EPO, said to me then. Everything in life happens for a reason.'

Two days before Papalanis arrived in Boston, Dedes had been insulted, in front of the TV cameras, by the then manager of the national team, Alketas Panagoulias. The coach had also confronted him in front of the players and threatened to have him thrown off of the bus for joking with another executive after the team had been defeated in a friendly.

During his visits to Athens, Rehhagel would spend many hours with Topalidis and their new team member. They would meet in Nea Smirni, 'have long conversations, eat together and go for drinks in the local bars'. Rehhagel went out quite often, as he wanted to get a taste of life in Greece so that he had an idea of the environment his players lived in. The tone of conversations made it obvious that the manager, mostly through his first private meetings with the players, had been researching the causes that led to the national team's miserable past.

Papalanis, with 34 years of experience with the EPO, would prove an invaluable source of information and personal assessment: 'We discussed everything. I mentioned who had hurt the national team and in what ways, who operated in a harmful or disruptive fashion.

I had already figured out what he was interested in from our first conversations. I had made sure to collect information for him, to learn how tough he was. Of course neither Rehhagel nor Topalidis were aware of people and situations in Greece. He entrusted me with all those things he considered self-evident from his time in Germany. We were supposed to operate according to his model, and I followed the instructions given to me by Topalidis to the letter and on time, which is why he started having more confidence in me.'

- - - - - - - - - -

ENGLAND 2 GREECE 2: TACTICAL ANALYSIS
Athanasios Terzis, coach and author of 12 football analysis books, will provide technical analysis, accompanied by graphical detail, of pivotal matches in qualification for the Euro finals, and a full rundown of all matches in Portugal. Here, he begins by outlining how Otto Rehhagel's strategy was applied at Old Trafford:

Rehhagel, after the heavy 5-1 defeat against Finland in Helsinki, decided to employ a cautious 5-4-1 formation against stronger opponents.

England manager Sven-Goran Eriksson went with his usual 4-4-2 formation.

Greece had numerical superiority at the centre of their defence with 3 vs 2. In midfield there was a balance with 2 vs 2, while England maintained numerical superiority in their defence with 2 vs 1. It was 1 vs 1 on the flanks.

With this formation, Rehhagel deployed Greece to neutralise the attacking game of the English, which, to a large degree, depended on attacks down the wings,

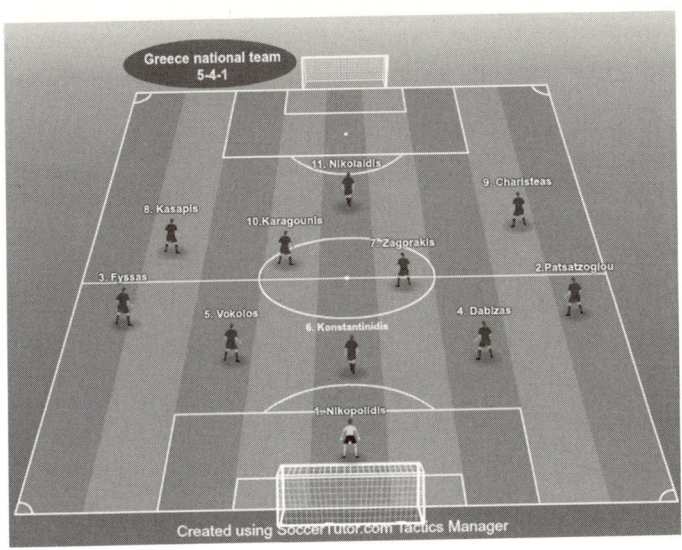

Greece vs England

especially from the right through Beckham. He was also
conscious of the danger presented by long balls.

In the early part of the game Greece did not press high
up but started defending from midfield. In spite of that,

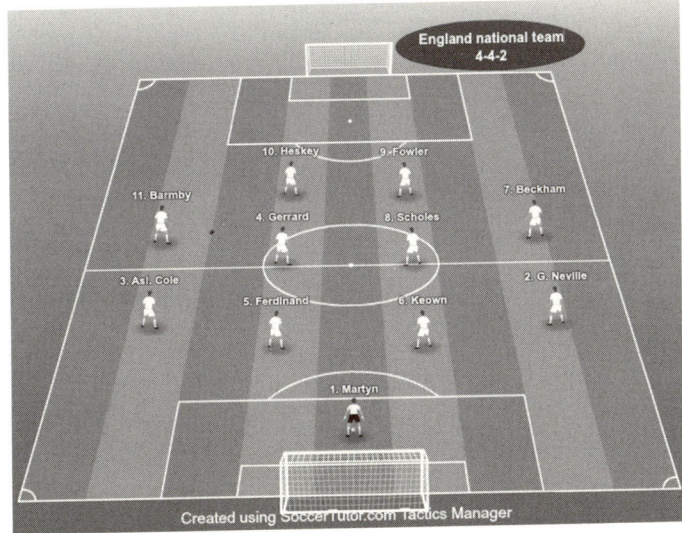

England line up

England did not attempt to take advantage of the light pressure and their numerical superiority at the back by sensibly advancing the ball with short passes. Rather, they sought to quickly get it forward with long balls. Those were either directed behind the defence and at the empty spaces between the defenders, or aimed at Emile Heskey.

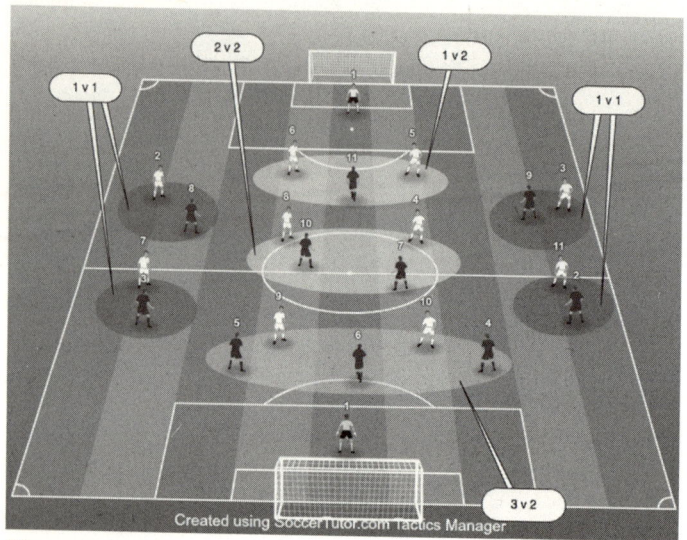

The matchups

However, the five-man Greek defence left very little space unattended. Vokolos, Dabizas and Konstantinidis' headers neutralised any potentially dangerous English attempts at reaching their forwards. Centre-halves Dabizas and Vokolos, as well as full-backs Fyssas and Patsatzoglou, marked opposition players within their area of responsibility, while Konstantinidis had a freer role and could come to their assistance as and when needed.

The man-to-man marking resulted in England making several errors, as the Greek players either reached the ball first or left little available space and time to the receiving opponents. No matter how many times the England forwards Fowler and Heskey dropped back to midfield in order to receive the ball and bring it forward, the Greek defenders would follow and press them energetically, restricting them.

Defender puts pressure immediately to prevent turning between lines

Created using SoccerTutor.com Tactics Manager

Defender puts pressure to prevent the turn

England tried to take advantage of the Greeks' pressing in order to create space on the wings for Cole and Neville, the two full-backs, by drawing Patsatzoglou and Fyssas out of position. They tried to do this by having Barmby and Beckham move towards the centre of midfield. However, the two Greek full-backs worked perfectly in tandem with Kasapis and Charisteas. The two Greek midfielders would follow the movements of the English full-backs very closely, never allowing them to take advantage of any available space.

When trying to go forward, Greece would pass the ball with Zagorakis moving between the middle and forward lines of the English, while Karagounis moved higher in an attacking midfield role, often acting as a second striker. This happened because Kasapis, as a left wide midfielder, had a more defensive role and would not advance. From the right, Charisteas would move as a second forward, assisting Nikolaidis. With this deployment, Greece avoided playing one-dimensionally when formulating attacking moves.

Whenever possible, Greece's play would start with Nikopolidis, the goalkeeper, passing the ball to his defenders and the ball would be transferred to the midfielders and forwards by taking advantage of their numerical supremacy (3 vs 2) in midfield. When under pressure, they would hit long balls to Charisteas who had a height advantage over Cole and won all the aerial duels. Greece were more patient and relaxed in their game in the first half and dominated possession. Nikolaidis helped in this by often dropping back, like a midfielder, thereby creating a 3 vs 2 numerical

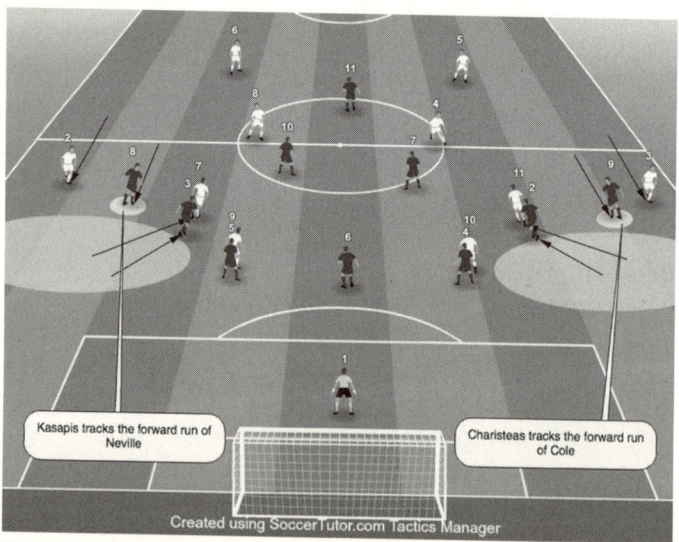

Tracking the runs of the fullbacks vs England

advantage in midfield and offering the midfielders and defenders an additional option when passing the ball. In those instances, Charisteas would also converge as a central midfielder and full-back Patsatzoglou would move up in order to maintain balance.

Rehhagel's plan seemed effective both in defence and attack.

After 30 minutes of play, England had had four shots on goal (the majority of which were free kick efforts by Beckham) versus Greece's seven efforts. This superiority was translated into a goal 36 minutes into the game, when Patsatzoglou crossed from the right, England defended poorly and Charisteas, reacting quickly, beat Martyn with a diagonal shot.

Spaces that the Greeks sought to exploit

After the goal, and because England could not find ways to open up the Greek defence, Beckham started drifting even further towards central midfield in order to have more

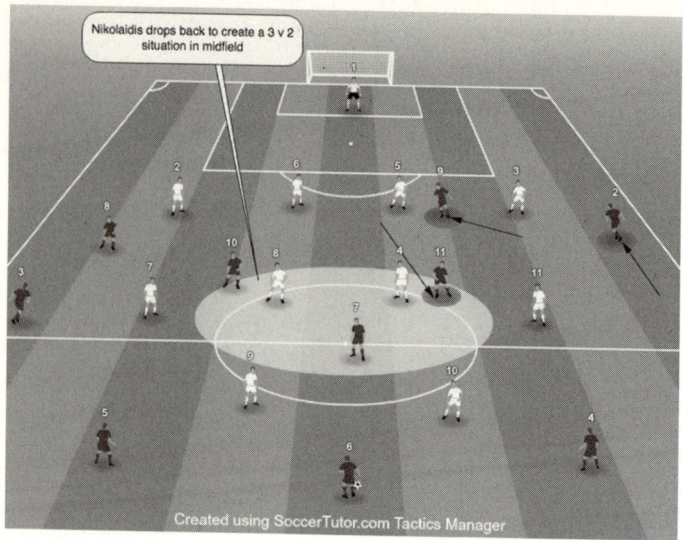

Nikolaidis drops back vs England

Charisteas goal

time on the ball. Because Fyssas would not follow him that far back, choosing to stay close to the other defenders, this gave England the opportunity to play 3 vs 2 in midfield with Scholes, Gerrard or Beckham playing higher between the lines. However, in the Greek defence, there was still a 5 vs 2 ratio, with Rehhagel's team solidifying its defensive line even more.

Numerical superiority allowed England more possession in midfield, without doing anything different to what they had been doing until that point. Combination play with fast and short passes seemed to be missing from their repertoire. No matter how many times the ball reached whichever of the three midfielders was furthest forward, Konstantinidis or the nearest centre-half would intervene and restrict them, while Fyssas' presence near the other defenders added one more player to Greece's defensive line.

Creating numbers up 3 v 2 in the centre

When the ball was passed out wide for a cross, the tall Greek defenders, working closely with their goalkeeper, would neutralise every threat. The end of the first half saw Greece with eight shots on goal to England's four. This underlined the fact that Eriksson's players were unable to find attacking penetration even after falling a goal behind.

England started the second half with Andy Cole coming on for Barmby. Cole took his position in attack next to Fowler, while Heskey moved to the left, where Barmby had originally been deployed. During the first minutes of the second half, Greece came under great pressure from England, who kept crossing the ball into Greece's penalty area until Nikopolidis dealt with England's first noteworthy chance. The Greek goalkeeper saved Cole's angled shot and preserved his team's lead.

Exploiting the 3 v 2 in the centre

Gradually, Greece started to retain possession of the ball, which prevented their opponents from maintaining their tempo. In addition, England had not attempted any tactical changes besides Scholes occasionally acting as a second striker. His efforts were countered by Konstantinidis. Karagounis then missed a great chance in a one-on-one with goalkeeper Nigel Martyn, following a header by Charisteas. The game followed the same pattern, with England attempting to attack using long balls, crosses, free kicks and corners and Greece increasing their share of possession as time went by.

Karagounis had another major chance midway through the second half after exchanging a one-two with Nikolaidis. This produced another one-on-one with Martyn, who saved once again. Almost immediately after that missed chance England equalised, in the 67th minute. Following a cross from a Beckham free kick, substitute Sheringham headed the ball into the net.

nikolaidis goal

It was the only header missed by the Greek defence, but the team's character was borne out when they responded two minutes later. Basinas, who had come on for the injured Zagorakis, crossed the ball. Dabizas passed to Nikolaidis, who fired in a shot from the penalty spot.

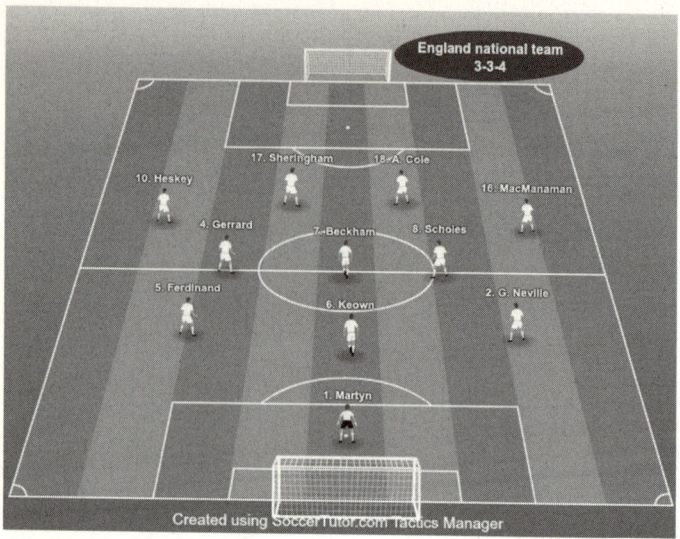

England line up 2

Eriksson's last tactical move was to substitute Ashley Cole with Steve McManaman 78 minutes into the game. McManaman became the right-sided forward, with England now playing with three defenders and four attackers in a formation that looked like 3-3-4. Beckham took on the position of central midfielder and Gerrard occasionally covered Lakis, who had taken over Charisteas' position on the right wing.

Despite all the positional and personnel changes, the home team continued in the same manner, and were therefore not particularly threatening, except from free kicks and corners taken by Beckham. In the the third minute of injury time, the Dutch referee Jol gave a free kick for Konstantinidis' challenge on Sheringham, just a few metres outside the Greek penalty area.

Beckham bent a shot on target and beat Nikopolidis, making the score 2-2, which would be the final result. England qualified for the 2002 World Cup on the strength of that goal, which was Beckham's way of atoning for his suspension four years earlier in the game against Argentina during the round of 16, which caused the 'Three Lions' to be eliminated from France '98. Greece, even though missing out on a prestigious victory, put on a great performance which signalled the start of the Rehhagel era and was a forerunner of its later successes.

Chapter Three

Integrity and Credibility

OTTO REHHAGEL'S main concern regarding infra-structure was the creation of a training centre. Giorgos Papalanis, settling into his role as team manager, understood his urgency: 'When he joined, we would go from Rizoupoli to Nea Smirni to any place that was available. On the first day of preparation for the opening match of the qualifying stage of Euro 2004, against Spain, the facilities in Agios Kosmas were not ready yet, so we started heading for a field in Markopoulos. It started raining really hard on the way there so we had to come back and miss our training. Rehhagel lost it.

'Everyone understood. They were worried. He would put a lot of pressure on [federation president] Gagatsis and that's how they somehow were able to finish the work and deliver him the new training pitch. Stelios Manolas really looked after that field. He was manager of the national youth team and a perfectionist, very tough. He threw out two agronomists because they were not able to maintain the turf. Rehhagel provided the blueprint for the structure, even the offices, and they put it together really quickly.'

Appearances mattered to the head coach. Rehhagel, like many individuals in similar positions across high-level sport, sought association with symbolic achievement. He insisted that only two photos be hung on the walls of the training centre; one was of the team that went to the final stages of Euro 1980, the other featured the team that took part in the 1994 World Cup. The increasing intensity of his demands was driven by a deeply personal vision.

'He started convincing Gagatsis, and of course myself, that in order to succeed, you have to treat your players like stars,' remembers Papalanis. 'They need to enjoy every luxury. The best hotels, the best food, the best flights, the best of everything. He considered that self-evident from his time in Germany. He wouldn't accept that his demands wouldn't be implemented. He was insistent. That was a fundamental ingredient of success. He was able to convey to everyone that the players, workers in general, had to enjoy luxurious comforts.'

Gagatsis, having already heard similar views from Iordanescu, started to accept the logic of Rehhagel's demands at a time when the EPO was not able easily to secure the necessary funds. For Gagatsis, however, money was not the only object. The German's most difficult requirement was the demand to completely isolate the team from the Greek environment, meaning federation officials, football union executives, journalists and the media.

Rehhagel effectively sought an exclusion zone. That entailed clearing the hotel, the plane and the training centre of executives and journalists, of indiscreet eyes and anything else that would distract or upset the players. He was offended, professionally, by hangers-on who would pile on to the team plane, or turn up at hotels, demanding to have coffee and be photographed with the players. Some even had the nerve to give him suggestions about the way he ran the team.

It was a political minefield. Rehhagel was effectively asking Gagatsis to displease his voters, the presidents of amateur Greek football clubs. This was at a time when he was trying to establish himself, broaden his voter base and become more popular so that he would be able to protect and ultimately utilise his authority. He wanted to distance himself from the controlling influences in Greek football, which had originally helped elect him back in 1997.

Papalanis used his own survivor's instinct: 'Otto already knew what he wanted because he considered all those things self-evident, coming from Germany. Also, because he wasn't familiar with the football environment here, he left all that to me, meaning, who or who not got to be close to the team. Agents, journalists, beggars, prostitutes, girlfriends, none of them found their way to our hotel ever again. Of course, I already had experienced that previously, in 1994 in the US. I had seen what had ruined the chemistry back then.'

The message got through to the players. Stelios Venetidis adds: 'He constantly said that he didn't want to see anyone else there, not our families, no one. If he noticed an agent, he would come to talk to us, as a group or individually. "I don't want your friends here. It won't hurt them to miss you for a day," he would tell us. He wasn't able to understand that need. "We are here for a reason. We're here for a mission that requires concentration."

'He placed a lot of importance on that. He didn't want anything that could, or would distract us. There are players that are not influenced by external factors, but some cannot do without concentration, they have no off switch. He was very protective of that. He would tell people off if he saw anyone distracting us. Most of all, he would lose it with agents. He would immediately want to know who they were. He would go up to Topalidis, who would go straight to Papalanis. "Don't bring agents, they create trouble, they don't know the team, we are a group, they don't have our best interest at heart."'

Gagatsis' decision to assign Papalanis to Rehhagel was not accidental. He first sent him to the national team just before Kostas Polichroniou's departure. Papalanis recalls: 'An English journalist had been waiting for him for some time for an interview, the press officer went to remind him and the manager replied: "Leave me, can't you see we're not done yet?" He was playing backgammon. I immediately saw what was happening so I left.'

He was similarly underwhelmed when asked to assist Iordanescu, who left before he did, and was subsequently sent to work with Daniel: 'We were playing a friendly abroad. It was midday. I was responsible for the team and the players started asking where the manager was as only his assistant was there. The manager had left to have lunch with some EPO executives at a restaurant several kilometres away. As soon as we returned to Athens, I told Gagatsis I was leaving.'

The EPO president saw in Papalanis an administrator who possessed the ability and experience to support a personality like Rehhagel's. Papalanis saw his chance. He came up with his own job title, christening himself team manager, thereby creating a position that did not exist in the organisational chart of the national team. He told

Rehhagel: 'I'm going to get an Oscar for my role.' The little messenger boy from 1967 now had the opportunity to develop into an important executive.

He was determined to seize it: 'Gagatsis held me in high esteem, he trusted me. He placed me with the junior national teams in order for me to progress. When he sent me to Rehhagel, I thought that he was trying to "burn" me, but it wasn't that. He had figured out the German manager. He sent me because he considered me capable of satisfying his demands and fulfilling the mission.'

Following the game against England, Rehhagel faced ten months without a competitive fixture until the beginning of the qualifying stage of Euro 2004, in September 2002. During that time, Greece played eight friendly games, seven at home and one in Romania. The change in culture became apparent with every match. Players started noticing the improvement in services and the attention paid to them by the EPO. Their sense of self-worth and professional value was enhanced.

Demis Nikolaidis remembers: 'I don't recall ever catching myself thinking "we are bound for success this time". That wasn't what had been missing. What had been missing was feeling good about being part of the national team. In order to feel special about that we had to see what was different for ourselves. We did start feeling good when we joined up with the national team. The difference was that you could tell that they had started to respect us and take notice of us. It only took small steps on the part of the EPO. No more executives near us. We boarded the plane first in order to get settled in and travel comfortably. We stayed in good hotels. They indulged us. We felt important being in the national team.'

Nikos Dabizas was another convert: 'A football person with so much experience, who came from a country with a national team of such a high level, it made sense for the coach to have a plan and standards that we weren't aware of because we had never had them. When simple, basic, self-evident things happened, we thought they were extravagant. That's when we became very enthusiastic and wanted to give back. We felt calm. All of that helped.'

Newly found comfort and the improvements in work conditions were not the main reason behind the players' enthusiasm. The principal motivating factor was the feeling of security and fairness that had been fostered by Rehhagel's player selections. The German manager would drop insubordinate players and disruptive elements. His selections showed that he wasn't giving in to outside pressures. His choice of players was dictated by his own mind and not by random executives inside or outside the EPO.

'We would see news reports that were critical, perhaps justifiably, regarding players that should have been called up,' Dabizas acknowledges. 'But the manager, with his attitude, showed that he didn't change his mind. He didn't give in to pressure. That kind of integrity, as far as the choices were concerned, was instrumental. It mattered more than anything. It sent the message that, even if he has made a mistake about you, it's only because that's how he perceived it, he didn't leave you thinking that there might be some kind of politics behind it. An organisation's credibility – I have experienced this as both a player and an executive – is a crucial factor in the decision-making process.'

Nikolaidis enjoyed knowing where he stood: 'He did what he wanted. Seeing the call-ups, you realised that it wasn't a public relations exercise and that he was trying anything that came into his head. He didn't make "politically correct" choices. This slowly dissolved any remaining suspicion among the players, which had always been an issue and poisoned the national team. We slowly started hanging out together. My own relationship with the other forwards was terrific, regardless of who was on. There were no doubts between us; 99% of the players didn't complain, no one had anything to say about the manager. As bitter as you could be for not playing, your mind didn't wander.

'We would think, "He didn't use me because he didn't want to use me, not because someone told him not to." That made us feel better, both towards each other and towards the manager. Our relationships became really good and that was the national team's biggest weapon. Rehhagel never had to urge us to hang out together. He didn't have to because he had already managed it with his attitude. He knew what he was doing. No one would ever slam him during conversations among us players. That's what he felt like, we would say. We didn't trash him. That was the most important step towards us becoming a team.'

This was not just about football. This was the creation of the first Greek public institution in which you didn't have to pull some strings to be hired, to work, to advance, to become established. Rehhagel achieved this with an EPO which, according to Papalanis, 'was not interested in ability, they were always looking for people with no backbone. The EPO was rife with nepotism. Fathers would bring in their sons, brothers their sisters, their sisters-in-law, uncles would bring in their nephews, members of parliament would bring in their protégés. There were those shackles holding it down forever. It was Greece in microcosm.'

This new state of affairs was a breath of fresh air for those in the previously diseased dressing room and was greeted enthusiastically by pivotal players like goalkeeper Antonis Nikopolidis: 'During his conflict with Georgatos in Finland, the important thing was that he didn't back down, he simply dropped him. This showed the rest of us that there was a man here who didn't care about the pressure he would be put under, who wouldn't be influenced by the president. He said no and that was it. Straight away he showed he was a man to be reckoned with. This made the players feel secure that he wouldn't be controlled, that he did what he believed in. He started gaining the trust of the players.'

Assistant coaches tend to have the ear of senior players. As a trusted source of advice and perspective, they are in the best position to take the temperature of a dressing room. Giannis Topalidis was a case in point: 'The game in England, him dropping Georgatos, counted in his favour. The players themselves told me this. Otto showed that he had guts with that decision. He has never said a word against Georgatos. If Georgatos had thought to meet him and apologise, he may have reconsidered. He never told me anything negative about him. Nothing, ever.'

Pivotal personalities like Theo Zagorakis were fully on board: 'If the guys who left because they made mistakes had experienced this situation, they would have definitely wanted to still be members of the national team. But someone had to pay the price. In the past, none of us had been 100% professional in our attitude towards the national team. So, in reality, the question was who would pay the price, who would make a mistake big enough for the manager to drop them in order to make an example out of them for the rest of us. His decision to leave out some big names had us all shaken. We realised that there was something happening, that we must get our act together.'

Zagorakis paints a vivid picture of the change in behaviour, and therefore of mentality, of the players: 'The main reason we felt at ease was that, when he didn't pick us, it had been clearly his own decision. I would lose it and complain to Topalidis, but in private. Before that, we would do that out in the open, at the managers. We didn't take it out on Rehhagel, because we knew we would be out.'

Chapter Four

Confidence and Trust

THIS MIGHT seem counter-intuitive, given the lazy assumptions formed in the aftermath of the triumph at Euro 2004, but Otto Rehhagel's original concept, that he would fine-tune his Greek team in the friendly matches before the qualifying stages, was based upon the development of an attacking style.

'Rehhagel was considering playing offensively because, as he said, all his teams played offensively and he had the best forwards,' says Giannis Topalidis. 'We played really well in the friendly matches, so we started to believe, but we also conceded many goals. Two against Estonia (4-2 win), two against Cyprus (1-2 defeat), two against Sweden (2-2). We then travelled to Patras in March 2002 to play against Belgium who had qualified for the World Cup. Belgium led 2-0. We turned it around in the second half, beat them 3-2. That result caused a sensation, but the manager was still concerned about all the goals we were conceding.'

Despite the praise for the character and resilience shown against Belgium, memories of the home defeat by Cyprus and the draw against Sweden were toxic. It did not take much for certain sections of the Greek football scene to forget the performance at Old Trafford and doubt Rehhagel once again. This unease would provide those within the EPO who opposed Rehhagel, or rather those that were opposed politically to Gagatsis' choice, with much-needed ammunition.

Gagatsis was elected president in July 2001, during which period he had started to distance himself from the team that had won the EPO elections in 1997. Those elections caused a major scandal in Greece which almost resulted in criminal proceedings. In 1998, Gregoris Peponis, the district attorney for Piraeus, ordered a preliminary investigation into a case of alleged vote-buying by Thomas Mitropoulos during the EPO elections.

In December 1999, Piraeus prosecutor Maria Tsirimokou indicted Thomas Mitropoulos for charges of bribery, the vice-president of Olympiakos FC Giorgos Louvaris for instigation of bribery and Gagatsis for complicity in attempted bribery. Gagatsis responded at the time, 'The charges are without foundation. The investigation will prove my innocence and I will definitely be cleared.' Eventually, all three were cleared of the charges by ruling of the Piraeus Magistrates' Court. The case was subsequently closed.

Gagatsis' decision to distance himself from the system responsible for the election win bothered many both inside and outside the EPO. The national team was one of the main areas of contention between opposing factions. While Gagatsis chose to support Rehhagel, there were many who would try to force him to have the German removed and replaced with someone more pliable, who would listen to the football power-brokers before making his call-ups.

Gagatsis recalls: 'In the beginning, for about a year, I was under constant pressure to kick him out.' The media, following a narrative driven by specific journalists, were prominent in this sphere of influence, in supporting the faction agitating for change. As Rehhagel was no one's yes man, reports that fostered or cultivated an impression of his inflexibility were designed to multiply doubts about his character. Impressions were distorted in an attempt to create the necessary conditions for a change of manager.

Giorgos Papalanis recalls the situation vividly: 'On the day of the friendly with Belgium, I knew very well that, if we lost, Gagatsis would face unbearable pressure to replace him. They already had a replacement lined up, and they were laughing with glee during half-time. But Rehhagel started the second half with Vryzas, who scored two goals in the next ten minutes and saved the day.'

How did he know that? The national team was his 'second' job, as he spent every morning in his office at the EPO, as 'General Director of National Teams and Refereeing'. Papalanis held that position for 12 and a half years from late 1997 until 2010. He had his finger on the pulse of the plotters.

Rehhagel was pragmatic, and unafraid of big decisions. He had taken full advantage of the series of friendly matches, to make the players understand the essence of his concept of a productive playing style. His concern about the concession of easy goals drove him to formulate a more defensive game plan.

Stelios Venetidis comments: 'At first he would say, "OK, you tell me you're top level players, what is your level compared to Spain? Can we count on that level to win, if we play a quality game against big teams? No. We have to find a different way, different elements." He would say that from the very start. That alone shows he was an intelligent man, who went on to give a country its own identity in football. That counts more than giving good tactical advice.

'He had seen us, the players of Panathinaikos, during the Champions League and decided to call up our defence to the national team. He counted on our experience. His rationale was simple: "I've got their defensive tactics. I also have Zagorakis, Nikolaidis and Charisteas. I have built a solid framework and I will create something different." He was creating the framework. That was his plan: as long as the defence works, the goals will come.

'We didn't have elaborate offensive combinations and plans. Our orders when we had possession were to cross from the sides. We followed the logic that we have some tall guys, and we will score. The main target was to not concede goals. That was the plan. That was the main thing. "Yes, let's do that," we would say. He would say, "Fine, if anything happens, we will use Tsiartas who can help with free kicks and corners." Those were his alternatives. We agreed, even though we could have complained that we were playing too defensively, that the plan didn't inspire us. We continued like that.'

Antonis Nikopolidis emphasises the extent of the buy-in from the players: 'After England we had a series of friendlies and the results were proving us right in our decision to support his concept. We were winning, not easily but we were winning. I remember the match in Romania. I've never been so tired. They had us locked in for 90 minutes, but Giannakopoulos had scored a free kick from 30 metres out, so we won. That's when you gain confidence and trust.

You think that we can go ahead, even like this. That's how his plan and our trust in that plan, was created.'

Rehhagel gained the players' trust by his willingness to drop players because he had doubts about their mentality. That sense of strength and fairness helped form a nucleus of players who rallied the team around him. Stelios Venetidis explains: 'After everything that happened in Finland, he said that next time he would bring those that really wanted to be part of the team and that he would change what had been going on until then. We immediately realised that this man wanted to create a team.

'As soon as he let two or three problematic cases go, because he was so intelligent – which is his biggest advantage – right away he bonded with some of the guys in order to form a core. His rationale was, "When these two or three disruptive individuals go, I will keep some people close who can create a feeling of solidarity." With Zagorakis as leader and Karagounis with his unbelievable passion for football and the national team holding the fort in the dressing room, the attempt to create a new mentality began. This combination of moves was critical.'

Giorgos Karagounis was one of the first players to be won over: 'Yes, I was part of the original core he created. According to Topalidis, I was Beate's favourite … just kidding. Maybe the fact that I scored a goal during his first game, in Finland, played a role – he was like that. I don't know, I am just speculating. If someone made a mistake, that was it. I scored a goal during his first game, so he saw me differently. That's the German mentality. Moreover, he hadn't missed any of Panathinaikos' games in the Champions League, and like many of the other guys, I had some very good games.

'I remember we were in the hotel in London for a game against Arsenal and I had nothing to do, so I went down to the lobby and I saw him there sitting in a corner by himself. He had come to see the game, without us knowing. That also played a role, I suppose. Besides, he would see how crazy I got during training. That was the beginning. I was one of those who had been there since his first game. Maybe that explains why he saw me differently.'

For a reforming manager like Rehhagel, Karagounis possessed the ideal attitude. He had been a genuine and staunch fan of the national team from the first day he wore the colours: 'This sentiment had been cultivated within me from very early on because I was lucky enough to join the national youth team at the age of 14 and a half, two years under the designated age. The coach Alekos Sofianidis had taken me to play as a forward for a tournament in Poland and I was top scorer with four goals. I saw how nice and different the national team was, so I loved it very much from the start.

'I came to love the team even more because, for me, it was a way to show what I could do. I played for Panathinaikos, where if you were Greek and young, you had to be able to play like Maradona to say the least before they let you play. You weren't taken seriously before you reached the age of 20. I remember Vardinogiannis, the owner, always telling me, "Kid, don't get ahead of yourself." I would hear that all the time. It didn't matter if you deserved to play at 16, that's what they believed in Greece.

'With the national youth team, we came third in Europe, but no, you can't play for the club yet. The youth team beat Holland 5-0 in Litohoro and I scored two goals. Yet a month earlier, Wouter and Musampa, from that Dutch team, had played for Ajax against Panathinaikos in the Champions League semi-final, while I was in the reserve team. It wasn't that we couldn't play. It was just what they believed.

'So I saw those tournaments with the national youth team as a chance to show my worth. All that made me love the national team very much. It was a special feeling. I used to think that even if I ended up at Barcelona, it would still rate lower than the national team. I always thought that, despite playing for big clubs as my career progressed. Not many saw the national team that way. The big clubs rated higher. Everything would collapse after the first bad game. There was no real spirit. Everyone would watch out for their clubs first. There was no national consciousness before Rehhagel.'

Unknowingly, Rehhagel had stumbled upon a generation of footballers who wanted to change the attitude around the national team. Some were reaching the twilight of their careers, but hadn't had a taste of success because they had missed the 1994 World Cup. They were mature enough to realise the dynamics of the situation. Some were playing abroad and had their minds opened sufficiently to realise what impact the success of the national team would have on their contracts and careers. Others were young or poorly compensated and therefore hungry for a successful run that would change their careers.

Nikos Dabizas remembers: 'We were ready for a change. For sure when we came across a new order of things, when the generations changed, those of us who had played abroad and saw what could be gained by playing in the national team made an attempt to give back to the team what it had offered us. We started conveying that to the other guys too, that the national team reflects on us. This caught on. The team would be held in higher regard and people showed concern for its improvement. We started laying the groundwork in 2002 and it took time. Our first impression of what Rehhagel stood for as a person was crystal clear. We realised who we had to deal with after the first few meetings. He was very different to what we were used to, very intelligent. He understood what was happening around him. Over time, we started to realise how he operated on and off the pitch.'

Takis Fyssas saw the value of self-analysis: 'We took a look at ourselves because we saw that we could succeed that way, go to the Euros, which we had only seen on television. "Enough. We are good footballers but Greece has no respect for us," we would say. In the eyes of the people we were not great players, few of us had become established. So we decided to see what we could do to achieve all that.'

Year after year, call-up after call-up, Rehhagel would drop anyone he believed would not change their attitude. Fyssas explains the impact of such decisiveness: 'This manager, who was so different, kept the players that had another kind of attitude. I didn't join the squad with that attitude already in place. Neither did Karagounis, Giannakopoulos, Dabizas, Demis or Tsiartas. It's not like we suddenly said, "Hey guys, let's all be friends." This all came out so naturally through the inspiration we drew from that man, Rehhagel. If it hadn't been for Rehhagel, who retained and brought into the team those whose attitude suited him, this generation wouldn't have made a change. We would say that nobody believed in us, nobody wanted to change how this works. But this man did. He had a choice and he made it and he benefited from us.'

Traianos Dellas recognises the subtlety of the process: 'I don't know if Rehhagel himself communicated it with words, that we have to be a team, or if it was the combination of his manner and our character that made the difference. We somehow realised that this manager was different than the ones before. I don't recall him ever saying "guys, make sure to become a team because I don't see us having any luck otherwise". That happened by itself as we came to see a man who was secure, who would not be swayed, who did not adopt the old mind-set. Another factor was that several of us were playing abroad, so we viewed the national team as a chance to be together again and not as a way of getting away from our clubs' problems. Also of course, the results played the most important part.'

Rehhagel spent less than 30 days in Greece during the ten-month period between the game in England and the start of the Euro 2004 qualifying campaign. His contract included rented accommodation and the EPO paid 5,000 euros a month for a house in the suburb of Psyhiko. 'About ten months later he comes and says, "You are paying so much money for the house and I'm never there. Leave it and find me a room at the King George Hotel in Syntagma Square so I can stay when I'm here and see the Acropolis,"' recalls Vasilis Gagatsis.

The Acropolis had enchanted him from the first time he laid eyes on it with Beate, during a trip they had made before the position with the national team had opened up. The view from the King George was a definitive image, shared with Norbert Kuntze, author of the book *Otto Rehhagel*, when he outlined his first impressions of life in Athens: 'It is special sitting on the balcony of the hotel and seeing the Acropolis just half a mile away, all lit up. One feels like the whole world comes together at that point.'

Gagatsis was coming to terms with the fact he had employed a singular man: 'When he asked to stay at the hotel I told him we provided the house because I thought he would be coming to stay with his wife. "My wife can't stand the heat, I told you," was his answer. That was his position. He didn't want to stay here and I respected that.'

Papalanis, as ever, had an acute insight into the situation: 'Rehhagel had made up his mind about the Greek football scene and the Greeks' relationship with the sport. He wouldn't open up to anybody and he didn't want to stay here to avoid being pestered and influenced. His routine was to be in Athens three days each month. He would arrive two days before the game and leave the day after. He didn't want to have the slightest contact with the football community, the unions, or the EPO board members. He wouldn't go to meetings with the club managers either. He would send me; he wouldn't even send Topalidis.

'From very early on he realised that if he chose to stay in Greece, he would receive a lot of pressure. They were trying to tell him who to call up. They complained because he wouldn't call up more Olympiakos players. They would ask me to help sway Topalidis. I was even approached by agents. I would tell Topalidis everything so that they wouldn't suspect or doubt me. I wouldn't speak to the journalists that approached me. I knew who didn't have the team's best interests at heart so I tried to keep them away at any cost.'

Fyssas went on to assist Rehhagel for the 2010 World Cup campaign after retiring as a player in 2008. He knew the territory well: 'I was aware that he would have been under enormous pressure had he been staying here. He was, they told him things. Even the president had said "call up so and so". But he didn't want that, he didn't want to have to listen to them and be put on the spot.'

Dabizas, one of Rehhagel's early confidants, gives a flavour of their conversations: 'I remember that someone had told him, early on, that they had called him "the German Elephant". He would still pay attention to what was being said and written at the time and that affected him. I told him not to get caught up in that and get upset. If he had found out about everything that was being said, we wouldn't get anywhere. Smart man that he was, he switched it off. He kept his team of close colleagues small. It was something like self-defence on his part. He didn't form relationships and friendships to stay away from all that. He liked being in Greece. Living in Germany, he wanted to be in a pleasant environment with sun and sea. I thought the whole "my wife can't stand the heat" thing was a ploy. He just didn't want to be here, to avoid being pestered.'

Topalidis, his assistant, was notably protective. 'There were many who tried to influence him but they were not successful,' he explains. 'People from the EPO would ask, "Why isn't he looking at this or that player?" They wanted to pressure me into telling him. One time, someone from the EPO approached me really angrily and asked, "Don't you talk to him?" From the very beginning, they asked me to "stay in contact" with them. But we came to Greece and said we will do what the manager wants. If he had been Greek, all that may have affected him.'

The circle of trust was tight and had, at its centre, Gagatsis, the coach's greatest advocate. When he informed Rehhagel of his intention to leave the EPO in 2008, the German coach invited him to dinner. 'I'll tell you why we succeeded,' he told him. 'According to the contract I was supposed to spend nine months per year in Greece. You never pressed me on that, you set me free. That, which I imagine was a conscious decision, was the secret.'

Why didn't Gagatsis press him? 'He had explained the rationale by which he picked players based on their mentality. He chose those that played at bigger clubs or abroad, because they were more open-minded. So I didn't see the point in keeping him here in order to watch the rest of the games in the Greek league. Moreover, I saw a man thinking with a clear head, who didn't get caught up with the media and I realised that if he lived here, he ran the danger of being swayed. So why poison him? I saw a man who never wanted to make friends in Greece. He never brought Beate to spend even a month here. He was a special individual, very different, with an unusual attitude. I didn't have the right to try and change him and bring him closer to us, because that would create the risk of his thinking and judgement being affected.'

'It is sort of like that,' reflects Rehhagel. 'I had told Gagatsis that success came because he let me live in Germany. Besides, I knew very well what was happening in Greece when I was in Germany.' He didn't know exactly everything, but enough. Topalidis and Papalanis made sure of that. The two, his most trusted staff members, became very close from the beginning. They spent hours together, so they came to understand each other very well.

The pair had a common basis, their mutual interest. Both were desperate for the national team to succeed for personal as well as collective reasons. Topalidis realised that staying with the team was his best prospect if he wanted to live well in Greece. Papalanis placed all hopes of advancing in the EPO and becoming established in Greek football on the team succeeding. Such incentives are powerful in football.

Chapter Five

Crisis and Conviction

THE OPENING match of Euro 2004 qualifying took place on 9 September 2002, at the Leoforos Alexandras stadium, the preferred ground of both the manager and the players. 'The Cage', as Rehhagel called it, has stands that are close to the pitch and he hoped to exploit the atmosphere that created. They would be playing against Spain in front of a full house.

Eight minutes into the match, a defensive error gave Spain the lead with a goal by Raul. Greece did not crumble. They remained patient, retained possession of the ball and created chances, until the game was taken away from them by a second Spanish goal, by Valerón after 76 minutes. 'It was very difficult to react against such a formidable opponent,' recalls Giannis Topalidis. 'We were shaken.'

Crucially, however, they regrouped without seeking a scapegoat. Angelos Charisteas captured the post-match mood perfectly: 'All the guys went up to Dabizas, who had made the error that led to the opening goal, in order to encourage him. There were no recriminations, which was a change from the past, when the players would

75

draw attention to errors and confront each other. We had already started to gel together.' Demis Nikolaidis added further perspective: 'We had had a good game, we were not disappointed.'

Little more than a month later, on 12 October, the team played Ukraine in Kiev. This was seen as a pivotal test, since they were regarded as Greece's most significant opponents in the group. Many believed it would come down to the two teams for the second qualifying place behind Spain. Greece started well in front of 50,000 people in the Olimpiyskiy stadium, and the defensive plan worked well until Vorobey scored 51 minutes into the game. Greece were unable to respond and eventually conceded a second goal in the first minute of injury time by Voronin.

Already, the vultures were beginning to circle. Giannis Topalidis recalls: 'We played well in the Ukraine, despite the defeat, but a journalist wrote something about "Rehhagel's Crimes". He would ask what the Greek newspapers wrote but I wouldn't tell him because the comments were really negative. This statement, however, had been conveyed to the German press by his former translator, with whom he had parted ways. Otto wanted to resign after this. "Crimes? How can they use that word for a manager, for a football game?" he would ask. He lost it. He kept repeating, "Is this what they will be reading about me in Germany?"'

Giorgos Papalanis also sensed the danger. 'Two days later, we were in the hotel in Athens because we had the next game in three days, and he went to get a German newspaper. In it they had reprinted a statement by former manager Nikos Alefantos to the Greek sports newspaper *Fos*, which talked about Rehhagel's "crimes". He welled up. He was furious. I explained that this was the guy's style, that he had said the same about Iordanescu. The players and Topalidis had to talk to him and persuade him to stay.'

Vasilis Gagatsis, the federation president, met the plotters head on: 'Following the defeat against Ukraine, five EPO board members came to my office. "Is it perhaps time to start thinking about the next manager?" they asked meaningfully. "I will leave before he does, this cannot go on," I replied. I was there, I lived through it, I knew what was going on. They had never worked like this before as a team. I went to the training sessions. I kept saying that what he had been working towards is going to bring results.'

Crucially, the players remained supportive, though, as Stelios Venetidis recalls, 'That's when the seed of doubt entered. We saw that the way we were playing, which wasn't spectacular, didn't bring the results we wanted.' Theo Zagorakis, a positive voice and an influential presence in the dressing room, emerged as a unifying leader.

'The team hadn't played badly against Spain, but they were on a different level,' he reasons. 'We never doubted the manager over those games. The entire country did, but we kept saying "moving on, we're doing OK, the results will come". Also Gagatsis had his back, which wasn't an easy thing to do because EPO administrations are always vulnerable. We were all concerned, but we hadn't played badly in Ukraine either. The match could have gone either way. So we said that the schedule of games was better for us from then on. That was what showed the administration that they had to soldier on. We said that we would lose to Spain, overtake Ukraine, and see what happened. We considered ourselves better than Ukraine.'

Antonis Nikopolidis, another seasoned player, and future manager of Greece's under-21 team, also led by example. 'I never had doubts about the team,' he stresses. 'Not that I was sure that we would qualify, but I didn't doubt that we were a good team. We would get over it. We had seen that Ukraine weren't anything special. That's why I rate Gagatsis for not backing out and replacing him. Despite all the pressure he had been put under, he gave him a second chance.'

Such praise for Gagatsis is shaped by hindsight, because the rift between him and the players, following the Ukraine defeat, was serious and sustained. Due to the political pressure heaped on him by rivals within the EPO, Gagatsis had attempted to offer additional incentives to the players before what he considered to be a crucial match. He explains: 'Before the game, after the manager's speech, I offered them a bonus of about 30,000 euros each if they won. I never did that again, it was a mistake. It put additional pressure on them and I realised after the game that it hadn't helped.'

Had he kept his counsel the situation would have been recoverable. Yet on his return to Athens Gagatsis blamed the defeat on the players in a radio interview and dismissed the team as a 'fourth division neighbourhood outfit'. Within a few minutes, the players had found out that the president had called them disorganised and lazy. He reasons: 'The team needed a shock. I thought I'd hit them where it hurts in order to shake them up.' But the consequences were far-reaching. As he wrote in his book: 'After that they wouldn't speak to me. They wouldn't even look at me.'

Gagatsis has not regretted his decision, which he still perceives as having been necessary at the time. It is certain that he paid a big price, given that the players refused to see him until October 2003, when they were celebrating the team's qualification. It took some time for them to welcome him back into the fold; the rift was not fully healed until they had started preparing for the Euro finals in May 2004.

Giorgos Papalanis confirms: 'Until we arrived in Switzerland for pre-tournament training, the players hadn't spent time with Gagatsis. They didn't want to see him in the dressing room or the hotel.' Traianos Dellas expands the point: 'That statement by Gagatsis after the second game, that we were disorganised and lazy, was a turning point.'

Four days after the defeat in Ukraine, Greece played the third game of the qualifying group, against Armenia. The crowd was down to 6,000 from 17,000 for the opening game. Though the performance was far from convincing, the team easily achieved its first win in a competitive match under Rehhagel, with Nikolaidis scoring two goals.

Three friendly games followed, the first a 0-0 draw against the Republic of Ireland at the Leoforos stadium in Athens. A 2-1 win against Cyprus in Larnaca was followed by a single goal win against Norway in Irakleion. After the third game, Rehhagel asked to see Gagatsis. According to the former president's book, Rehhagel told him: 'I have received a magical offer from Bayer Leverkusen to join them as technical director. After everything that has been said and written, isn't it better for you if I go?'

Gagatsis repeated his conviction that the team would qualify for the Euros and Rehhagel decided to remain in his job. Despite his ambitions to return to his homeland, he decided to give his Greek project more time. 'I knew that back then he was interested in going back to Germany, to a club,' recalls Giannis Topalidis, who is backed up by Giorgos Papalanis: 'Rehhagel's dream was to return to

Germany. It was always on his mind during those first few years.'

Before the fourth qualification match in Belfast against Northern Ireland in March 2003, Rehhagel decided to take the players to Germany for a week and play a final friendly in Graz against Austria. Antonis Nikopolidis recalls: 'The manager then did something unbelievable, which showed his guts. After we had scored two goals at the start of the second half, we conceded one and the team lost its concentration.

'Rehhagel was on his feet, trying to say something to Konstantinidis, who was in the starting line-up and the person he spoke to the most because he spoke German. Konstantinidis made a rude gesture towards him and that's the first time we saw the manager so angry in the dressing room. We went to Ireland, he was in the starting line-up again and then he dropped him. When that happened, when we saw him dismiss the player he had been closest to, we realised that he just didn't care.'

The team flew to Belfast with the plane clear of executives and hangers-on for the first time in history. At the same time, the team had their own bus and they had changed hotels. They stayed at a luxury hotel in Vouliagmeni, which would be empty of other guests during their stays, so that the team would not be disturbed and each player would have his own room. The EPO paid for this convenience.

On the eve of the game against Northern Ireland, the manager got personal, and utilised a fundamental method of introducing the players to his philosophy, through one-to-one meetings. He would invite them to his room, or in the hotel lounge, or during the morning team walk, whenever he saw fit. That was his way of feeling out the collective mood of the team or an individual player. He talked about his principles, conveyed his instructions for the next game, and shared his experience. As he explains: 'My philosophy is to encourage and uplift my players, to talk to each of them individually and as a group. In order to reach our goal, we needed to be as tight as a fist.'

Angelos Charisteas admits: 'I carried a lot of mental pressure over that game. Rehhagel and Topalidis had told me during our meeting that if we lost they would have to go, so they asked me to do anything I could to help.'

His impression, that a crisis point had been reached, was shared by Stelios Venetidis:

'There had been a lot of doubt following the defeat in Ukraine and the mediocre performance against Armenia. So when the Northern Ireland game came along, there was a lot of pressure. He felt it too, I could tell. He had the ability and the intelligence to convey his anxiety about the importance of the games without burdening us. The atmosphere was boiling in Belfast. Everything he had created was threatening to collapse. Even the complaints of those who wouldn't be playing hit home.'

Before the start of the game, a large group of players gathered around Rehhagel. They discussed the importance of the result, fully aware that the preservation of the atmosphere that they had come to love hinged on it. Charisteas' eight-year stint in German football allowed him to be able to compare Rehhagel with more typical examples of German managers of the time.

'The team didn't need a "pure" German manager,' he reasons. 'Otto isn't your typical German. He is a bit weird, a strange man. He affords you so much freedom that you start thinking, "If we lose, we will also lose this freedom and we cannot lose what we've got now." We got together before that game and said that there's no way we can destroy what we had, we would have been foolish to do so. We didn't want a change in the status quo, we were doing great. But there was so much stress about the game in Ireland.'

Charisteas scored the two goals that gave Greece the much-needed win. He made brilliant use of Vassilios Tsiartas' through-ball to score the first goal only three minutes into the game. Then early in the second half, he won the ball following some aggressive pressing by Greece and went on to score the second, handing Greece a 2-0 victory.

'That's when this kind of special relationship with Otto began,' he recalls. 'He told me, "I'm going to use you. I need you to help me." So I did the job, I was in good condition. I was really stressed but I did help him with those two goals. The game went our way and Otto never forgot. That's how this bond between us became stronger. The same thing would happen every game, with different players. That game was also the start of his relationship and bond with Tsiartas.'

Giorgos Papalanis vividly expresses the hidden stresses of a tempestuous match: 'Otto had a serious case of nerves for the first time in Northern Ireland. He had had a fight with their manager, who had called him "a fucking German" or "fucking German Nazi" and wanted to beat him up.' For Rehhagel, under so much pressure, the slur of being called a Nazi added insult to injury.

His birthplace, Essen, had suffered considerably due to Nazi intransigence and the hardships of war. Rehhagel grew up listening to stories about the night three months before he was born, on which the SS entered the old synagogue in the centre of town, set it alight and murdered 91 people. The Helene mine where his father worked belonged to Gustav Krupp von Bohlen und Halbach, who was a personal friend of Hitler's and wore the golden Nazi Party pin with pride.

In early March 1943, Essen experienced its first serious bombing. Rehhagel, curled up in his mother's arms at the age of five, would hear the Allied bombers and the air-raid sirens. Explosive and incendiary bombs destroyed half the city leaving 80,000 people homeless. Essen, an industrial city, was a target of Allied air raids until March 1945. In early April of that year, when the American troops invaded Altenessen and attempted to find lodgings for the thousands of homeless, they stipulated that each adult was entitled to a room and that every two children under 12 would share a room. Otto found himself crammed into a room with his sisters Clara and Roswitha, in a house shared by ten families.

Rehhagel told his biographer Norbert Kuntze: 'When we lost dad, mum retired and the kids were working. I thought, "No way. I have to do something with my life, away from all these ruins, hunger and misery." Football was the only way out.'

He became a painter at a Coca-Cola factory in order to avoid working in the mines, where his father lost his life when Otto was 12. Football rescued him at the age of 22. His difficult childhood experiences ensured he regarded a career in professional football as a blessing. In later years, he would convey that gratitude to his players at every opportunity in order to remind them that they, too, owed their lives to the game. Stelios Venetidis was among those players moved by his manager's conviction:

'He would look for reasons to show us that what we were doing was special, a blessing. Football has huge potential. It is so influential. When he took us running in the morning, in order to motivate us he would have us gather around and say, "Look at this worker there. You wake up and run, do your hobby, which lets you live a comfortable life. You are important. You play for the national team. Look at those who wake up in the morning and struggle for a day's wages." He would say this having experienced it himself, and it would shake you up. He helped you understand that what you're doing is special. That was great life advice.'

Chapter Six

Band of Brothers

FOOTBALL IS a succession of sliding doors moments. Otto Rehhagel's arrived in Zaragoza in June 2003, in the second qualifying match against Spain. Having warmed up with a 2-2 draw against Slovakia in Zilina, his team were burdened by an assumption of inferiority that he knew could be personally costly. This would be the match that changed Greek football history.

Giannis Topalidis understood the consequences of failure: 'When the time came to play in Spain, they had already decided to have us replaced if we lost. I knew it and I knew who the successor was going to be. The manager knew as well. We had managed to convince him to stay one last time, but if we lost in Spain that would be it and he knew it.

'There were other complications that I can't go into. We won in Northern Ireland and we said that we needed to win the home game against Ukraine. Then it was a case of seeing if we came second. As it turned out, Spain was the key game. It changed our trajectory with the team.'

Giorgos Papalanis, as ever, also had his ear to the ground: 'Topalidis knew that Stratos Apostolakis would be in Zaragoza to watch the game on behalf of Giannis Kyrastas. Kyrastas had been in talks with the EPO to take over with me as assistant, if the team lost in Zaragoza. I was already working with the youth team but I would join Kyrastas at the senior national team.'

Apostolakis revealed in an interview with *sdna* 15 years later: 'Kyrastas and Dusan Bajevic were the main candidates in the minds of those who had been pressuring Gagatsis for change. Some had approached Kyrastas, who had accepted, and some Bajevic. It had all started to go wrong for Rehhagel after those two initial defeats. So they were discussing changing the manager and Rehhagel found out.'

Rehhagel was prepared. His foresight did not simply help him in running game scenarios, which shaped selection and strategy. It also allowed him to be a step ahead in his professional life. In a revealing report published in the *Frankfurter Allegemeine Zeitung* in July 2004, two days before the German coach would be crowned European champion, the journalist Michael Horeni wrote: 'Rehhagel had kept negotiations open with Bayer Leverkusen, who wanted to take him on as manager or sporting director, until the unforeseen victory over Spain, at which point Rehhagel discontinued them.' Leverkusen had not hired a new sporting director in anticipation of Rehhagel's reply.

A single goal, and what a goal by Stelios Giannakopoulos, sealed Rehhagel's future. It shaped the destiny of the team and of the 23 players who became European champions. It led an entire country to take to the streets four times in the summer of 2004 to celebrate one of the greatest sporting achievements of all time and the greatest unifying event in Greece's modern history.

The senior players and those who formed part of Rehhagel and Topalidis' core group had become aware that a negative result would drive the manager away. 'It would have taken a single defeat to replace him with Kyrastas,' remembers Giorgos Karagounis. 'Before the match in Spain we knew we would be going to the final stage with a different manager. I had talked to Kyrastas. But the main thing was that, even though many of us knew, the situation did not affect us.'

Antonis Nikopolidis adds: 'It had to do with our motivation, but also with the fact that many of us had 40 Champions League games under our belts. We knew what we were up against. It wasn't the same for the guys a decade earlier, who didn't play often under conditions like these and were therefore affected by them. We had the experience, we knew how to handle the game and execute the plan. We were looking to see what we could take from there; the atmosphere did not affect us.'

'I first heard they had shaken hands with Kyrastas on the eve of the match in Zaragoza,' recalls Traianos Dellas. 'I don't remember even considering that he would leave if we lost. I remember us saying that it was a landmark game, that if we didn't lose we still had a chance. We had a lot of faith and I remember the training sessions being intense. We were in great condition, we would bet on which side would win during training and would kill ourselves trying.'

That game was a testament to Rehhagel's man management work in Greece. The players travelled to Zaragoza 25 days after the 3-0 win of Olympiakos over Panathinaikos, which decided the identity of that season's champions. That game was staged in a warlike atmosphere both on and off the pitch. The Panathinaikos players were terrorised, the object of continuous attacks that started even before they had disembarked from the bus and which continued on the way to the dressing rooms and the pitch. Videos of the event are still making the rounds, accruing thousands of views even today.

What followed in Spain, however, was the clearest proof of what Rehhagel had been able to achieve. In less than two years, the German manager had attained his initial goal; 'To persuade the Greeks to place the national team over and above the clubs and distance it from what went on in the Greek championship.' The goal he had mentioned during his introductory press conference – 'to unite the players that played for the bigger clubs because that was the only way to success' – was fulfilled spectacularly.

Takis Fyssas puts the unlikely unity into perspective: 'Travelling to Spain after the game in Rizoupolis, us Panathinaikos players felt persecuted and disappointed. We had been through a lot, chased by Olympiakos fans, by our own fans. They had stolen the title from right between our fingers and we have to go play alongside Olympiakos players Giannakopoulos and Venetidis. Yet we're all a family.

'We are bitter and they have been crowned champions even though we were the favourites. [Panathinaikos would have won the title if they had lost by anything less than the final three-goal margin.] So we go there and we give it our all, together. Rehhagel played Venetidis and Giannakopoulos on the left side. He would take everything into account, our psychology as well. But there we were with Venetidis and Giannakopoulos, celebrating like brothers. The way we handled all of that proved that the team had reached a different level.'

How did the team reach this level of solidarity? A statement to his biographer at the time that his agreement with the EPO was announced shows that Rehhagel had done his homework: 'Some clubs boycott the national team, so I've heard, I don't know details yet. The big clubs will have to lend a hand in order to achieve the common goal. The slightest disruption will bring failure.'

He trusted those who had outlined the prevailing state of affairs within the team. They helped him form his first impressions. It took him two trips, to Moscow and Helsinki, to confirm he had located the root of the greatest problem faced by the national team during the previous two years or so. He decided to touch on that in public. 'The fundamental problem is that the team plays second fiddle to the big clubs,' he stated in an interview with the German newspaper *Die Welt* in September 2001, just before he watched the game in Finland. 'If this mentality doesn't change, we will not qualify for the final stage of any big tournament. Everyone has to be convinced that the team is very special and commit to treating it that way.'

As he had always done in his career, Rehhagel invested a lot of time in communicating with his players in private meetings. He was direct in insisting that club issues had to be separated from the national interest. After Finland he had communicated to the team through his selection policy, which proved he would keep insubordinate or disruptive elements away.

He did not need to make speeches. He was economical in his behaviour and his words, preferring to make his points by call-up after call-up. He chose players who put the team first. This is how, in the space of a year, the squad went from being a web of personal animosities to becoming a group of friends comprised of smaller groups of friends. Zagorakis, Nikolaidis, Dabizas, Fyssas and Karagounis played the biggest role in achieving this.

Kostas Katsouranis explains: 'Rehhagel united AEK and Panathinaikos players, whom he trusted because of their appearances in the Champions League during that time. What he did was very clever. That no one brought up the clubs within the national team was Rehhagel's achievement. He had shown trust in those who approached him and he tried to select players who wouldn't carry club problems over to the national team.'

Stelios Venetidis adds: 'He put a lot of stock in solidarity. He would observe people's behaviour. He would read everything in our body language thanks to his emotional intelligence. He was the one who solved the puzzle, who brought about camaraderie and good cheer. "The team is created in the dressing room," he would always say. "It is difficult to become a team when we meet once a month." He asked us to work on that. "I want to create a homogenous and solid team. I need those two elements to exist in a team that I get to meet twice a month."

'He put a lot of stock in the character and mentality of each player he chose. That's why he would not easily accept new players in the team, despite the pressure he was under. It was more like a closed club. "Yes, that's what I will create, a club. We are a family, a team; I will not bring new players into the family willy-nilly. I want to see their character, their mentality, if they have the potential to be disruptive." He would pay attention, learn everything and that was also the role of his assistant. To learn, to protect him, to protect the team itself.'

'Zagorakis was very important,' reflects Antonis Nikopolidis. 'He was the stabilising influence both on and off the pitch. There were 12 captains in that team, me, Basinas, Demis, Karagounis, Dellas, Tsiartas, many of us. But it was Zagorakis who would communicate with the president. It was a balancing act. We wouldn't judge him even when he would get angry during a game and yell at us, because we knew he had the team's interest at heart, he wasn't being selfish. So we accepted his role on the pitch and that was fundamental.

'But Zagorakis wouldn't shut down Dellas, for example, when he had something to say. He was respectful. He knew they had valuable experience from the Champions League and just wanted to help the team. But nobody, even Demis, who is a difficult guy, would give him trouble because they were aware that Zagorakis was responsible for balancing everything out. Of course the sense of security and justice fostered by the manager played a role but, at the same time, this sort of homogeneity was largely created by Zagorakis – he was instrumental. If Zagorakis had been with us in 2008, we wouldn't have had all that infighting and tension, he wouldn't have let it happen.'

It was significant that Nikopolidis' sense of perspective should come not just from the triumph of 2004, but the troubled preparations for Euro 2008. At the time, AEK and Olympiakos players were just back from the championship. AEK had lost the title due to the Valner case, an objection by Olympiakos regarding the ineligible participation of one of Apollon Kalamarias FC's players during a game that Olympiakos had lost. All that tension, in which Vasilis Gagatsis was also involved, was carried over to the national team.

Giannis Topalidis recalls: 'In 2008, the players wouldn't even speak to each other. We almost left. The manager had reached the end of his tether. I call the players to training and instead they have a fight and head back to the dressing room! It was all because of the Valner decision. Rehhagel was speechless. "It's the first time this has happened to me, to be ignored by the players. We are leaving," he said. We would have done well at Euro 2008 if it hadn't been for all the club drama.'

Zagorakis had helped filter such animosity out of the system. The captain had already made a point of associating with players from all clubs before Rehhagel's arrival, but after the new beginning he had additional responsibilities. He was responsible for helping each new member become integrated into the team. Fyssas was extremely popular and was often the link between groups. Dabizas and Vryzas would bring close groups of players that they had played with before they had moved abroad. Venetidis, Georgiadis and Kafes were low profile types and were liked by most.

Nikolaidis and Zagorakis belonged to the same group as Nikopolidis, Basinas, Karagounis and Fyssas. Giannakopoulos and Nikolaidis were more extrovert and friendly, compared to their pre-Rehhagel time with the national team. Lakis, Karagounis, Venetidis, Kafes, Dellas, Seitaridis and Charisteas, who had played together in the youth team, were on more than good terms with each other. Like that, with neither the manager nor the players having to try too hard, the group gained in solidarity. They developed into a team, which fed on and gained strength through positive results.

Giorgos Papalanis who observed the group closely, states: 'They were good boys, of good character. Dellas had a forceful personality and his opinion was respected. Demis and Tsiartas, too. Karagounis helped Topalidis feel more secure. All managers have insecurities: it's the nature of the position. Karagounis played a major role in that. I saw another very intense personality during the Euros, Basinas. Seitaridis, Kapsis; they were all very decent guys.

'None of the substitutes would complain, or at least they didn't show their disappointment. They were all on good terms. The leaders? Whatever Nikolaidis said mattered. Nikopolidis was always calm, his opinion counted. Zagorakis was not originally part of the starting line-up but he went on to establish himself not only as a player but also as the accepted captain. Fyssas would calm the team down. He was a good mimic and helped them unwind. Chalkias was a quiet man, like Georgiadis. Giannakopoulos, Venetidis and Vryzas were also very nice people. There came a time when they all became a single group of friends.'

Vasilis Gagatsis offers his own analysis: 'Zagorakis was a thinker, he made good decisions. Nikopolidis, too. Dellas was a character. He had a quiet strength. Basinas was instrumental when it came to managing a game. Karagounis was crazy as usual. Fyssas was the team mimic. Kapsis was really quiet. Katsouranis was the most intelligent Greek player. There were some commanding personalities. Demis was important because, while not in the starting line-up during the Euros, he behaved impeccably. He was a big name, had been in the starting line-up in the qualifying stage, hats off to him for his conduct. I won't say the same for Tsiartas.'

One of Rehhagel's mantras every time he is called upon to analyse the miracle of Euro 2004 is 'we were lucky we had good generations of Greek footballers at our disposal'. The older generation, the Men, were ready to change their mind-set about the team because they were tired of taking part in failed attempts to qualify. They were aware of the fact that this could be their last chance. Then there was the younger generation, the members of the youth team who went on to the senior team. They were more advanced compared to the older players who had gone to the senior team straight from the under-21 team.

Kostas Katsouranis explains: 'Guys who belonged to my generation, who were incorporated with the older players, made a larger contribution than the one they assumed we would make. They didn't expect to gain so much from us. That didn't used to happen. Me, Seitaridis, Charisteas and Dimitris Papadopoulos, all born between 1979 and 1981, had been playing in the youth team. Charisteas came up really early, as did Patsatzoglou and Kirgiakos, who didn't play in the Euros due to injuries. We had a lot of confidence and no risk awareness.

'We had grown up differently. We had demystified the foreign players. Seitaridis and I played in the Champions League. Charisteas and Papadopoulos played overseas. We had been exposed to different things. We had already faced some of the great players we would go on to play against with the national team. Giourkas and I had a different mind-set. Everyone realised that we would help the team immediately. Dellas, Nikopolidis, Zagorakis, Nikolaidis, everybody. The game in Spain was my first game in the starting line-up but the rest weren't worried about that. AEK and Panathinaikos had been very competitive in Europe and their players formed the basis of the national team. It was very serendipitous.'

Giorgos Karagounis recalls: 'It was good for us that we went to Germany and spent some time with each other for a week before the game in Northern Ireland. We bonded, we came closer and then went out and won a key game.' He is backed up by Antonis Nikopolidis: 'The days before the game in Northern Ireland, the bonds between us grew stronger, we came closer to protect what we had. We believed that we could get to the final stage, we wanted to get there. We had the motivation and the solidarity, we started getting closer.

'I always kept apart. I have always been like that. But I didn't think it was wrong for four or five players to hang out in a room and spend more time together. Such things never bothered me. They would have only if I had started to see them affect our behaviour on the pitch. These guys liked each other, they were younger, they spent time outside the team as well. I never thought it was a clique. They used to think like that in the past. That had been the mentality before and it had been one of the biggest problems with the team. We, the older players, accepted these relationships. If you accepted that it was simply friendship it didn't bother you. These bonds started becoming stronger in Northern Ireland. It was natural that each time we were vindicated by the result, like after Spain when we started having first place in our sights, we came closer together.'

At one of his greatest moments, the evening of the victory against France at Euro 2004, Rehhagel summed up his method regarding the team's trademark solidarity during the tournament. He did it in a single sentence when answering a question for the *Frankfurter Allgemeine Zeitung*: 'I explained to the players that inter-club rivalries have nothing to offer the national team.'

In Zaragoza, Rehhagel gave his players an early indication of the strategy they would follow during the final stage of Euro 2004. His game plan for the match against Spain was, as has been proven subsequently, a platform for the fundamentals which created European champions. Only he didn't know the potency of the plan when it was unveiled. It was only during the game that he discovered the recipe for success.

'We identified Spain's key players,' explains Giannis Topalidis. 'In our view, those were the forwards, so we tried to block Raul. Kapsis was the one who took over that role.' Michalis Kapsis, tried for the first time in that match, in La Romareda, had impressed Rehhagel in an epic 3-3 Champions League draw between AEK and Real Madrid at the New Philadelfia stadium. As Gagatsis recalls, the German manager had not been convinced until then: 'I would say, "my man, we have an amazing centre-half at AEK, Kapsis", and he would reply, "OK, it doesn't matter". He didn't pay attention. But when he saw how effective he was against Raul, Figo, Morientes, Zidane, Guti etc, Rehhagel finally did pay attention.'

Kapsis was lacking one of the fundamental characteristics of the 'controlled offensive', Rehhagel's concept of the profile of his team. He was too short for a centre-half. But he went on to check him out in the away game in Madrid as well. AEK managed to get a 2-2 draw in the Bernabeu, where Kapsis performed very well against the Brazilian Ronaldo. Convinced by AEK's performances during the group stage of the Champions League, Rehhagel called him up for the first time for the game against Northern Ireland.

He kept him out of the starting line-up in Belfast, but threw him in at the deep end in Zaragoza. A debut in such a pivotal match was a test of nerve, durability and character. Kapsis, however, was 30 at the time. He had been playing for AEK for five years and had been ready for some time. He quickly developed into Rehhagel's principal weapon when it came to countering the opponent's centre-forward.

'Michalis didn't expect to be called up,' remembers Kostas Katsouranis, who had also been selected for the same game. He explains: 'He trusted him after he saw AEK play so he started him off right away. Rehhagel could read footballers. He had noticed that he was the best when it came to man-to-man defence in Greece. He would watch your game, read it and realise if and where your attributes matched what he had in mind for the team and his own game plan. He visualised Dellas as a sweeper and Kapsis on man-to-man. He saw what he wanted to do.'

Kapsis, with the disarming truthfulness that is his trademark, talks about his experience in a way that is instructive and which also corroborates Katsouranis' account: 'I interrupted my holidays because of the invitation to join the team, which came about a result of Paraskevas Antzas' injury. I was under the impression that I would simply be there as a placeholder. We went to Spain and during training Rehhagel and Topalidis wouldn't pay much attention to me. Nothing happened to show that I would be starting in the game, no one attempted to encourage me or assess my psychological condition.

'The evening before the game Theo Zagorakis passed by my room. We played together at AEK. He was captain of the national team, and wanted to see how I was. "Are you ready, big guy?" he asked. I answered "Yes, why?" "Because you never know with the German. He's nuts, he could play you. Expect everything," he said and I laughed.

'An hour and a half before we left the hotel for the game, we get together for the manager to talk to us. He draws ten circles with the name of each player and he has left one blank, next to Raul. Suddenly he says "Kapsis". Everyone was giving me looks. I was looking back at them. Then he says very off-handly, "I saw you during the games with AEK. You played very well. Well done. Do the same today." Nothing else. No one-to-one meetings, nothing. I was given some advice later by the other guys.'

Rehhagel's emotional intelligence had led him to the correct assessment that he was a player with a special kind of mind-set. Not only did he not appreciate long talks, but it helped and relaxed him when the manager showed him trust and then left him alone: 'Maybe that was good for me, showed that he put faith in me. It had crossed my mind that he wanted to use me against Raul in order to embarrass me. I was doing well in Europe with AEK but he wouldn't call me up, despite pressure by the media. I didn't know him yet, so it crossed my mind that he would do that. But it wasn't like that.

'After the game against Spain, the press asked about me and he said, "He stuck on Raul like a stamp." Four days later, we would be facing Ukraine and they expected him to play me against Shevchenko. He announced it on the eve of the game, during training, "I want you to play opposite Shevchenko, like you did with Raul." No meetings, no directions. No further requirements he may have had regarding marking him.' Kapsis became a fixture in the team without ever receiving special directions from his manager.

'Rehhagel realised, based on my behaviour, that I was introverted. I just wanted to spend time by myself. I didn't want to go down to the lounge for chit-chat. I just wanted to go to training, then dinner and then back to my room. He had realised that helped me so he would leave me be. I knew that he had confidence in me. He didn't want to press me. We still have the same relationship, 15 years later; it's like "hello, how are you?" Nothing else. He still views us as his team and he behaves in the same way.'

Topalidis explains: 'Strategy is the set of conditions that you determine before you go on the pitch. We will play offensively or defensively, I will cover left or right. For the game in Zaragoza, the original strategy was to play defensively and keep worrying the opponent with quick counter-attacks. We put our faith in Tsiartas' long balls. Otto showed me the line-up and I told him I found it more attack-minded. He said that, yes, he wanted to play more offensively because if they laid siege on our defence from the beginning, we would definitely concede a goal.'

Traianos Dellas still sighs at the memory of the pressure the team had been under for the first 30 minutes: 'The game starts and the Spanish are killing us. As the game progressed, they created many chances, so the manager reconsidered.' Topalidis remembers: '"We need to pay attention to the defence," he said, and we agreed, so we made the changes.' Thirty-five minutes into the game Rehhagel substituted Lakis for Charisteas, whose selflessness was not immediately apparent to outsiders.

'In Spain, he had me play while I was running a 38.5 degree temperature,' Charisteas admits. 'He knew it but he said he wanted to play me. The guys were urging me to ask him to have me replaced but he was aware of it and had asked "for 20 minutes at least". And you never said no to him. If you did, you lost your place on the team.'

This was an absolute condition of Rehhagel's, which carried the ultimate penalty, expulsion from the team. He needed to feel that his team consisted of players with blind confidence in his plan, and blind obedience to his orders. As Antonis Nikopolidis confirms: 'If Rehhagel asked you to change positions you had to obey. If you didn't play as well in a different position he would blame himself, not the player. That was up to the player to realise. He wouldn't explain that, he would show it with his behaviour and decisions. It fell to you to process and realise it.

'If you said "No, I won't play there," you lost him. He would cross you out. This is what happened to Tavlaridis, who refused to play in a different position during the Confederations Cup. He never called him up again. When he made the choice to put you in a different position, he would take responsibility. "I am placing you there. It's my responsibility not yours," was his principle, which is why he didn't put up with refusals. He wanted players that trusted him implicitly. "Don't worry about anything, I'm there for you and I am above all of you." You realised that, and you never said no.'

Kostas Katsouranis was also aware of the need for compliance and versatility: 'There were times when he would ask a wide midfielder to play as a right wing-back and if they said no, he would never call them back. That was the rule, even if you'd never played in that position before. He would test you to see if you were ready to sacrifice for the team. He looked for players who would play in multiple positions. It was on his mind.'

In Spain, he also tested Stelios Giannakopoulos, using him on the left instead of the right side of the attack. 'Those inspirations were part and parcel of his tactics during a game,' explains Stelios Venetidis. 'He would read the opponent, see what their advantages were compared to ours. Then he would choose to play around with the players' individual attributes and not with the formation. He wouldn't explain what our or the opponent's problem was, or what we had to do. He would look at the players' attributes, what their strengths were or what side they play better. And he played around with that. The case of Giannakopoulos in Zaragoza is a typical example.

'He had already mentioned his thoughts, so we go to Spain and there, during training, Stelios cut inside and finished the move. Rehhagel told him, "You will do that during the game, too." We were together in the room with Stelios, figuring out how to play on the left, me further back and him in the front. That had been the manager's inspiration. He would use Charisteas wide in some games because we needed someone who could run. It was educational. You had to be brave, to experiment. Angelos was a typical forward. We didn't believe that he could shine in the Euros by playing wide, helping out both in defence and attack. We didn't expect a forward to display the attributes of a midfielder. But Rehhagel did. He was looking for that, which is why he urged you to try. That's how he played, with individual attributes, with inspirations.'

Topalidis' face still shines with admiration towards his manager today: '"Stelios, play there, on the left and then cut inside towards the centre and shoot with your right foot," he said during a meeting with Giannakopoulos. He believed that Salgado, the Spanish right-back, had difficulty marking with his left. Stelios had his reservations but he didn't refuse and it worked out for Rehhagel.'

The band of brothers were in business.

Chapter Seven

Lieutenant Topalidis

OTTO REHHAGEL blindly trusted first impressions and relied on his emotional intelligence. Everything was seen through the prism of his thoughtful, penetrating character. In the words of Stelios Venetidis, a player he admired for his solidity and solidarity, 'Rehhagel was aware. That was his gift.'

Venetidis extends the thought: 'His method was "hold on to the result and restrict the opponent if I can". That's where his head was. That's why he used me as a midfielder during the Euro final, to restrict the opponent. He would continuously think about "who am I going to use and for what". All the things that seemed random to us, like using Kapsis and Katsouranis and the changes for the game in Spain were the inspiration, his gift of awareness. He was perceptive. He read personalities and processed images. He would talk to the guys, come down to the hotel lounge to communicate with them. He wouldn't hear what you said, he watched you. He was assessing your condition.'

Any manager must have complete faith in his assistant. He had sensed the fit with Giannis Topalides from their introductory meeting in Berlin, even with his natural caution. They would work together in 106 matches for Greece: it was an occasionally complicated relationship founded on professional respect and an acceptance of order.

'What I admired in Rehhagel was that he knew football,' reflects Topalidis. 'He had an eye for the game. A very shrewd manager. When we talked I would express my opinion but I would always defer to him because I bowed to his experience. When the draw for Euro 2004 took place, he said to me, "It is not such an easy group. We might make second place."

'In the beginning, when he was having difficulties with the team, he kept thinking about returning to Germany. We hadn't started well, and he said "I shouldn't have come to Greece. Language is my greatest weapon and I cannot communicate here." But when we started doing well, he started being more confident about our working together. He is a difficult man. It takes skill to be with him.'

Rehhagel was very honest about that. He had always considered that his greatest asset as a coach was his skill in communicating with players. It was the basis of his philosophy and method: 'I live and work because of my language. I want to speak the same language with my players and communicate with them directly,' he would state when he worked in Germany and the press asked why he didn't move abroad. Ultimately, results overrode everything, including his reservations about the language barrier.

'He never said that he had been considering learning Greek,' Topalidis explains. 'He would ask me to write a few words. We pulled off something clever too: he learned the national anthem. When ERT [Greek State Television] came to do a feature with him in Germany, he sang it and it went down very well in Greece. The people felt closer to him. He didn't consider taking lessons. He was old and had grown comfortable with me. If anything went wrong, he could blame it on me, and my interpreting. This worked for him, everything went well. He had a nice life with Greece.'

Rehhagel told his biographer, Norbert Kuntze, 'I was always of the opinion that one has to speak the players' language in order to communicate correctly with them. But there is a lot that one can achieve with one's personality and expression, and a good interpreter, of course.' Topalidis was his human shield and, inevitably, came under heavy fire. The manager's enemies used criticism of his assistant as a weapon against him.

'They would accuse me of not translating correctly,' Topalidis recalls. 'I never withheld or altered anything he said. I just said it in my own words. I wasn't an interpreter, as such. I did that because he entrusted me with it and I was aware of the obligation to do right by him. Plus, it was in my interest to do it properly. In the beginning, I was responsible for interpreting for the players but after a couple of months he wanted me to be responsible for communicating with the media as well. He didn't want to have more people around him.'

That preference for a small, trusted team with proven self-reliance was maintained until the 2010 World Cup, the only finals of his career. There he had an additional staff member, Takis Fyssas, who had taken over the position of technical director on his retirement as a player. Just before he left for South Africa, Rehhagel explained his rationale in an interview with Weser Kurier: 'I always tell my close colleagues, we will never have talks in public spaces and we will never publicise our discussions. The media will always seek to learn what we talk about. But my experience has proven me right in my decision to keep my staff as small as possible.'

Fyssas recalls: 'We didn't have the know-how or the organisation. We had a two-person staff. He didn't want to work with many people and his logic was, "I achieved the impossible and made you a team and I did it with only one other person, Topalidis, whom I trust. I don't need more people." It was difficult for him to trust people. When I took over as technical director I wanted to increase the staff and told him how I wanted to do it. "You are the coach, I am a former footballer of yours and I have some ideas. I want a trainer, a goalkeeper coach." It was very hard to do that. He only trusted me because he considered me as one of his people.'

Even though he had accepted Fyssas, when Rehhagel left Greece following the tournament, he thought his decision to extend his staff had been a mistake. Topalidis recalls: 'When we left the national team he would say, "It's your fault. You wanted more people. Everything was better when it was just the two of us." He didn't trust people easily. But I had gotten tired of doing ten different things at the same time. Translation, training, schedules, scouting, everything.'

His versatility was noticed and valued by the players, as Katsouranis acknowledges: 'He was a trainer. He did the warm-up. He would analyse the opponents. He was assistant to the manager. Along with Papalanis, he did everything at the same time. He was prepared to argue with the manager, as any assistant should. He put forward his opinion. It was like having two coaches sometimes.'

Fyssas understood his influence: 'Topalidis, with his skills and his good fortune, just went for it. He managed to be close to the players and encourage them. He conveyed really positive things. He was the trainer: he had played as a right-back. He was the manager's eyes and ears. He never badmouthed anyone or caused any intrigue. Hats off to him for that. There were many things that were going on that he never shared.'

Topalidis' greatest service to the national team was his determination to act as a filter between the manager and the players. He was very selective about the information that he passed on to Rehhagel about the prevailing situation in Greek football or in the dressing room.

'The players didn't understand Rehhagel, they understood me,' he explains. 'I had to be careful about how to translate and convey what he said. When he said something hard, I had to watch how I would say it. I would phrase it more carefully. At the same time, I protected the players. I never sold any of them to the manager.' Charisteas observed, in an interview with *Kicker*, that 'Topalidis would sugar-coat Rehhagel's words.' The assistant smiles in response: 'I simply knew what the Greeks are like.'

Charisteas expands his point: 'Topalidis was shrewd. He knew how to manage the situation, how to soften the manager's words. He wouldn't say everything. Sometimes Rehhagel would say words that could offend a player but Topalidis would soften it and the player wouldn't take it wrongly. The thing with me was that I understood and it would bother me when the manager called me out. But I couldn't explain to the rest why I was bothered by words that hadn't seemed hard to them in translation.'

Topalidis knew his brief: 'Otto's biggest issue with communication was language so he didn't come into contact with the media. He would ask me to speak to the press, and I did as I was told. I never told them what they wanted to find out. I never gave out any information, so they got angry. But I wasn't the top man. I couldn't speak on his behalf. I didn't have the right to speak about things. I also didn't tell him all that the press wrote about him in Greece. When he called and asked me how things were, I would say "All good, coach", so he remained calm. The bad thing was that some of things that were being written in Greece would be picked up by the German press, so he read them there – and some of it was offensive.'

Rehhagel had never been a media darling in Germany, and in Greece the search for popularity bothered him even less. Giorgos Karagounis remembers: 'Before the play-off against Ukraine for 2010 World Cup qualification he was the object of severe, levelling criticism. As captain, I would say, "Go say something too. They are eviscerating you." He would reply, "That's not important. What's important is how we're going to score goals without conceding any. Journalists cannot save goals and they cannot score them." He had said everything in that one sentence, how we have to think and act in relation to the media.'

Topalidis considers Rehhagel's decision to live away from Greece beneficial: 'He spent most of the time in Germany and that turned out to be great. It's a good thing that he didn't make any friends in Greece. They would have been filling his head with nonsense. It had often been the case that random people or even football people would stop him and ask me to translate utter nonsense. So he would call and I would say "all well" and he would be fine. I always said that we shouldn't "fill his head with stuff". We went to Xanthi once and a football person who used to work in Germany comes up to him and says, "You made a big mistake coming to Greece!" These things would affect him.

'He would say, "You know what you have to do and if there are any problems you'll say Rehhagel told me so." So I did what I thought was right, which made me unpopular with the EPO, even though I was only acting according to his directions. But internally, many were jealous of the success.'

Fans were more direct, as Topalidis discovered when asked to join Rehhagel on a stroll around the Kolonaki district of Athens before qualifying results improved: 'When the team wasn't doing well and he asked me to join him for coffee in Kolonaki, I didn't want to go because people would curse and call him a "tourist" and other derogatory terms. They would yell at him. It put me in a difficult position. He would ask what they were saying and I told him, "Oh, complaining about the results, don't pay attention." I mean, what else could I say?'

Giorgos Papalanis tagged along to offer moral support, but knew he wasn't needed after the win in Spain: 'That's when they started going to Kolonaki again,' he says with a smile. 'After that victory, they didn't need me to escort them. They had become famous. People wouldn't take their money anywhere. The same people that had believed the manager to be a disgrace, would suddenly buy him coffee.'

Topalidis was a true disciple. He was associated with a famous German manager, attached to the Greek national team, and living the dream. He was desperate to succeed for various reasons, professional, financial, family, and romantic. Like his mentor, Topalidis was a self-taught assistant. Through his choices and behaviour, he managed to please everyone – the players, the administration, his collaborators – and make his teacher happy:

'Some time after the start of our collaboration, Rehhagel told me, "We were lucky to get you. It was a good thing that Wolfgang called me and I set up an appointment to meet you." I admired him from the start, so I didn't even consider doing anything other than what he wanted. Sometimes I would say, "The newspapers are writing about such and such a player, how about we call him to have them on our side?" He wouldn't give in.

'He would tell me, "I am not going to select anyone just to satisfy whoever. Who am I going to use, someone the people want or someone that I want?" He felt very strongly about that and who was I to doubt him? He had won three championships and had finished runner-up seven times in the Bundesliga. He had done it with small teams in small German towns. Beyond all else, I admired him, and I still do, because when he started his career he suffered a heavy 12-2 defeat and he still managed to recover and have a great career. Anybody else would have crawled away and holed up at home forever after something like that.'

That defeat, by Borussia Monchengladbach in Dusseldorf's Rheinstadion, took place during Rehhagel's eighth year as a coach, towards the end of his second year with Borussia Dortmund. It was the final game of the season, and Gladbach had to inflate their goal difference if they were to overhaul Cologne. Jupp Heynckes scored five of their 12 goals. Rehhagel was sacked the following day, when he also had to appear in front of the prosecutor, investigating if the result had been 'clean'. The case was quickly closed and the Dortmund footballers cleared, but Rehhagel had to live with the nickname 'Torhagel' (Goal Hailstorm).

Topalidis was encouraged by the Greek players' response to Rehhagel: 'He had his players' full respect right from the start. After a while, the players started to see what he was talking about. His orders and decisions were bringing results. Because he loved and respected them, which they were able to see for themselves, their relationship was great.'

Yet, according to Papalanis, the assistant deserved his share of the credit: 'Topalidis played a very important role in building the relationship between Rehhagel and the players. He got that Karagounis was crazy. He was fair with everyone and brought them close to the manager. He would update Rehhagel fully about each player. When Otto was away, Topalidis would do all the work, so he was committed. He wanted to prove himself. He was also lucky to work with me and not someone who would have taken advantage of him. At the time when Rehhagel was only here three times a month, Topalidis was going through many personal problems and I was right there to support him.

'I've never seen a better assistant to a manager. Rehhagel was a very good coach but he didn't have a Greek mentality. His was more Teutonic, which is why he couldn't have a career here by himself. So Topalidis deserves an Oscar as an assistant. If it hadn't been for him Rehhagel wouldn't have remained, he would have abandoned us long before the Euros. Topalidis was very honest towards Rehhagel. He spoke to him on the phone ten times a day in order to keep him up to date about everything, to help him make decisions and intervene whenever he saw fit.

'Neither the players nor Rehhagel would have kept on anyone unsuited to the task. That's easy for everyone to understand. Topalidis, however, went above and beyond in order to promote that model and make it work. Rehhagel would tell a player "Why don't you go smash rocks, you're not suited for this," and Topalidis would paraphrase. He would be attacked by the press about his translations and yes, Topalidis did paraphrase right from the start in order to protect him.

'If you asked me who was more responsible for that achievement, I would say Rehhagel first and then Topalidis. Giannis worried about Rehhagel constantly. Rehhagel would lose it when things didn't go his way. I saw him come close to losing it and smashing the place up at least five times. But everything was always great between them. It bothered Rehhagel when he heard Topalidis being referred to as an "interpreter". He considered him his assistant, his partner, and that's how he treated him.'

Peter Hess, a German journalist for the *Frankfurter Allgemeine Zeitung,* was on good terms with Rehhagel, and said it all about Topalidis, in a sentence that he most probably took from his interlocutor. He wrote on 16 June 2004, the day Greece had drawn 1-1 with Spain in Porto: 'The fact that Rehhagel's principles can be rendered from German to Greek is down to Giannis Topalidis. A Greek who grew up in Germany and studied at the University of Cologne, he acts as assistant to the manager but, above all, as a sympathetic interpreter. He has even adopted his boss's body language. Their relationship is the framework for the success of the Greek national team.'

'Was your colleague what you expected when you were looking for an interpreter?' I asked Rehhagel. 'Careful, I want you to translate correctly,' he told Topalidis who was there with us. 'He was very important to me. I convinced him and then we convinced the team together. He was very important because of the language, but also very important to me in general. Giannis is a Greek. The Greeks invented democracy. It is not easy to assert yourself in Greece because the Greeks know everything.'

Rehhagel was clear-headed and decisive under competitive pressure. He shaped that pivotal win against Spain in Zaragoza as early as the 37th minute, when, two minutes after the first substitution, he made a second change, substituting Karagounis for Tsiartas. This changed the whole aspect of the game. Vasilis Gagatsis, the federation figurehead, was hugely impressed: 'That's when I realised that this manager didn't care about reputations, fans, the press, criticism, nothing. I said, "This man doesn't even care about God himself!"'

Nikos Dabizas recognised the strength of leadership: 'He identified the issue, balanced the plan and we relaxed. That is the lesson here. The original plan didn't work, and yes, I do have strong ideas about how the game is supposed to start. But I cannot be dogmatic about it or selfish to the point where I can see disaster looming and still insist that I have read the game correctly. His adaptability and perceptive ability were among his strong traits. He would go ahead and prove that he was strong but if circumstances demanded it, he could adapt. That was a major lesson.'

Kostas Katsouranis recalls: 'Things were tough during the first 20 minutes in Zaragoza. We were lucky to not concede a goal. That's when the coach showed that he had character, when he made two substitutions fairly early. It is not easy for a coach to do that, but the substitutions worked. Karagounis was fearless and the great thing about him was that he conveyed this audacity to the rest of the team. He would say, "Come on, I've played them before. Don't be scared, that guy is nothing, if I can pass him so can you." His enthusiasm and faith were infectious. Stelios' goal had worked in training and the coach had stopped us and said, "You'll do that tomorrow, too." Not that we worked on it, it just happened so he told him to try it again during the game. He was like that. He would see certain moves in training so he would ask us to try them in the matches.'

Gagatsis was coming to terms with the man he had employed: 'Rehhagel was selfish and he had a big ego but he would ask me to point out his errors. Of course, he never admitted that he made an error. He would always justify his actions but he would also retain what you told him in the back of his mind.'

The end justified the means. That gives Topalidis, the trusted lieutenant, the luxury of being able to indulge his imagination today. 'What if all that hadn't worked out and we had lost 4-0, with those substitutions?' he asks. His smile tells you he knows the question is irrelevant.

- - - - - - - - - -

Spain 0 Greece 1
Tactical insight

For the match against the team with the best attack and the strongest playing resources in the group, Rehhagel chose a 5-4-1 formation with an emphasis on secure defence.

Ináki Saez, the Spanish coach, on the other hand, selected a 4-4-2 formation. Greece were numerically superior with 3 vs 2 in defence, the two teams were equal in midfield with 2 vs 2, while Spain had an extra player in

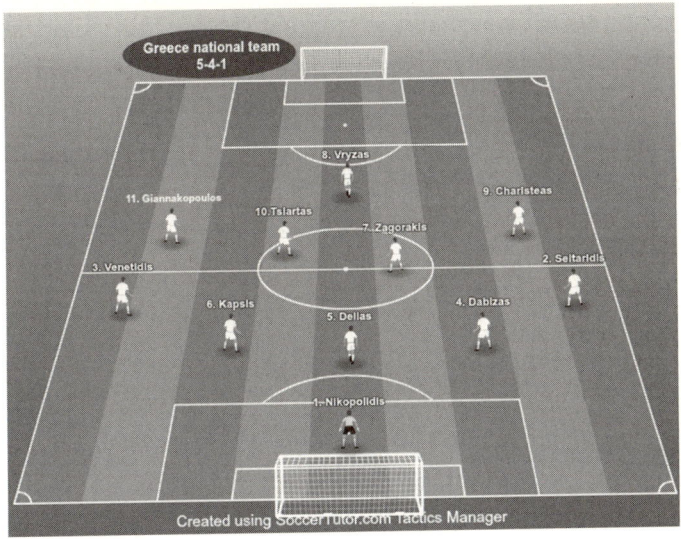

Greece vs Spain qualification stage

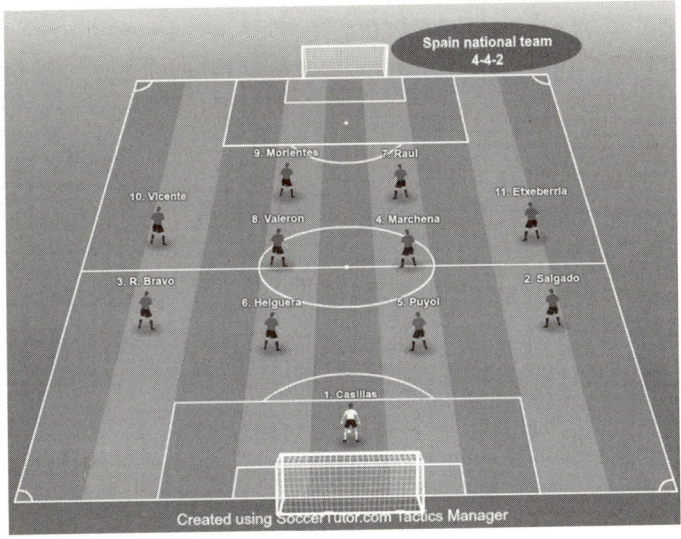

Spain line up qualification stage

their own defence with 2 on 1. On the wings, there was a 1 vs 1 balance.

Rehhagel went for a reinforced defensive line with Dellas being the extra player. The decision to play with two centre-halves was made on the grounds that their personal attributes matched those of their opponents. Thus, the faster and more explosive Kapsis was chosen to contain Raul, while Dabizas, being stronger and more capable in the air, played opposite Morientes.

In the first half Rehhagel's intention regarding Greece's defensive shape became clear immediately. The players had been instructed to mark individual opponents. Not just the centre-halves and the full-backs, but also the midfielders. The only ones who did not have a specific player to mark were Traianos Dellas, in his role as sweeper, and Zisis Vryzas who was free to pressure either Puyol or Helguera, the two Spanish centre-halves.

The area of responsibility of the Greek players was very wide, since both Kapsis and Dabizas would follow their men up into midfield. In addition, there was never a change of marking target. The two centre-halves crossed paths many times by following each other's personal opponent. In

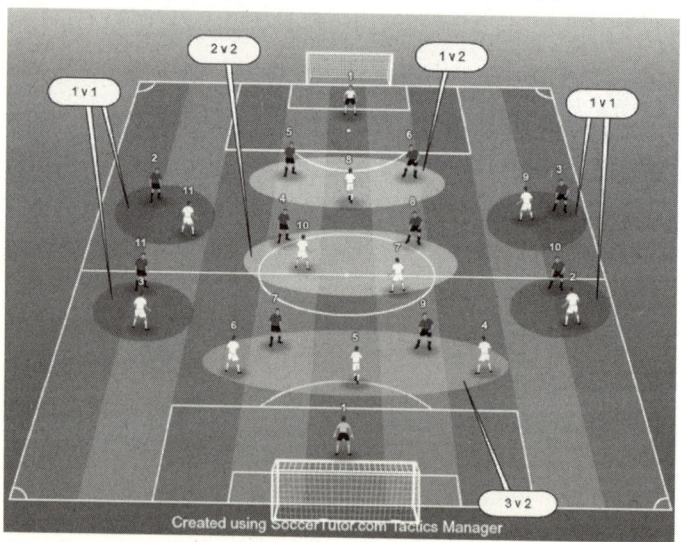

Spain vs Greece: the matchups

midfield, Zagorakis was always close to Valerón, who had a more creative role, while Tsiartas had Marchena under his supervision. On the wings, Seitaridis and Venetidis had assumed the responsibility of marking Vicente and Etxeberria respectively, whom they would follow each time they converged towards the centre and assumed midfield positions. The full-backs Raul Bravo and Salgado were shadowed by Charisteas and Giannakopoulos.

Spain started the game with the intention of scoring quickly. In the first few minutes, Etxeberria caused several problems for Venetidis with individual attempts. Fortunately for Greece, the first shots were not on target. The Spanish sought to maintain a fast pace using long balls and wall passes in order to overcome Greece's man-to-man marking. Forwards Raul and Morientes frequently changed positions, while midfielders Vicente and Etxeberria often converged in the centre to draw Seitaridis and Venetidis away from their positions and to create room for Bravo and Salgado. This tactic was effective on the left wing, as Charisteas was not consistent in his marking, resulting several times in Bravo receiving the ball and crossing into the Greek penalty area. However, the crosses were routinely dealt with by the Greek defenders.

Man-to-man marking can be an effective way for a team to defend their opponent's attacks, especially when all players carry out their responsibilities properly. But losing personal duels in facing a team with superior technical ability can create many problems. Greece, however, after the first few minutes, defended effectively. This was partly the result of good teamwork and timing between the players after lost duels, which were not that frequent in any case. In particular, when either Seitaridis or Venetidis were

Pairs of players in man to man

beaten, the nearest centre-half would challenge whoever had the ball, while Dellas would mark the other forward.

When one of the defenders lost a personal duel, sweeper Dellas would move to cover and immediately block the Spanish striker. The nearest full-back would also contribute to this, leaving their assigned player and shifting to the most immediately dangerous opponent. Lost duels, while few in number, neutralised the numerical advantage of the Greek team for a few seconds. However, as the reaction of the Greek players was immediate, Spain did not have the necessary space and time to exploit them.

Greece struggled to keep possession in attack and to lower the tempo of the match in its early stages. Their main objective was to move the ball, mostly via long passes by Tsiartas, to Vrysas or Charisteas in order for them to find an unmarked team-mate. This tactic brought results after 20 minutes, when Charisteas found Vryzas, who attempted

Dabizas leaves Morientes free and closes down Vicente, while Dellas moves to mark Morientes

Vicente wins the 1 v 1 with Seitaridis

Created using SoccerTutor.com Tactics Manager

Defenders work in synchronisation to cover the attacker

Raul wins the 1 v 1 with Kapsis

Dellas provides cover and immediately closes down Raul with the help of Venetidis

Created using SoccerTutor.com Tactics Manager

Defenders work in synchronisation covering the attacker

a shot which was blocked by Puyol. Spain continued to have the upper hand, with close to 70% ball possession, but did not become particularly dangerous. Rehhagel reacted by making his first substitutions early, in the 35th and 37th minutes. He first substituted Lakis for Charisteas, who had problems marking Raul Bravo. Two minutes later he put on Karagounis for Tsiartas, choosing Karagounis' energy and runs over the creativity of the former Seville midfielder. These changes had the desired effect. Seitaridis received some much-needed help from Lakis, making the team better able to press centrally in midfield, while Karagounis stayed close to Marchena. Moreover, the team started to move the ball more effectively and was thus better able to disrupt the pace of the home team.

Just before the end of the first half, in the 43rd minute, following a passing build-up, Venetidis found himself with the ball on the left wing and shaped for a cross. Vryzas moved behind Puyol to take position in the penalty area and Marchena followed him. Venetidis passed to Giannakopoulos however, just outside the penalty area. The Spanish midfielders were not close enough and the Greek international found himself with a clear shot on

Giannakopoulos goal

goal. Puyol failed to stop him and the ball ended up in Casillas' net.

Spain started the second half without any changes in their line-up but modified their tactics, with a view to scoring quickly in order to equalise. The first opportunity came in the 50th minute following an error by the Greek defenders who could not clear the ball following a cross by Bravo. The ball ended at Raul's feet by the penalty spot, but Kapsis and Venetidis were able to block the shot. For the next 30 minutes, the only dangerous situations for Greece came from direct free kicks. The first one was by Vicente in the 55th minute, while a second one by Del Pedro in the 61st minute was saved by Nikopolidis.

Saez made his first two substitutions on the hour mark. He took off wide midfielders Vicente and Etxeberria and put on Del Pedro and Joaquin. The Spanish coach did not change the way his team attempted to create chances tactically; he was seeking to bolster his team's energy and speed. As time passed, Greece managed to retain more possession. This was helped by the fact that most of their passes were directed at Vryzas' feet. Aided by his size, Vryzas used his body to shield the ball, allowing his team-mates to move up and support him before passing it to them.

Karagounis did an effective job in this area as he kept the ball and won free kicks, giving his team some much-needed breathing space. Saez attempted to make his team more aggressive by bringing on the more creative Sergio in Marchena's place in the 77th minute. But what really gave the hosts a bigger boost was Venetidis being sent off three minutes later. Immediately, Rehhagel instructed Giannakopoulos to fill the gap on the left-hand side of

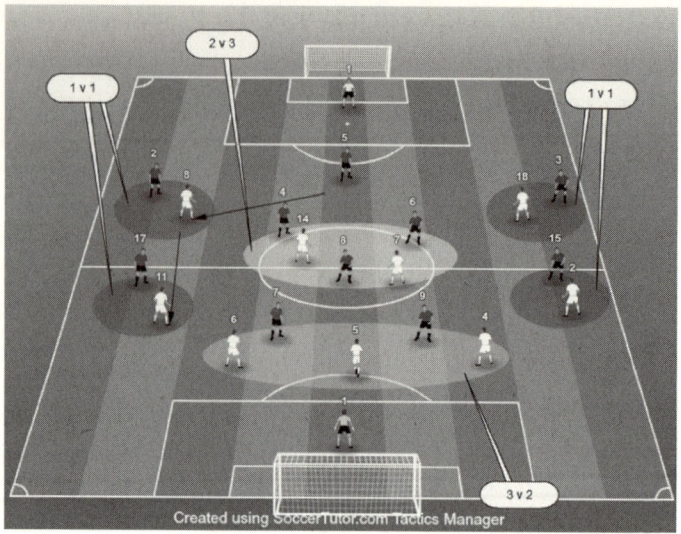

Players match up - Greece with ten men

the defence, while Vryzas moved to the left of midfield opposite Salgado. Saez responded by leaving Puyol alone in defence, moving Helguera into midfield.

In the remaining time, Spain sought to take advantage of the extra player in the centre and to pass the ball behind Zagorakis and Karagounis, to get a final pass or shot. To overcome the numerical advantage of their opponents in midfield, Karagounis and Zagorakis applied zonal defence. Moreover, the two Greek midfielders took positions closer to each other along the defensive line to limit the space that the Spanish players sought to exploit. Where the ball was passed to one of the Spaniards behind the central defence, Dellas immediately intervened to pressure and limit both the opponent's field of vision and space. After 84 minutes, despite Greece adjusting well to the situation, Sergio found room behind Zagorakis and attempted a shot from just outside the penalty area before Dellas managed to intercept him. Nikopolidis was able to parry the ball, countering the best and final chance Spain had in the second half. In the last few minutes, despite the pressure, Greece were not in danger. They even came close to scoring a second goal when Seitaridis intercepted Sergio's pass and three Greek players found themselves against two defenders. Seitaridis dribbled past Puyol, but Salgado successfully tackled him and blocked his shot.

Chapter Eight

Turning the National Team into a Club

OTTO REHHAGEL is not one of those managers who favour grand statements or empty rhetoric, so when he announced Greece's win in Spain as a 'result that is going around the world' we knew the significance of his satisfaction, and the extent of the achievement.

He still left celebrations to others: 'We achieved a historic victory, which stands high in my own career too,' he said, in the immediate aftermath of the win. 'The Greek players are not of the same calibre as the Spanish. However, tonight we can claim that we have become a team and that we can achieve great victories. But now we have to win in Ukraine next Wednesday, otherwise this win has no value.'

Giorgos Papalanis saw a man of substance at work: 'Rehhagel is not a man who is thrown off balance,' he says. 'Even when he was happy or sad he would stay calm, thinking clearly. On the bus on the way to the stadium in Zaragoza, we would keep up to date about the match between Ukraine and Armenia, which interested us. It ended 4-3.

'Armenia were leading at first. A cheer went around the bus. When Ukraine equalised we were all down. Armenia scored again, so we celebrated again until Ukraine equalised. I would go back and tell jokes to lighten the mood. I even had Kapsis laughing. The manager would encourage me in this but he would stay calm, like he had his blinds down to all this.

'He would call Beate and say, "Everything is OK, under control. We're in a great mood." Calling Beate was the last thing he did before he went on the bus and the first after entering the dressing room, no matter what the outcome of a game was.

'The miracle is what happened up to that victory against Spain. It happened without any money. After that everyone believed in the team, in Rehhagel, in the team qualifying. Until that moment, no one else had known about, understood or experienced Rehhagel's project besides Topalidis and myself. And I'm not referring to the 90 minutes that the games lasted.'

When I asked the manager to single out the game that left him most satisfied that he had done the most to help his team succeed, Rehhagel furrowed his brow and replied: 'A manager helps his team the same in every game. It's not just the 90 minutes on the pitch, what people see at first sight. It's everything all the time, every day, every minute. That's the most critical part of the project, the preparation that goes into those 90 minutes. That is a dynamic process, which progresses day by day.'

Theo Zagorakis acknowledges Rehhagel's success in fostering this mentality in his players: 'It wasn't that we didn't love the team before. But, before Rehhagel came, the team and the games ahead only worried us when we got together at the hotel. We didn't communicate with each other between matches to discuss our obligations, our games or our opponents' games. But after he came, we started thinking about the team in the meantime as well. That was Rehhagel's doing, us talking to each other about the games. We had become a team, like a club.'

What was Rehhagel's secret, in his first job as an international manager? He was a genuinely empirical and self-taught coach who came up with patterns and shapes and developed them over the course of his 30-year career. He arrived in Greece without a tried and tested formula. The idea to turn the team into a club hadn't been on his mind.

It started to form relatively quickly, when he came to the conclusion that in order to build the team, he would have to select players who played in big clubs or abroad only. He was fascinated by Panathinaikos' appearances in the 2001/02 Champions League and impressed by AEK in the following season's Champions League. He identified which players playing abroad fitted the pattern.

If he brought all those pieces together and insisted on retaining the same core, time would bring him a team. Rehhagel wanted cohesion, homogeneity, good communication on and off the pitch and healthy relationships among the players. All of these he would build on the framework of 'no second-guessing, no suspicion between players, I make all the decisions'.

'The idea to turn the team into a club by limiting his available choices came later, it wasn't there from the beginning,' Giannis Topalidis remembers. Vasilis Gagatsis, the federation president, takes up the story: 'We had a discussion. "I will take players from Panathinaikos, AEK,

Olympiakos and PAOK because these players have been exposed to European games. You tell me I should call up a player from Xanthi" – we were having this discussion about Vasilis Torosidis, who played for Xanthi then – "and I am telling you that I will only after he gains experience in Europe."

'I would read reports and talked to him about them and he would say, "I have a philosophy. I am not concerned with the smaller teams. I am building the team based on the available material. What am I to do? It's not like the best players in the world are born here for me to have more options."' The players understood.

'I remember him saying, "I saw Panathinaikos in Europe and I want their defence and whoever else suits me,"' reports Antonis Nikopolidis. 'A Greek manager couldn't do that. He was German and didn't worry about the number of players from each club. The EPO would point out that he should not overdo it with players from a single club, but he didn't care. Then the results would back him up and he could do no wrong. He would end up calling up injured players and no one would bat an eyelid.

'It wasn't a simple task to try and keep his head on the game with so many attempts to influence and sway him. They had even invited him to watch one of Olympiakos' Champions League games from President Kokkalis' suite. They had told Topalidis that there wasn't enough room for him, so that Rehhagel would have to go by himself. He refused to go and that gave him his edge, his stubbornness. He wouldn't care.'

As Giorgos Karagounis adds: 'Even his mistakes were his own mistakes, they hadn't been dictated by someone else.' Giannis Topalidis offers further context: 'In Greece everyone acted based on affiliation but Rehhagel never did, he would never go by that logic.'

In an interview with *Frankfurter Allgemeine Zeitung* before the start of Euro 2004, Rehhagel was asked about his blueprint: 'I focused on bringing together footballers from the three biggest Athens teams, who played in Europe, who had worked together before and who worked well together. Some executives told me that I had to watch the percentage of players from each team. I replied: "Gentlemen, this is not the SPD [the Social Democratic Party of Germany]."'

Antonis Nikopolidis saw consistency and purpose in his manager: 'Even later, when he selected new players, he wouldn't upset the team's balance. He was aware that we depended on psychological bonds and he didn't want to disrupt that element. This was in contrast to Claudio Ranieri, who would use whoever did well with their club at any given moment. Rehhagel placed our cohesion above all else. He would take out someone who was growing older and replace him with a younger player, so the core remained stable. It made the players feel that the manager is always there for them, protecting them.

'When there is a massive influx of new players, the rest lose their motivation because they lose that sense of security and trust. The manager invested more in that feeling of trust and fairness, in character and homogeneity than in tactics. Yes he may have been fortunate as he says, to have had good generations of players to work from, but he picked them. I used to wonder what the essential criterion was when it came to picking players. Was it talent, character, how we blend in together or a bit of everything?

'I concluded that it was everything. It was all important to him. I remember watching him eat at our table. This was one large table and not many small ones as it used to be before he took over. He would scan the table in a subtle way, to see who was sitting with whom and how they communicated with each other. He would take all that into account.'

Traianos Dellas also refers to the human element: 'Rehhagel's greatest achievement was that he elected to call up those who were more cooperative, even if they didn't seem to be in the best of condition at the time. He wasn't out to get the hottest names of the moment, which had been the case before. He didn't perceive the team as an all-star team, but as a club. He would put stock in the players' mentality and character.'

Stelios Venetidis adds: 'He turned the team into a closed club. "I cannot call up anyone who plays at a lower level on principle. I want top tier players," he would tell us during one of his speeches, when he conveyed his philosophy. That's why he wouldn't invite new players to the team easily, despite the pressure he was under.'

Theo Zagorakis speaks of trust in the group: 'After a while, relatively early, he had made his decisions regarding the squad plus or minus a couple of players. That's why we were not concerned that he didn't live in Greece. We also knew that he was constantly being kept up to date. The atmosphere in the dressing rooms was the be-all and end-all for him and ourselves. Back then, when Rehhagel brought a new player in, he would look for an excuse to say that "they don't fit in the team". He would very rarely call up someone new to the squad. It was a big achievement of his that the team operated like a club.'

Angelos Charisteas had spent time talking to Rehhagel in order to become more familiar with his way of thinking. 'Teams are built around stable players,' he reflects. 'We can't all be in top condition all the time. Otto would not be affected by that, he knew what he could take from us. He had the idea to make the team operate like a club. This wouldn't alter the character of the team. He was a clever man … we didn't realise all that until much later.

'He knew that it wouldn't do to alter the team's chemistry, its heart, which was Basinas, Karagounis and Zagorakis. This is why he would not use Zikos and Stoltidis. It's not like this is a country where everything works like clockwork, so he couldn't expect that all those changes would not affect the way the team worked. He did not want to risk stability in order to experiment.'

Nikopolidis cuts to the heart of the matter: 'The whole meaning of this fascinating story is the rationale on which the creation of the team was based. How he maintained balance within the team, how he kept a clear head despite all the pressure, how he showed trust to the players he selected and how he managed these resources. The competitive part was the icing on the cake. He included us in his plan and it didn't take much for us to do the job.'

Rehhagel told me: 'Thanks to the positive results and the success we were having, over time we were able to create a team consisting of players from all the bigger Athens clubs. Thanks to the victories all this continued to develop.' Four days after the triumph in Spain, Greece hosted Ukraine at the Leoforos Alexandras stadium. On the eve of the match, when the bus arrived at the stadium for the final training session, something happened which revealed the level of solidarity and the strength of the bonds between the players.

Giorgos Papalanis takes up the story: 'It had been a month since the showdown in Rizoupolis, when Panathinaikos had lost the title. Panathinaikos players had been chased by their own fans afterwards. So we arrive at Panathinaikos' home stadium for training. The bus alights right outside the dressing room entrance and I am the first to disembark. That's when I see 50 Panathinaikos fans moving towards us in a threatening manner. I almost burst into tears.

'As soon as the players realise what's happening, Dellas moves first. He pushes me to the side and all the players line up behind him, no exceptions. They were ready to jump the fans. If you only saw Dellas' expression and body language, you'd realise that. The fans backed away. There was no police presence but after that the manager insisted that we be escorted by police on motorbikes. The fans were not driven away by the police. It was the look on the players' faces that did it. The team was bonding, so much so that the players were ready to get into a fight with the fans to support their team-mates who played for Panathinaikos.'

Chapter Nine

Qualification

THE WHISPER was growing in volume and intensity. The word on the street was increasingly favourable. This was a team to get behind. Slowly, the Greek public was starting to believe. More than 15,000 fans turned up at the Leoforos Alexandras stadium for the return match against Ukraine on 11 June 2003, an increase of 9,000 from the previous fixture, against Armenia the previous October.

Adversity merely emphasised the national team's renewed character. Takis Fyssas, exceptional throughout, won a penalty after 15 minutes. Giannakopoulos, the scorer in Zaragoza, took it, only to be denied by Shovkovskiy, the Ukrainian goalkeeper. The Greeks were not discouraged. They retained possession and created chances without finding a finishing touch.

At the other end Antonis Nikopolidis denied Shevchenko one-on-one and Seitaridis stopped Kalynychenko with what felt like a goal-saving tackle that led to referee Frank de Bleeckere waving away Ukranian protests. Then, with four minutes remaining, they found salvation.

Tsiartas, who had replaced Zagorakis, sent a magical cross towards substitute Angelos Charisteas. The forward, then in a key phase of his three-year stay at Werder Bremen, put the ball into the net. Greece saw out a 1-0 win, and suddenly, Rehhagel was running on to the pitch, to celebrate with his players. The goalless draw between Northern Ireland and Spain in Belfast, already confirmed, meant that Greece had taken first place in the group.

'You know what Rehhagel had done?' Charisteas asks. 'He had invited Werder technical director, Klaus Allofs and my coach Thomas Schaaf to watch the game. He had let me know before the match so I knew they would be watching me play. He had given me an additional motive. Otto paid attention to details like that. He put me on in the second half of the game against Ukraine. Tsiartas makes the cross and I jump.'

Fyssas found context: 'We had been able to build upon the victory against Spain. Those two games were milestones. With Spain tied at 0-0 and our victory against Ukraine, we are in first place and the tough games are behind us.' Nikopolidis added: 'That's when we said, "Let's finish first so that we don't play in the play-offs." In the space of ten days we were first in the group, where we had been six points behind a year before.'

Giorgos Karagounis highlighted the importance of unity: 'We had started to become very close with those two consecutive wins. Success builds morale and creates team spirit, so the celebrations after the victory against Ukraine were very fervent. That's what made us a team.'

Rehhagel's pride was mixed with pragmatism. 'My team has always been accused of failing at defining moments,' he said after the Ukraine game. 'We talked about that. I told the guys that we can win the tough games and they proved on the pitch that they are winners. After the victory against Spain, I had to bring them down. They made an exceptional appearance against Ukraine, faultless, but the goal we are dreaming of has not yet been achieved.'

Giannis Topalidis shared that sense of pride, and was aware of the mood swing behind the manager: 'We were now first, so no one could move him. The entire country was behind him. We couldn't lose first place. We had two more victories and went six games without conceding a goal in the qualifying stage.'

Morale was maintained by a 2-1 victory over Sweden in a friendly on 20 August which was the precursor to a golden finale that came in two parts. Firstly, on 6 September, Armenia were beaten in Yerevan, where a 36th-minute goal by Zisis Vryzas, following a cross by Dellas, separated the teams. Then, on 11 October, in the Alexandras stadium, they found fulfilment.

The game ended with 15,000 fans 'ole-ing' in celebration with Rehhagel's players. It had been a nervous wait, but made all the sweeter by such uncertainty. The only goal against Northern Ireland came in the 70th minute when Vryzas won a penalty, which Tsiartas coolly converted, left-footed. Greece were in their first European Championship finals for 24 years, and the nation was exultant.

The centre of Athens and all the other big cities echoed with cheers and car horns. No one knew at the time, but this was a dress rehearsal for the street celebrations that awaited in the summer of 2004. 'It is a historic day for Greek football and another landmark in my career,' Rehhagel said. 'I managed to unite players from all three great Athenian clubs under one roof and make them proud of appearing in the national team. Now we can celebrate all night.'

Even today, to his mind, what he was able to accomplish during the qualifying stage was a much tougher job than what he did in Portugal, in winning Euro 2004: 'Qualifying was much more difficult. We were more carefree in Portugal. We had nothing to lose. We were already happy and did not feel pressure. Qualifying was the hard part.'

Before lowering his raised fists in front of Mikis Theodorakis and other celebrities from the worlds of arts, politics and business who were in the stands, 'Rehaklis' coolly stated his next goal: 'We don't want to go to Portugal and be a punchbag.' At the moment of the greatest achievement of their careers, the manager was communicating to his players that they could not be complacent.

They had to aim higher. The very least they had to demand from themselves was to 'prove to the rest of Europe that they are competitive, that they didn't qualify by accident, that they are not the poor relations of the tournament'. This attitude would immediately be evident in the players' victory interviews in the dressing room of the Leoforos Alexandras stadium.

Rehhagel had not used the punchbag metaphor by accident. Boxing was the favourite example, employed during his pre-game speeches to the players, particularly before matches against theoretically superior opponents. He would put on a show, with Topalidis as his co-star. At the end of each training session he would gather the players around them and start pretending to be in a boxing match against his assistant.

'It was his favourite metaphor for a football game,' Fyssas remembers. 'If you are cornered by your opponent, you have to remain on your feet and protect yourself, defend yourself. You avoid getting hit and bide your time until you find your chance to throw a solid, technical and very strong punch that would knock out your opponent. He would really get into it, as would Topalidis, and end up throwing a punch at Topalidis. We would burst out laughing each time. In reality, while we thought that he was entertaining us, he was building our sporting mentality.'

Topalidis played the straight man: 'Otto would use the boxing example particularly in reference to stronger opponents. "You have to hit hard and move away, don't stay close and get hit." We would laugh. Rehhagel's speeches were always funny. That isn't something that every manager can do if he is not of a certain age. Otherwise he runs the risk of being misunderstood by the players. He had many such humorous examples. He had a great sense of humour.

'During training we would divide the players in two teams of roughly equivalent strength. I would mix up those we intended to be in the starting line-up so that no one knew what it would be. We would let the first two sessions be open to the public and press but the third one would be behind closed doors. He would say, "Where is everyone?" "It's a closed session," I would reply. "Why?" "So no one understands how we are going to play." He would then reply, "The way we put the teams together even we don't understand how we are going to play. How are they going to figure it out?"

'During the matches, the opposition manager would have a player start warming up, so I would go tell him, "He is preparing so-and-so, he is going to use him." Nothing. I would tell him again, "Coach, he is using so-and-so." He would just look at me and say, "Don't stress. No matter who he uses, it'll still be 11 vs 11." He used his sense of humour to get him closer to his players, though more than anything else, positive results achieved that. The victory against Spain, the six victories without conceding a goal during the qualifying stage, and the 18 months we remained undefeated were decisive, but his style definitely helped.'

'I saw a man that was real, genuine,' Nikos Dabizas remembers. He goes on to explain: 'The genuine quality of his character did not fit his expressiveness, nor the typical German stereotype. He isn't your average German. He is a very intelligent man who grew up in a very specific culture. A very special man. He wasn't afraid to ruffle his image. He could be talking about the most serious thing in the world and he would then combine it with a funny gesture. He was unique in that, very genuine. And people respond to genuine.'

Chapter Ten

King Otto

THREE DAYS after the victory against Northern Ireland which sealed the team's qualification for Euro 2004, Rehhagel met with Vasilis Gagatsis, the federation president, to discuss his new contract. Under the original one, which dated from 2001 and had been automatically renewed until the end of 2004, the German manager's annual salary was 420,000 euros after tax.

'We came to an agreement in no time,' Gagatsis boasted publicly after the meeting. The new contract called for a 40% salary increase and would end in the summer of 2006. The federation also agreed to Rehhagel's request that his assistant's contract be extended; Topalidis saw his monthly salary rise from 4,000 to 12,000 euros. 'I had no complaints whatsoever,' the president confirmed. 'I was very satisfied with Topalidis' work. He was able to strike a balance between serving the manager and the EPO and sometimes that was very demanding.'

Rehhagel's only demand regarding the automatic extension of the original contract beyond November 2003 to July 2004, was to determine the size of the bonuses for each stage of the tournament in Portugal: 'We agreed on that, and he wanted to determine one for winning the Championship too. I told him: "Are you crazy? I'm not putting that in the contract." He insisted, so I said "OK, go ahead and win the trophy and I will do whatever you ask."'

Giorgos Papalanis saw the balance of power shift: 'As soon as the team qualified, because he is such a clever man and he was in a win-win situation, Otto started to ask for a lot, many things. It was not just his own money. It was also the demands over team support, comforts, everything he imagined he needed and had trouble securing earlier. Gagatsis granted everything he asked for.

'When he realised that the EPO did not have the experience and infrastructure to put together a quality preparation for the final stage of the Euros, he asked that his agent take over that project. That's how we found ourselves in Bad Ragaz in Switzerland. It was the ideal choice for the team.' Wolfgang Fege's company, IFM, took over the preparation project and the Italian Franco Moretti became project manager.

The EPO announced that the contract had been signed on 13 November 2003. In public, Rehhagel did what he had always asked of his colleagues, and kept personal and professional considerations away from the press. He immediately 'forgot' about the situation that prevailed during the first two years, the times that he got close to leaving, the information that reached him regarding moves to have him replaced. 'It has been a pleasant two years and we want to continue together,' he stated. Summarising the reasons for his renewal of commitment, he added: 'I like Athens, my relationship with the players is very good. Success and my wife Beate are the defining factors.'

Gagatsis' statement shared the same tone: 'We wanted to extend the contract regardless of the outcome of the final game. We wanted to do it even before the game took place. We are absolutely satisfied with Rehhagel's work and we never doubted his abilities.' Papalanis, the veteran of the system, understood the dynamics: 'Rehhagel was a star, a king. The strength of the results enhanced the manager's power. When he secured qualification, he asserted himself.'

Preparations for the finals began in earnest two days after the contract was confirmed publicly. Greece played Portugal, the Euro 2004 hosts, in Aveiro, and found themselves down to ten men after half an hour when Karagounis was sent off. They remained unfazed, taking the lead two minutes into the second half following a three-man move initiated by a throw-in. Venetidis crossed, and Lakis headed in.

Portugal equalised a few minutes later with a great strike by Pauleta but Greece were able to withstand the pressure and see out a 1-1 draw. Antonis Nikopolidis, who saved a penalty by Figo in the 30th minute, remembers: 'That game was good for us. We got to see what the Portuguese were like. It was also good for our morale that we didn't lose despite heavy pressure.'

The team were in more familiar surroundings for their next game, a 2-0 win over Bulgaria at the Leoforos Alexandras stadium on 18 February 2004. Interest was gathering: Andy Roxburgh, UEFA's technical director, visited Crete for a seminar the following month, and watched them beat Switzerland in Heraklion, with a goal by Tsiartas.

Roxburgh had been given the responsibility of heading a high-powered team of eight managers, tasked with analysing the Euro 2004 finals. He was joined by Roy Hodgson, Gerard Houllier, Anghel Iordanescu, Gyorgy Mezey, Holger Osieck, Josef Venglos and Berti Vogts. At the end of a stellar Greek performance against the Swiss, Roxburgh sought out Theodore Theodoridis, who then headed the EPO's public relations department and is now general secretary of UEFA.

'That's a fantastic team Rehhagel has put together,' the Scottish coach told him. 'I wouldn't like to come across them in the Euros if I was managing another team. Good luck to those who will be facing you there.'

Rehhagel had asked Gagatsis to organise a challenging friendly during the build-up to the finals. 'How about Holland?' asked the president following communication between the Greek and Dutch federations. Rehhagel agreed. On 28 April, Greece lined up at the Philips Stadion in Eindhoven. They played very well in a goalless first half. Rehhagel made five changes at the interval; Dick Advocaat, Holland's coach, made only two. The Dutch scored three goals in 11 minutes and added a fourth in the 89th minute. The 4-0 defeat was a wake-up call for a team that had remained unbeaten for 18 months, since the loss against Ukraine in 2002.

Gagatsis remembers: 'We head back to the hotel after the game, and he asks if I was unhappy. I said, "You did that on purpose. You wanted to bring them down to earth, didn't you?" We had remained undefeated for 15 matches after all. When he said that no, that wasn't the case, I challenged him again: "But you've never made five changes at half-time [he had in fact done so once before, during a friendly against Sweden in 2003, when Greece came from a goal down to win 2-1]. Don't tell me you didn't do it on purpose."

'Again, he insisted, "No, everyone had to play." He never admitted it but I am certain. Topalidis confirmed it indirectly long after the game. The result shook them, however. After the game the players thought differently. A manager does not do that easily.'

Takis Fyssas admits: 'The defeat scared us. It was the best thing that could have happened to us. We were shaken. Things could have been different if we had not been shaken up, but I don't think the manager did it on purpose. If anything, his confidence may have suffered because of that game.' Nikos Dabizas reasons: 'It was a way for him to assess things before the tournament. What he did with the changes made absolute sense from a footballing point of view. I think the friendly with Holland was the last time I saw him so worried.'

Giorgos Karagounis comments: 'The friendly against the Dutch may have deflated us a bit. It may also have been doubly good for us because the result may have lulled the Portuguese into a false sense of security before the opening match of Euro 2004. After that game, many thought that we would suffer the same heavy defeats as the World Cup team had in 1994. Those who judged based solely on the result, and there were many, had already written us off. That score gave a false impression and it may have been deliberate on the manager's part with all those changes.'

The night before that game, five of the players had a memorable conversation. They hypothesised about winning the Euros, in a conversation which reveals how far they had come mentally, spiritually and competitively. They were evidently ready to exceed their limits in a tournament which was only six weeks away.

'On the eve of the game I got together in a hotel room with Nikolaidis, Katsouranis, Zagorakis and Vryzas,' recalls Traianos Dellas. 'We were relaxing, talking about the game against the Dutch and the importance of a good performance. Someone, I don't remember who, asked, "Guys, if we go to Portugal and win the Euros, what shall we ask for?" I said that I would like to have the White Tower of Salonica named after me so I could live there.

'Zagorakis said that he would have the Thessaloniki airport named after him, Katsouranis that he would have the Rio-Andirio bridge named after him, Nikolaidis mentioned Kifissias Avenue first and then the Acropolis. We all mentioned something outlandish that evening. We lost 4-0 the next day and were back at the hotel saying, "That's it, we drowned. We wanted the Euro, but we got four Dutch goals instead." Our mediocre performances over the last few friendly games did us good; we became worried and that kept us very sharp before we even landed in Portugal.'

Kostas Katsouranis adds: 'We may have had that conversation as a joke but it showed that we believed we would do well. By "well" we may have meant something less than the trophy. It could have been a single victory, which Greece had never been able to achieve during the final stage of any tournament in the past. We had not been specific about it, but we believed we would achieve something important. That is why we had ended up joking about what we would be asking if we won the Euros. The team believed it would do well.'

Time has given Antonis Nikopolidis perspective: 'That was the toughest moment for us during those 18 months. Despite that 4-0 defeat, however, there were no issues among us. If anything, it was good for us. It was a much-needed wake-up call because we had been on cloud nine until then. I also thought that he may have led us to that defeat. Knowing him as I do, though, I don't believe he did it on purpose, he just wanted all of the guys to have their time on the pitch. I don't think that he caused it deliberately.'

Stelios Venetidis valued that wake-up call: 'After the result against Holland we were like, "Let's not lose it. If we don't fight well, if we are not united and organised, we will be a laughing stock." We realised that it doesn't take much for us to ruin everything we have built. "We are not a superior team. We simply do what we do well." That was the message for us then. I cannot say that the manager did what he did with the substitutions on purpose, but he did bring up that game in later speeches. That shake-up kept us on our toes regarding our fundamental principles. Like Zagorakis used to always say: "If we play like this we will be humiliated."'

Greece had only participated in major tournaments twice before. The experience was so foreign the Greek media naturally identified it as a historic event. Besides Rehhagel, his number two Giannis Topalidis and the 23 players he had selected, the delegation for Portugal included Vasilis Hatziapostolou, an EPO board member and president of the technical committee. Support staff consisted of Giorgos Papalanis (team manager), Haris Christopoulos (doctor), Michalis Tsapidis (press officer), Tassos Tsougos (physiotherapist), Kostas Paravas (physiotherapist), Nikos Kalamaras (physiotherapist), Antonis Skandalis (assistant), Nikos Koromilas (assistant) and Nikos Diplas (assistant).

Just before they took off for Portugal, Rehhagel had a short but meaningful exchange with his assistant manager.

Topalidis recalls: 'Someone met us at the airport and said "tell him that you will be humiliated in Portugal. It will not be his fault but that of the players". That is the kind of stuff we had to put up with in Greece. I told Rehhagel and he said, "We know something that he does not." "And what is that?" I asked. "That we have a good team, Giannis. We know that, he does not. There is no way we will be humiliated."

'It's not like we claimed that we were going to win the trophy, but it was in the back of our minds like pretty much everyone else travelling to Portugal. Everyone has dreams like that when taking part in a major tournament. Another time, a former international player told us that we were going to be humiliated in Portugal because the Greek players were not in great physical condition. Rehhagel said, "What does that even mean? They're not lazy and they're not indifferent. How is that even possible when they do so well in Europe?"

'Rehhagel would not abide by such talk. Some believed that the team needed the support of a psychologist. He would say, "They are young guys, they do not need a psychologist or special assistance. They make a ton of money. They do not have a care in the world. It's just that there is so much money going around that everyone wants a piece of the pie."'

The team suffered their second consecutive defeat on 29 May, losing 1-0 to Poland in a friendly in Szczecin, through a 17th-minute own goal by Kapsis. The players expressed their concern over the team's performance and a series of untimely injuries.

Papalanis wrote in his diary: 'The players asked Topalidis to hire a first team coach and a goalkeeper coach. They also complained about the manager's insistence not to allow physiotherapist Christos Karvounidis back on his staff.' During the Euros, the players covered Karvounidis' travel and accommodation costs at their own expense. They put him up at a hotel opposite the one in which the team was staying. The players would visit him there at Rehhagel's sufferance.

'It must be some kind of world record being the only national team with a two-person technical staff. It's never happened before,' boasts Topalidis. The next smallest technical team at Euro 2004 numbered five. 'The manager was adamant in his decision not to hire more people. "We do not need them," he would say. When in Germany, he would point at me and say, "He is part-German, part-Greek," meaning that I was German first and foremost. He would say, "If we took on more people, what would they do that we won't?" When we had a coach, he would say, "What does he do that you wouldn't do?" He did not want more people around him because the more people there are, the more they talk.'

Nikos Dabizas, who had discussed the issue with Rehhagel, recalls: 'He wanted as few people as possible in order to be able to keep things watertight. He didn't make friends in Greece, so he could stay out of football politics. This was another reason why he created this core of players that he trusted. He wouldn't allow others into the team easily.'

Karvounidis was one of the better-known physiotherapists in Greek football. He had worked with the national team previously, and travelled to the USA World Cup in 1994. Since he had also studied at the Frankfurt University Clinic and spoke German, one would expect that Rehhagel would not oppose his inclusion in the travelling group. On top of that, he enjoyed the trust of the majority of the players in the team. Rehhagel, however, was adamant.

Papalanis recalls: 'Rehhagel had met with Karvounidis when he first came to Greece. Karvounidis knew that Rehhagel would have a private meeting with Nikolaidis in order to convince him to return to the national team. When Rehhagel came out of the room after that meeting, he was met by cameras and reporters, so he blamed Karvounidis for leaking that information to the press. He did not want him involved with the team after that.'

As the saying goes, if you come at the King, you had better not miss.

Chapter Eleven

The Protector

THE NEXT phase of preparation began on 30 May, when the team arrived at Bad Ragaz, a village of some 5,000 residents in the canton of St Gallen in Switzerland. Rehhagel had previously travelled there with Topalidis because it was his preferred spot to prepare with the German teams he had managed. He decided that the team would prepare at the Bad Ragaz Grand Resort, a five-star hotel complex with two football pitches close by.

'The players had already become accustomed to a comfortable life so they were impressed by the hotel right from the start,' Giorgos Papalanis recalls. The team manager, 51 years old at the time, was responsible for creating the team's daily schedule and ensuring that it was followed. Rehhagel relied on him to operate within established parameters and apply fundamental rules of operation. He also had the liberty to take any initiatives he believed improved the well-being and operational environment of the team.

'This was a position that did not previously exist within the EPO and it covered a wide range of responsibilities,'

Papalanis explains. 'I developed the nature of the job and its responsibilities empirically over time. Once I realised how Rehhagel wanted me to operate, we spent hours talking privately in English because I did not speak German. After that, I started planning any actions I thought enabled him, his assistant and the 23 players to perform better.

'The routine was the same for the entire 40-day duration of that magical journey. The manager would come down to breakfast and would then reappear for the team stroll. If we didn't have a video to analyse after that, they would meet up again for lunch later. They would then rest until they had to meet up again for the afternoon training session. They would finally come down again at 9pm for dinner before withdrawing to their rooms to sleep. We had been following that same schedule for three years by the time we went to Switzerland. Of course, for the support staff, this was an ongoing project. Nothing was left to chance. We made sure that everyone had what they needed when they needed it.'

Papalanis was one of those who had been inspired by Rehhagel. He would go above and beyond the call of duty because he had realised that this was his chance to stand out and succeed. Anyone who has had even the slightest experience of competitive sport can appreciate the importance and difficulty of having to support 25 people with various and pressing needs and demands. It is a deliberate, often undervalued process that often goes under the radar.

Everything from finding an HDMI cable for a footballer's gaming console to locating a dentist in the middle of the night in a foreign city goes through the team manager's hands. He needs to multi-task, because he is likely to be making the following day's travel arrangements at the same time. These may sound like details to some, but they can mean the difference between winning and losing.

'Football is show business. They are all stars,' Rehhagel would tell Papalanis, who along with Vasilis Hatziapostolou and Vasilis Gagatsis, would try to satisfy those demands at a time when the EPO did not have the financial or human resources to support such a high-level undertaking.

'I would ask our support staff not to be in the hotel lobby between 9pm and 11pm or in the morning after breakfast,' Papalanis recalls. 'Doctors, physiotherapists, and assistants all had to be in their rooms so the players could locate them if they needed anything. I wanted the lobby to be a distraction- and worry-free zone for the sake of the players, so they could unwind and relax there. That had been my idea, my initiative. The manager would disappear into his room after breakfast or dinner. He would spend hours talking to his wife, psyching himself up. He was like a star who needed constant encouragement. At the same time, Topalidis would spend hours watching videotapes of our opponents' games and analysing their game plans. He was really driven to succeed.'

Papalanis had started working at the EPO in 1967 at the age of 14, when Greece was still under a military dictatorship. 'The board of directors consisted of military officers,' he recalls. He finished night school in order to be able to work there in the mornings. Starting as an errand boy, he gained experience in a variety of positions during his time there: 'I knew that all of that would come in handy one day.'

In 1987 he left for the US, where he studied and worked as an optician. He returned seven years later in 1994: 'I got back in March and the EPO hired me on 1 May as a liaison officer. I was responsible for looking after foreign referees, beginning with those who officiated in the Champions League Final in Athens and subsequently those who would referee the Greek teams' home Champions League games. In 33 games, I counted 30 victories, two draws and one defeat. Naturally, I would come across those same referees during Euro 2004.'

At the very beginning of his relationship with Rehhagel, even before he had even met him properly, Papalanis would be approached by EPO administration members who would tell him that 'that German will drive you crazy and you will all have left within two weeks'. However, after five interviews with the manager, he had been convinced that this was the best career prospect he ever had. He was able to work with an exceptional manager and participate in a successful run to Euro 2004.

'I quickly came to realise that what I was dealing with was a lord and his assistant,' he remembers. 'I proved that I was on their side in no time. I believed that, if the team did well, I would be rewarded and would have a better career.' The pattern of their collaboration was quickly established: 'Rehhagel would arrive two or three days before each game. He would also travel occasionally for EPO events but that would be it. It was me and Topalidis who would deal with everything most of the time.'

Papalanis had been promoted to national teams and officiating director in 1997. That afforded him the opportunity to become acquainted with the Greek football scene. 'Rehhagel was very fortunate to have worked with me at a time when I was on the lookout for opportunities. I had spent my entire life in the EPO so I knew what I was getting into. At the same time, I was also fortunate that Gagatsis gave me that opportunity.'

It only took Papalanis a few months to realise that he would be working with two very honest colleagues: 'Rehhagel is a very decent man and Topalidis a very honourable guy, if a guy who was rather gun-shy at the time. Topalidis required support and training and the project demanded serious commitment for the next three years before we got to where we wanted to be.'

When it came to the politics of Greek football, Papalanis was more than forthright with Rehhagel and Topalidis. He picked sides. 'Over time I sided with Rehhagel,' he says. The result was that as Rehhagel became unpopular within Greek football and as Papalanis did not appear to be reasoning successfully with him, so did he. He admits: 'The press was merciless. The fact that I kept away those that I knew did not have the team's best interests at heart bothered people.'

The period from October 2002, after the defeat against Ukraine, to June 2003 during which Gagatsis was pressured to replace Rehhagel, was a trying one for Papalanis: 'When I started to realise that they were after him I chose to side with him. Rehhagel was lucky to have found Topalidis and myself. I could have undermined him if I had been on the opposite side but I did the opposite. I tried to persuade Gagatsis not to do anything rash. Topalidis was very protective of him too, but if he hadn't been such a good coach and didn't have such good players ...'

Papalanis' stance during those critical nine months, as well as the support he received from Gagatsis, allowed

Rehhagel's plans for the team to come to fruition. Gagatsis, at a time when he was not yet the dominant figure in Greek football, held on to his position and managed the situation without having to let go of the German manager. He could have simply removed Papalanis and forced Rehhagel to resign. 'It was mayhem. I read so many articles critical of both the coach and myself while he was in the Alps with his friends and Topalidis was in Stuttgart to see his children,' Papalanis remembers, and his face darkens.

In those three years, he had taken care to learn Rehhagel's habits, in order to make his manager's life easier and to communicate more effectively with him: 'Otto loves sweets. Topalidis was his guardian angel. When I wanted to cheer him up I would sing some Elvis Presley and Tom Jones songs and he would join right in. "Patience, step by step" was his favourite slogan. We would always have a chat during the final training session before a game and he would be really relaxed. He always watched what he ate. He would have a chat with Beate before and he would have a glass of wine.'

These are not casual reminiscences. Papalanis took careful, exhaustive notes in hotel notebooks during the team's travels. They read, alternately, like a therapy session and a management manual. Over time, Papalanis had evolved into a competitive sport support specialist: 'I lived the dream as a spectator. I didn't play but I was there and I supported it. I loved that role. If Rehhagel, who was very intuitive emotionally, had deemed me worthless, he would have kicked me out in a day.

'He is a genuine person and I lived for him. I lived for my role, to see the players smiling. I did my job to the letter. I was, or tried to be, their guardian angel. No one bothered them and I never spoke to agents or members of the press.' Rehhagel's job was to lead the team with Topalidis' assistance. Gagatsis' responsibility was to protect and support the team and Papalanis was his man on the ground.

Papalanis resigned from his post as team manager during the return flight from Portugal, following the win in the Euros. 'They had promised me a bonus which I never received. I got very angry once I realised I had been messed around with and also because I needed the money at the time, so I decided to leave,' he explains.

What had Rehhagel's reaction been to this? 'He asked Gagatsis to pay me my bonus but he wasn't very insistent. When he realised that the chemistry wasn't the same because I was still resentful about the money, he didn't press them further.' The players, aware of his contribution to the team, put pressure on the EPO president and ended up giving him money out of their own pockets after the team's return from Portugal.

Kostas Katsouranis speaks about him with respect, and admiration: 'He played his role. He would cheer us up and help build our confidence, especially the older players like Zagorakis, Tsiartas, Nikopolidis or Demis. He would tell jokes and instil faith in our ability to win. We all gave him a bonus after we won.' But political reality proved more powerful than such well-meaning generosity.

At a time when he was still justifiably insecure about his own position, Gagatsis saw Papalanis, a man he had helped create, gain in popularity among the players and become accepted by Rehhagel. He was afraid that Papalanis' opinion would carry more weight than his own when it came to the national team and that the situation would catch up with him in the future. He therefore decided to rid himself of Papalanis.

He suffered the inglorious fate of all office workers who take on extra work but are never paid any overtime.

Chapter Twelve

The Myth of 'Anti-football'

'IN THIS business there is only one truth. The ball must go into the net.'

Rehhagel's favourite motto gained increasing relevance as the tournament edged closer. He found himself in the classic dilemma of a club manager, preparing for a new season with precious little time in which to ingrain his ideas and improve his team's collective technique. He worked them intelligently in a week-long camp in Switzerland before, on 6 June the group travelled to Portugal, where they would hone preparations for their opening match, six days later.

The final phase, then, spanned a fortnight, not nearly enough time to teach his team a new game plan, given that even when a team is in top condition it takes three to four weeks of work to do so. Rehhagel, however, was clear-sighted and determined. He did not intend to change tactics; he was interested in long-term strategy. And the basis of that strategy was defence. Nikos Dabizas explains things, from a player's perspective: 'During the qualifying stage, a manager will not attempt many complex things.

The core of the team is there and he is more interested in deterrence. He believes that a goal can come out of a set piece or a player's initiative. That was his approach, defence and individual skill. Rehhagel's logic was very specific, his plan revolved around a specific formation. He knew which substitutions he would make and his patterns of play were not overly complicated.

'He was pragmatic and cynical in that he knew that, as a team, we did not have the philosophy or identity to play in a different style. Everything would be the result of someone's individual skill level. Each of us had skills in different areas. He was able to recognise that and base our playing style on that. Set pieces, a solid defensive line in a specific formation and directions on how to operate defensively. What we did in the qualifying stage was very simple and clear. He wasn't one to over-analyse and change tactics. He leaned more towards simplicity.'

During the training camp in Switzerland, Rehhagel elected to consolidate rather than change the team's playing style. 'We didn't change anything during preparation,' Dabizas explains. 'We had achieved what we wanted so we felt secure enough – both him and ourselves – to continue in the same manner. Time was too short to try new things and we were all content with what worked for us. We trusted each other and we knew that, if we stuck to what we knew there was a chance to come out of a match smiling, so we didn't try anything different.'

Stelios Venetidis, now a manager in his own right, understood: 'There are times when a player is not aware of everything his manager does. A manager's job is multifaceted. It is not just about tactics. Rehhagel did not place much emphasis on tactics but he did so much more. He gave a sense of identity to our style, even if it was more defensive in nature. That was very important because previously there had been no identity whatsoever.

'During the qualifying stage, he put a lot of stock in the result. His goal was to win so he wasn't interested in us playing great football so much as playing defensively. He paid a lot of attention to set plays, both defending them and executing them. He wasn't interested in taking risks and he wanted to instil that in us. As far as our attacking play, he didn't spend much time on tactics. He left us room for spontaneous creativity and imagination. His rationale was that, as long as the team is solid defensively, we will be able to depend on individual initiative and set plays in order to score goals.

'The important thing was not to concede any goals. When it came to our preparation, even though some of the players had been strained by injuries, we didn't spend much time on fitness training. The sessions were structured around playmaking. His aim was for the team to be combat-ready for the first few games. He counted on his experience for that, not statistics and metrics. He wanted us to have fun with the ball because his concept was that we should have freedom of movement within specific parameters established by him. He didn't want our freedom to affect the overall plan of the team.

'Our areas of responsibility were clearly delineated. If we didn't adhere to that, he would get rid of us. That was most apparent when it came to our defensive duties. We had to be aggressive, challenge the opponent. He urged us to go for the ball when they were attempting crosses into the penalty area, not turn our backs on them. If we did less than that, that was it. We had lost him.'

Angelos Charisteas amplified the respect of the group: 'Otto had a very clear idea of what each of us was capable of, so he would ask very specific things of us individually. He would tell Seitaridis that he should exploit his speed in order to get forward and shoot because he had a good shot on him. He would tell Fyssas to cross to me for a header or Zagorakis to pass the ball with Basinas and Karagounis in midfield. It was like he ran the entire game in his head. As a result, we all knew what he expected of us and that those things meshed and comprised a cohesive whole.

'What he hated, and still does, was for someone to do something completely different from what he expected of them. He would lose it then. But that happened very rarely since we all knew what we had to do, so it never got ugly with anyone. Otto was in a class of his own – and I have worked with a lot of people. He had a quality that's rare to come across. He knew how to make the most of the material that was available to him. Other managers spend hours trying to put together their starting line-up. Otto would do it almost instinctively.'

Traianos Dellas is another player-turned-manager who has been influenced by the logic of Rehhagel's actions: 'The manager would have players who work well together play close to each other. For example, he wouldn't use me and Dabizas together because he tried it and realised that we don't fit. His logic was to use pairs of players on the wings, in midfield, in the centre of our defensive line, etc. As a manager, I do that as well. I try different pairs of players during training to see who complements each other better.

'As a player I wasn't aware of it but as a manager I realised that it makes a lot of sense. Otto showed us a lot of trust. But it's not just about that, it's also about what the players do with that trust. Do they take advantage of it, are they selfish about it, do they use it effectively? Manuel Pellegrini used to say: "I show the players trust and I expect them to return it. I expect it but I don't know if I will have it." You decide whether to show trust judging by someone's character, his skill, his ambition – you take everything into account.

'Training was just "warm-up, possession drills, small-sided games". There was no real plan about our game against a specific opponent, unlike with other managers or as I do now as a manager. That may have actually been beneficial because training was never boring so it may have helped get us in top condition. Defensively, we were very solid and cohesive due to his insistence on using the same core of players but there was no offensive plan.

'Watching some of those games now and seeing how I played, as a manager, I wouldn't use myself. I don't like seeing that I simply kicked the ball long when it came my way. We followed simple directions and tactics when defending, like keeping close to each other, not leaving empty spaces, how to converge, how to send the ball forward. That's pretty much all he asked for. In terms of attack, there were no tactics. We did what we could in the circumstances. Strategy is the path you want to follow and tactics is the means you employ to achieve that. We did have a strategy and that was: "Do not concede goals and try to score at least once."'

Antonis Nikopolidis saw strength and consistency: 'His orders never changed. I knew how to play with the ball at my feet but whenever he thought I overdid it, he would point towards Charisteas or Vryzas indicating that I should try long balls towards them. He didn't like to see the goalkeeper take risks. He would shake his finger at me.

He also advised against dribbling or short passes at the back, he wanted the defenders to play towards the taller players at the front.

'This philosophy remained unchanged even when they would have a player play on the other wing because they had seen that the opponent's defender was shorter on that side. His instructions would remain the same. Pass the ball forward to Nikolaidis or Charisteas, cross the ball from the wings. That was it. No combination play. He put more stock in our defence. When attacking he was mostly interested in how we would win the ball and move it forward quickly. Our instructions were not complicated.'

Rehhagel was employing the fundamental principles of the philosophy he developed with Werder Bremen, with whom he won the Bundesliga and cup twice, three UEFA Super Cups and one UEFA Cup Winners' Cup. The *kontrollierte offensive*, the controlled offensive, as he called it, was a style which relied on players' individual physical traits. The formation would always call for a sweeper, two or three centre-halves, wide midfielders and a 'target man', meaning a forward whom the goalkeeper and the defenders would be aiming for when clearing the ball in defence.

'"Controlled offensive" was his favourite catchphrase. We heard it countless times during his speeches,' Charisteas recalls. 'He was controlled in everything that he did, training, speaking, analysing the opponent, providing instructions.' Rehhagel never paid much attention to technological aids. He relied on his eyes and brain to read and analyse a game. Even after his retirement from coaching, he insisted that football should not depend on digital technology.

In an interview with the German newspaper *Blick* in January 2017 he said: 'Football is evolving but I always say, "Don't make football a computer game." Football is the definition of unpredictability. If, for example, someone had told me before the 2016 Euro semi-final between France and Germany that Schweinsteiger would concede a handball in the penalty area causing France to win, I would have thought they were crazy! Yet there it was, a penalty for France [executed successfully by Griezmann paving the way for a 2-0 victory]. This cannot be reduced to a computerised description. People go to see football matches because they do not know what is going to happen. If you gave them a piece of paper saying "30th-minute penalty, 80th own goal", no one would ever go.'

Giannis Topalidis adds the insight of a valued assistant: 'We didn't have enough days to practise tactics, so Rehhagel would give the players instructions individually most of the time. That was on top of what we were able to try during training. He didn't want to pester them with details: "What should I say? They are international footballers. Am I going to have to tell them how to cross the ball or shoot? They know better than I do."

'So we confined ourselves to instructions regarding positioning. He would let them play fast small-sided games during training, but he would stop them and explain what he wanted if he didn't like something. He wouldn't tell Tsiartas where to shoot but he would enumerate his preferred options. Germans didn't attempt to fully control their players' movements back then.

'Rehhagel would say that, "There are a thousand different situations that can happen during a game. Who am I to foresee and explain all of them in advance? Strategy is the overall plan and tactics are how we achieve that during a game. Strategy is what is important." He would also say that "the game sets questions that you are called to answer, to react to. It is your decision." The manager would convey this responsibility to the players and would then leave them free to get on with it. The most critical thing the manager does is pick the right line-up. We wouldn't encumber them with excess information. The more we said the less they would absorb, that's what psychology teaches us, so we gave them the gist.

'Rehhagel cut his teeth by leading a very small club to victory over really big teams and in really big games. This is why he looked for players with similar experiences. He would say that Panathinaikos players were very aggressive and we later saw AEK lead Real Madrid 3-1. He put much stock in that. He knew his football so he couldn't be swayed in his decisions. He was very headstrong and he had never been proved wrong in his decisions.'

Theo Zagorakis, another self-taught manager, found it an enlightening experience: 'We didn't practise tactics during training. We worked a lot on set pieces. He started that during the qualifying stage and we kept on doing it until the final stage of the tournament. He had a plan, meaning that he knew what he wanted. He would talk to us about deployment. It was his personality that made Rehhagel a great manager. He was able to get 100% out of a player, not for his job on the field but for his character.

'Moreover, he had studied all those situations. He had experience of them, unlike us players who were not able to read everything straight away. We didn't fully understand everything that he had us practise. He would say, "You will never make risky passes at the back so that we don't concede any goals, do what you want when attacking." He knew the type of players he was working with. Our communication on the field was near perfect. That had to do with the fact that we were all passionate about football.

'We could run and we could play well. It was to his credit that he picked us. He chose some great midfielders and he drilled us at set pieces, for which we had some great takers like Tsiartas and Basinas. He was also able to convey his enthusiasm to us, which is why we learned to come to each other's assistance and sacrificed ourselves for the team. We all ran like crazy to cover for each other, which helped us defend with greater ease and precision. We left our opponents baffled.'

The Greek team's constant mobility was the talk of the European football community during the tournament. Many attempted to justify the Greek team's success by arguing that players of other national teams were exhausted because they played for bigger European clubs. Among them was French national team manager Jacques Santini. Arsene Wenger debunked that argument, however, in a statement to the *Guardian* on 4 July 2004: 'I have spoken to the French players. They deny that exhaustion had been an issue for them. They told me that they did not feel tired.'

In its report, the UEFA Development and Technical Assistance Committee touched on the issue as follows: 'What is the answer? Instead of massaging tired legs perhaps we should be working on tired minds. Which is the real issue, mental burnout or physical exhaustion? At the end of a challenging season, could it be that factors such as behaviour and motivation affect the performance of a team more than the players' fitness level? Is a new approach to preparation required in order that those teams that come from countries with intensive championships combat the phenomenon of low performance levels during big tournaments that take place at the end of the season?'

As if in reply to the above, Greek psychiatrist Anastasia Kokkali, of the 251 Greek Air Force Hospital, and neurologist Vaso Zisimopoulou, of the 251 Greek Air Force Hospital Neurology Clinic, attempted a psychological approach to the phenomenon of the Greek team's performance during Euro 2004. They wrote in an academic style, but posed the sort of questions a layman can understand:

'Was burnout, the athletes' "professional exhaustion", which has been studied in most career fields but only nominally in sports, an impediment for the rest of the teams? Could it have been that a good psychological make-up improved the performance of the Greek footballers? First of all, let's define occupational burnout syndrome. Until recently it seemed to mostly affect doctors and nurses, the kind of professionals who are in contact with human suffering. Newer data indicates burnout in athletes as well, defining it as physical/emotional exhaustion, sporting devaluation and reduced athletic accomplishment.

'Researchers looked at the relationship between optimism and burnout in 217 athletes, men and women, also monitoring the role of stress as an intermediary in the above correlation. Results showed that optimism is a powerful protective factor against stress as well as against occupational burnout syndrome. Increased performance adequacy stress levels correlate perfectly with both optimism and burnout. Both in terms of exhaustion and sport devaluation, and partly with the sense of goal attainment in sports.

'With that in mind one could assume that in 2004, some achieved their highest sporting objectives and some did not. Not because of luck but perhaps because there was a substantial difference in the psychological status between the Greek national team and their opponents. Were the Greeks more optimistic, less exhausted from the demands of the previous season, thereby experiencing less physical and psychological exhaustion, or did they have less stress, always in relation to the two previous factors?

'Nothing seems to have been accidental in terms of psychology that year, since studies in sports have shown the importance of psychological stress and tension on the one hand and optimism on the other. It is what sports and football fans correctly point out when watching a game: "It was a matter of psychology. That's what decided it." In the end, the degree by which a competitive athlete will be able to outperform his opponent in order to win is a matter of psychology.

'Speaking of psychology, we wonder if the Greek players, both on a personal level and as a team, were simply more optimistic or if there may have been additional reasons for their success. Were they more determined to win than the Portuguese, the Czechs, the French or any of the teams that have traditionally done well in European tournaments and had big names in their squads?

'According to the self-determination theory, first described in 1995 (Deci & Ryan), a person tries to satisfy three fundamental psychological needs:

i)   Competence to control the outcome and achieve mastery.

ii) The need for interaction with others and the development of inter-personal bonds.

iii) Autonomy, not in the sense of independence but of autonomous action which originates in ourselves.

'Based on the macro theory of personal determination, researchers studied the correlation between motivation, defined by a feeling of personal determination, and the competence and autonomy towards the achievement of goals. Results showed that those of the participants who displayed higher determination and confidence showed fewer signs of burnout, while those who were less determined showed signs of burnout more often. Conversely, when the athletes who took part in the study had become tired or exhausted there was a notable decrease in their response to external motivating factors.

'In practice, this means that an athlete who "wants" to win enjoys a comparable advantage over an athlete that "must" win. No one had been able to predict the performance of the Greek players during Euro 2004. It was a historic moment for Greek and European football. They thrilled their countrymen and forced the experts to wonder which factors led to their success.

'It cannot be ignored that the psychological condition of the players of a team is fundamental in achieving victory, in the sense of inner strength and determination, as well as the burnout syndrome of the team or their opponents. This is why research, carried out today, aims to improve the training programmes of competitive athletes, thereby reducing or preventing the risk of incurring burnout syndrome and maximising athletic performance levels.'

Giorgos Karagounis, in his simple and empirical way, comes to the same conclusion: 'Our psychology was good from the start. The victories that followed and the time we had at the hotel cemented it. That came out in our game. Sometimes your psychology gives you additional power and we had it. Most of us were at the right age and also in great condition. So we ended up managing situations well and played better, like when the game against Czech Republic went into extra time or in the game against France.'

Giorgos Papalanis concurs, 'At the time, the players were in love, rich, successful, healthy, insulated against distractions and problems. Their mental well-being was off the charts.'

According to Traianos Dellas, it was not that the Greek team worked harder on the pitch but that they practised Rehhagel's defensive dogma to the letter: 'They said that out opponents were more tired. It does not follow that a team that is defending works harder. I would get more tired, as a player, when I played against smaller teams. When you are in possession of the ball against a tight defence, the midfielders have to be more active in order to create space, so they all have to run around more.

'What we did was not "anti-football". We defended all along the pitch. We all operated defensively, all the way from the forwards to the back. I mean, Charisteas tackled Lizarazu right on France's goal line. We were all contributing to the team's defensive operation. That's why it looked like we were working harder.'

For Giannis Topalidis, the arguments about exhaustion are unsupported justifications: 'Two years earlier, Germany and Brazil played against each other at the final of the 2002 World Cup. Both teams featured many players that played in the Champions League. How did they get to the final? How come they were not tired that time?'

Takis Fyssas reflected: 'We didn't study tactics but the manager would spend a lot of time talking to us. He wasn't like Santos, who would drill us on tactics. Neither did he analyse things methodically, but he would take you aside and talk to you. "I want you to do this, I will need you to be there, your opposite number has such and such attributes, etc." He would hand you your part of the game plan; he did that through many individual meetings.

'I remember coming down to the lounge and seeing Rehhagel talking to one or another of the players with Topalidis. That was his method. It was inspiring and convincing in that it showed that he had prepared for the game and he helped you understand things better. During conditioning, even though we had important exercises to do, the sessions were not very organised or strict. We were coming out of a heavy season, so essentially we just did maintenance work.

'We realised that he wasn't the kind of manager who would train us in tactics and that he only had very little time to drill us in certain things. The atmosphere was great however, and we did work on things like set pieces, despite the fact that at the time, we hadn't caught on to what he intended to do. It was like that movie, *Karate Kid*, where the main character had to paint a fence and only realised why he had to do that when the time came for him to use those same moves during competition. When we played small-sides games, I was up against Seitaridis, who was the best right-back in Europe at the time. Basinas would play opposite Karagounis and Tsiartas and our defenders had to play against Charisteas. We all became better players for that.'

Chapter Thirteen

The Human Touch

IN MANY ways, Otto Rehhagel was ahead of his time, in empowering his players. Once he had made it plain with his actions that anyone who went against his principles would be left out of the team, he allowed them to fine-tune the details of how they would combine on the pitch. Such freedom encouraged them to initiate, improvise and communicate. Their application of responsibility was powerful, and effective.

Traianos Dellas laughs, in making a serious point: 'There was a very high level of communication when it came to our defensive operation.

'My own example, which became a bit of an in-joke, was that I told Seitaridis the same thing just before the start of each game: "If you have to press up high and the ball gets past you, I will cover your back. If it gets past me, close in at the back. Do not come to help me out." 'I would tell him constantly so that we got to do it automatically, but by the end I also said it for good luck. Seitaridis ended up complaining to Fyssas that I always told him the same thing!'

Antonis Nikopolidis tailored the message to his principles and experience as a goalkeeper: 'I would explain to my team-mates what I needed. I would say, "When someone cuts in from the side to get a shot in, don't open your legs. If they score it will be my responsibility if the ball passes by your leg. I allow for the angle between your leg and my position. If the ball passes between your legs, I will be out of position." I have conceded goals like that. That's the kind of very specific instructions I would give them. It helped me and it made them less stressed.'

He also applauded the inspiration of Vasilis Tsiartas in organising the placement of the Greek players at corners: 'Tsiartas would tell Dellas or Katsouranis, "Go to the near post and wait for the ball." And they did. That goal against Czech Republic came out of Tsiartas' idea that we had been practising during training.' As Tsiartas explained in an interview with *SportDay* in 2006: 'Seeing that there were enough capable tall players, during training I would ask Charisteas, Dellas, Vryzas, Katsouranis and Dabizas to go to the near post and stay there.'

Rehhagel would ask the taller players to place themselves near the far post and start their movement from there, but did allow them to experiment. His team had his consent to try almost anything in the opponent's half. The latitude he gave them was based on critical experience, rather than a maverick's whim, since he operated in a similar fashion with Kaiserslautern when they won the Bundesliga in 1998, a season after being promoted from Bundesliga 2.

Top scorer Olaf Marschall told uefa.com: 'Otto would put together the team and say: "You don't change a winning team." He would give us freedom on the pitch when we were in possession and we did the rest. Our attitude was the key. Everyone, even us forwards, would run everywhere to help defend as soon as the ball was lost.' These words seem to reflect the character, attitude and performance of the Greek national team under Rehhagel.

Giorgos Karagounis' explanation is in the same vein, but also stresses the importance of the players' skill level: 'We were tight and worked very well together, which is a difficult thing to happen in the national team. But owing to Rehhagel's insistence in selecting the same players, we had started becoming as tight as a club. There was a core of about 30 players, on and off the pitch. We knew our team-mates' styles. It is very important to be aware of your team-mates' behaviour and style with or without the ball, which is why, offensively, we played almost without thinking.

'He didn't necessarily call up players based on their performance but often a team is more than the sum of its parts. I still believe that you need to have great players for the team to work and our team did. We had players that would have been playing for huge clubs if they had been born abroad. The fact that we had good players and a good attitude was pure luck. He was a good manager, but if he hadn't been able to find players with that kind of mentality he would have ended up with players who would have put their own interests before those of the team.

'Individual instructions wouldn't change. They were the same from day one. I remember that because I played on the left in most games, he would tell me to get a long ball through to Seitaridis, who was very fast, or cut in and shoot. He would only ever give me those two instructions, no matter who the opponent was. He insisted that we had our own personalities, so we could each do things by ourselves, create something new. Offensively, he would allow us a lot of freedom. Most German managers I had seen did not work on tactics so much. That's their mentality. I remember Felix Magath at Fulham, "What do you want me to tell you about tactics? How to play football?" he would say. There's a man who had won the German league with Bayern Munich.'

Nikos Dabizas, another key influence, adds: 'I realised the importance of what he was doing over time. Now I am better able to move past the initial, superficial reading of what was happening and analyse things in depth. Yes, our tactics were simple. However, what happened in 2004 clearly showed that it wasn't tactics but other elements that made the difference with our team. Rehhagel came and filled other, more fundamental, gaps. Not that this model could work over three or five years, but it was sufficient for the team at the time. Certainly there were still things missing, but he had brought so many other elements together that he was able to strike a balance.'

During training at Bad Ragaz, Rehhagel's main goal was to strengthen the bonds between the players and capitalise on the feelgood factor created by the team's qualification for the finals. None of them knew what to expect from an event of that magnitude, so he understood the importance of cultivating the collective spirit developed during the team-building process.

'Greek players are individualist by nature,' Rehhagel reflected in the final phase of preparation. 'They need to learn how to collaborate and cooperate as team-mates in the same way that they have to as members of a small community off the pitch. That's what we did during our pre-tournament training camp. We learned to work as a team.'

Basics mattered. The German coach stressed to his players that they needed to conform to fundamental principles like punctuality, order and thoroughness. Giorgos Papalanis explains: 'He wanted us to operate like a Swiss clock. He would show up five or ten minutes before training or before we had to get on the bus, but he wanted everything to be ready and in order. Discipline was one of the principles that he really believed in. Not the sort of discipline that is typical of German football but his own take on it. He would be tolerant and easy-going when it came to small things but severe towards what he saw as serious instances of indiscipline.'

Antonis Nikopolidis gives the players' perspective: 'I never saw him checking to see if someone was late to anything. We had our schedule and conformed to it almost without exception by ourselves. We usually scolded him for running late, not the other way around. In that sense, he was different to someone like Santos, who always checked because he believed that you are as punctual on the pitch as you are off it.

'He never displayed that sort of "German discipline". He would only be strict when he thought you were completely out of line. I remember him telling us, "Don't fight with your wives over insignificant matters." When it came to important issues he wouldn't back down, he was unwavering. But it never happened over details.

'When he dropped Konstantinidis, after the friendly against Austria and the game against Northern Ireland, he proved that he could be flexible until you crossed a line. Then that was it, you were out. That's how he was with our game as well. As long as we stuck to the plan, he let us play freely and be creative. However, that happened because he allowed it to happen. If we crossed a line, as with Konstantinidis, he would step in and take charge of things. He picked players by that criterion, how confident he was that they would never exceed the parameters of his plan. It was like an informal agreement, we proved with our actions that we agreed with what he set out to do and were there to serve his principles.'

Theo Zagorakis recalls: 'We had already started to settle down as a team. If anyone was late, we would fine them ourselves. We had been doing that since the qualifying stage and it was something that Rehhagel liked, because it proved to him that he did well to put his trust in us. That is how we established trust between us, because we all followed the rules. We lost that after Euro 2004 though. We all let things slip, him and us too.'

To Giorgos Karagounis' mind, Rehhagel did not have to put special emphasis on discipline because he had picked players that were well-ordered and mature: 'We were mature enough to accept everything that we had to deal with. After a point, it was like we were on automatic pilot, even at the hotel. The press was going on about Rehhagel's iron discipline but he barely went beyond the basics. Was it because he trusted us so much or that we knew where the line was ourselves?

'He created an environment where we would relax at the hotel. We could have a coffee with our families but when it was time to go training or to a game, we were there without fail. We all did what we had to do for the team. He was lucky to have come across such great people, especially once he had got rid of those that he considered harmful to the group. After that there was no reason for him to enforce any rules himself. Our hearts were in the right place.'

Demis Nikolaidis respected the implicit trust from his manager: 'It wasn't like he had to watch us all the time but we were disciplined. He worked with a terrific group of people so he didn't have to police us. I recall seeing him sitting and watching in the hotel reception area but that was it. Once he realised how consistent we were, he relaxed.'

As Kostas Katsouranis stresses: 'He had a plan and, as a professional through and through, he expected us to be professional about it too. He would say, "I want them down for a team walk after breakfast at 9:30am. If they went to bed at 5am that's their problem."'

Rehhagel proved his flexibility and tolerance during an incident primarily involving Demis Nikolaidis, which could have had a detrimental effect had a manager of less empathy and experience rushed to the conclusion it represented a breach of discipline. Nikolaidis had travelled to the Swiss training camp with a strained calf, which had showed no signs of improvement during two weeks' sustained treatment.

Nikolaidis explains: 'Christos Karvounidis, my physiotherapist, believed that the problem was with my back, not my calf. As he was not allowed to travel to Switzerland, he suggested that I visit Dr Helmut Schreiber, chief medical officer of the German track team, considered to be one of the best in his field in Europe. On our first day off, I decided to travel to Freiburg, a three-hour drive, with Kostas Katsouranis. We only realised we didn't have any documents or passports with us when we got to the border. The doctor was able to see me and explained that indeed there was a problem with my back. He asked how important it was for me to take part in the Euros and concluded that, in order to maximise the possibility of my being able to participate, I would need 22 injections. He went on to explain that the drug, while legal, had adverse effects, so he would provide the appropriate documentation to be submitted to UEFA.

'I had injections all along my right side, from my waist up to my right bicep and then down to my calf. On our return journey, we were stopped by the border police. We didn't have any documents with us except what the doctor had provided and our Greek national team tracksuits. They saw all that, contacted the hotel, and let us go. I was so stressed out on our way back, because I expected that the manager would be waiting for us and I had gotten Katsouranis in trouble as well.

'I hadn't informed him in advance because he was strict and he wouldn't allow me to cross the border on our day off. However, I knew that he wouldn't punish me because he had the best interests of the team at heart and the reason I went through with that was so that he would be able to use me. I was not penalised by the EPO either. As players, we had the option to have a sit down with the president and work things out.'

It was a delicate situation, since Nikolaidis had been a source of internal tension, but Traianos Dellas recognised maturity of management: 'That Nikolaidis played in that tournament was further proof of self-sacrifice for the team. Despite the fact that he had already decided to retire from football, he went through all of that in order to be there with the rest of the team.'

Rehhagel saw the bigger picture, though he was deeply unsettled by another incident, a fortnight before his team left for Switzerland, when AEK fans attacked players during training. At the time, Nikolaidis was in talks to take over running the club. He had asked the players to accept less money than they were owed by the administration in order to facilitate the transition. The fans had gone to the training centre in order to force the rest of the players to capitulate.

Tsiartas, who had been among the players under attack during the incident, considered Nikolaidis to be the moral instigator and stated: 'I really don't know how I am going to be able to look at him when we meet in the national team. I am sincerely sorry that both of us are going to be there.' Rehhagel asked both players to put the story behind them and warned that he would leave both out of the squad if their behaviour became disruptive.

Giorgos Papalanis remembers: 'We went to Tsiartas' house and I had them sit down and talk. I told them that, if they didn't work it out, they would both be accountable. From then on I was at Tsiartas' side constantly, to help him manage the situation for the sake of the team. During the preparation period, half the players sided with Tsiartas and the other half with Nikolaidis. Neither one of them ever even mentioned the issue though. They were both perfect gentlemen at all times.'

Theo Zagorakis also helped Rehhagel deal with the situation: 'I remember Tsiartas complaining about Nikolaidis going to get those injections. I knew them from AEK. Nikolaidis was really smart and Tsiartas was a really special guy. Rehhagel was aware of what had happened between them, but still elected to call both of them up and somehow managed the situation so that it never became an issue for the rest of us.'

Rehhagel put much stock in his players' comfort and living conditions. Before the team left for their training camp, he had gone to see Gagatsis to ask if the players could sleep in single rooms in Switzerland and Portugal. The federation president was impressed by his logic, and his attention to detail:

'He told me: "This is not a demand. It is a thought and I would like you to sleep on it. I would like the players to have their own rooms. Think about it, when we go on holiday with our wives by the third day we start bickering and fighting over trivial things. We will be in Switzerland for ten days and in Portugal for another 15. It's too many, so I would like them to feel at ease and be relaxed. See if the EPO can afford it. I know that the Germans are staying in double rooms but I just wanted to tell you. It's not a demand." So we went ahead and did just that.'

Giorgos Papalanis, the veteran operator, saw political pragmatism and a positive personal relationship at work. 'The EPO had already started to earn extra revenue before we left for Switzerland, thanks to Gagatsis' action,' he explains. 'They were also expecting some UEFA funds to come in, so they were better able to support certain initiatives.'

The plan went down predictably well among the squad. 'Gagatsis loved us footballers,' Demis Nikolaidis recalls. 'He was the best president the national team had seen during my years as a player. He was very capable and played a very positive role. He didn't antagonise us. Rehhagel would not have been able to work things out with anyone else in his place. They both really looked after us.'

Theo Zagorakis drew on his experience with Leicester City, between 1998 and 2000, as a reference point: 'Rehhagel was a manager in the English style. Only he could have requested those changes. He kept us isolated from all those people. He insisted on comfortable flights, upgraded hotels and services, even the single rooms, which was something we had asked for and he managed to get from Gagatsis. Of course, keeping isolated from the president's voters, so to speak, was not an easy proposition and it was the president who had to deal with the aftermath because he had taken it upon himself to satisfy the manager's demand.'

As captain, he had his finger on the pulse of the dressing room. Players have lives outside football to balance. As experienced pros, they were well aware that things tend to go wrong during pressurised pre-season training at club level; this would be the first time they would have to deal with this issue as members of the national team.

'It is never easy,' reflects Zagorakis. 'You think about your kid being sick while you're away, or how your wife is coping. But it was on our mind so we dealt with it. The single rooms had a lot to do with helping things. We never got into fights. Minor things only, easily manageable. That's because Takis Fyssas would tell jokes for almost two hours straight after dinner. That was our time to unwind and let off some steam, even when there had been minor misunderstandings among us.'

Kostas Katsouranis was comfortable with the culture the senior team had created: 'We would get together all in one room and hang out. There was such a great atmosphere among us. From the very first time it was like a family. We all hung out in the bus or the hotel. We would get together and vote for the worst player after training, things like that. It was like nothing that I had seen before.'

For Giorgos Karagounis, even the fact that mobile access to the internet was not yet as popular was beneficial for the team: 'The fact that we did not have computers or smartphones to isolate ourselves and spend time on social media was good for us. We would get together in a room and hang out. We would talk and share thoughts about upcoming matches or our work together, everything. We would play backgammon and listen to Fyssas' jokes and all of that strengthened the bonds between us, because we were able to communicate with each other. None of that would have happened today.'

The human touch was working.

Chapter Fourteen

All for One

OTTO REHHAGEL had done such a good job of planting the seeds of team spirit and a sense of solidarity among players working towards a common goal that they took it upon themselves to change the status quo. Money is a notorious factor in fracturing morale in football, yet the Greek team changed the bonus system for Euro 2004, to ensure each squad member received an equal split of any reward. Until then, the bulk of the cash had gone to the starters.

Stelios Venetidis put the initiative into perspective: 'Our time in Bad Ragaz was easy and relaxed, what with the superb training centre and the single rooms. It was very pleasant. That's when we started forging the bonds between the starting players and the substitutes. The coach had instilled that element of unity and togetherness. It was sealed with the decision regarding the bonus. I think it had originally been Zagorakis' idea to split it evenly among the entire squad.

'It is certain that had we not agreed on that, there would have been a rift between the starting players and the substitutes. We wouldn't all have had the same drive to succeed. It is only natural. That discussion affected the overall mood and changed our outlook and it happened at a time when we had started becoming more of a team. You have to realise that we were really spoiled. We never had to sit on the bench at our clubs. We were very immature, so that agreement helped us maintain a high level of teamwork and togetherness.'

Traianos Dellas captures the mood: 'That was a wise decision and it saved us a lot of confusion. We were all in agreement. As a believer in karma and positive energy as a player, I didn't like to think that there may have been someone in the squad who would rather we lost because they were on the bench. That happens in teams and it creates bad vibes. It never happened with us.'

Antonis Nikopolidis expands the point: 'We had a talk without even considering that we might win the trophy. We thought we would move to the next stage and maybe end up receiving 30,000 each. So why not accept 15,000 so that everyone gets the same amount and be happy? We would all spend the next month working together. Gagatsis had no issue with that. We generally didn't have any issues with each other before that either. There were no resentments because the manager didn't leave any leeway for us to complain or cause trouble.'

'I don't recall anyone objecting to the decision we made. It played such a big role for our psychology. We all felt like equals,' says Demis Nikolaidis, who is backed up by Takis Fyssas: 'I remember two or three of the guys mentioning that we should all get the same bonus and the rest of us agreeing to that. Zagorakis and Nikolaidis come to mind. Things wouldn't have been as good among us if we didn't end up getting the same bonus.

'We all thought "even if the other guy plays instead of me, we'll all get the same". Speaking as a starting player I felt genuine joy at the idea. Imagine us celebrating side by side with Venetidis for example, if I was about to receive five times what he would get. Now we all looked at each other in the face, as champions, no matter who did or didn't play. And that was magical.'

Theo Zagorakis was the conduit between the team and management: 'I have been on the bench myself, so I knew what that was like. So I thought, we will have been through the same shit together, why not receive the same amount? There were some reactions but no one was sure they would be starting so the majority immediately agreed. That conversation had taken place over fries and pizza. That was what gave us the trophy. I remember when Gagatsis visited us at the hotel before the game against the Czech Republic to discuss the bonus, he was blown away when I told him that we had all agreed to ask for the same amount.'

Nikos Dabizas explains: 'We had a sense of justice. Everyone contributed to the team effort so it makes sense for all of us to get our bonus. It may not sound logical for everyone to receive the same amount of money, since some scored or saved goals and some sat on the bench, but where was the logic in what happened? Our sense of fairness dictated that we all share in the good and the bad. If I am sitting on the bench during a game, I am still going through the same psychological journey that the guys on the pitch are going through. I wouldn't say, "they were playing so it's them that got knocked out". It is much worse feeling unable to help because you're on the bench. So that unity and team spirit made the difference. There were 23 of us, a closed circuit, an organism.

'I left Newcastle for Leicester in January 2004. My presence in the national team was jeopardised because I wasn't playing regularly at Newcastle, so I left. I was not used to sitting on the bench. It was hard to manage at the time but I now realise that the agreement we made regarding the bonus helped me get through it. When you know you're in the same boat with everyone, everything counts. The vibe on and off the pitch, the sense of support and solidarity, all help if they are genuine. That's what happened in Portugal.'

Rehhagel had asked for an easier opponent for the team's last friendly, and chose Liechtenstein, who were duly beaten 2-0, with goals by Zisis Vryzas and Angelos Charisteas on 3 June. He denied they were selected through superstition, though Liechtenstein were Germany's opponents in their final warm-up before they won Euro 96, but pointedly raised the possibility of becoming champions in his final speech, before leaving Bad Ragaz for Portugal.

Stelios Venetidis recalls the speech vividly: 'That was a decisive moment. Generally, he wouldn't say much but when he felt that he had to, he would gather us all out on the pitch. He started to speak about our presence in the tournament and that's when he brought up the possibility of competing and winning at the highest level to a team that were considered underdogs.

'He mentioned a statement by Scolari, from his time as coach of the Brazilian team. "I am not interested in playing good football. I am interested in winning. Progressing is more important than just playing. We are not a club taking part in a long championship. This is a tournament." Scolari was saying those things about Brazil, a team that came from a country with an incomparably bigger population and quality of football. So he said, "I don't want to play pretty football, I want to win. That's where we need to focus, on the result. That is what counts and we can go really far. We can even win the trophy."

'So he brought up winning the trophy to a team that was not looking beyond scoring a goal and winning our first match. We were all aware of how we got to where we were and where we could go. We knew that what we were doing was not enough to take us really far. We still carried the experience of the 1994 World Cup fiasco within us. As a result, we believed that he only said that to boost our morale.

'We didn't laugh out of respect for him, but that's what we believed. He brought it up again and again. He expressed what he believed we were capable of doing. He went through our qualities and asked us to pay attention to set pieces. It was a defining speech because it made us, even on a subconscious level, think that he believed in us, that we were going there to lay claim to the trophy.'

Chapter Fifteen

Lift-off

INTERNATIONAL FOOTBALLERS are creatures of habit, who demand the best because they consider themselves to be the best. The Greek squad landed in Porto on 6 June, and checked into the Santana hotel, overlooking the river Ave some 30km north of the city. For the first day the room plans assumed greater importance than the game plans for the group phase.

The delegation took 57 rooms, but the players were not satisfied until they had been given those with large balconies. Giorgos Papalanis, who had visited 15 other hotels, which were fully booked, smiles ruefully as he recites his notes from the day: 'The players are grumbling about the rooms. They do not like the change from Bad Ragaz.' The solution was relatively simple. 'Rehhagel had a talk with them, we changed some of the rooms and they calmed down,' says Giannis Topalidis. 'They loved it after that!'

The welcome was fulsome. Hotel manager Nestor Rodrigues had provided his employees with a list of Greek words and phrases to make the players feel at home, and wrote individualised letters to them, in Greek, in which he stressed '… we hope that the final will be a repeat of the opening game.' Since that was against the host nation, you could say he was covering both bases.

'The Greeks were very easy-going. They didn't have the strict discipline I noticed in other teams,' recalls Estefanio Silva, the hotel barman. Rehhagel would ask staff to keep their distance when he spoke formally to his team. His initial speech concentrated on the historic nature of their challenge, and the need for complete commitment.

His audience was responsive, according to Antonis Nikopolidis: 'It was good for us that we got to Portugal that early. We were the first team there. We landed on 6 June and our first game would be on the 12th. We got used to the idea that the tournament had started. The isolation helped because we were so far from anything Greek, even our families. It was just us.'

The tournament offered a more worrying distraction two days before the opening game, when Theo Zagorakis was informed that he was under investigation by the UEFA medical committee because he had tested positive during screening before the team left Greece. High levels of testosterone had been detected in his test, a familiar story that had also cropped up in 2001 and 2002.

He had been able to prove that he suffered from relapses of cystic acne 'which is an indication of increased production of testosterone by the body'. Unlike Zisis Vryzas, who suffered from the same issue, Zagorakis had not gone through the series of tests that would help him provide UEFA with the appropriate documentation. Thodoros Theodoridis, the EPO public relations executive, made an appearance before the UEFA medical committee to present translations of Zagorakis' medical history, in order to secure his participation in the tournament.

'That whole testosterone story on the eve of the game with Portugal really upset me,' the captain remembers. 'I would be missing the tournament that I had been dreaming of playing in for so long. Rehhagel was in a quandary because we didn't know if I would be taking part. We finally found that I could do so on the eve of the game and Rehhagel used me without hesitation. I ended up being man of the match.'

It fell to Greece to open the tournament, at Estádio do Dragao. These showcase occasions can inspire or intimidate: Cameroon, who memorably defeated World Cup holders Argentina at the start of Italia 90, remain the best example of an underdog team raising their game in such circumstances. Rehhagel did not shy away from the consequences of what he called 'a game that will be seen around the whole planet'. He expected his players to realise and assume their share of the responsibility.

'Rehhagel taught you to confront your responsibilities,' acknowledged Kostas Katsouranis. 'If that was to man-mark someone and you failed, you knew that there was a chance he would not call you up again. What he did do was state the facts and force you to face your responsibilities. He would say, "You need to prevent your opponent from scoring," or "There's two of you and two of them in midfield. You will not allow them to dominate. They've got two legs like you." Given our level of tactical sophistication in Greece, that was exactly what we needed.'

The background noise was irritating, and required a response. For days prior to their departure from Greece, all the players heard or read about was their duty not to repeat the abysmal performance of the Greek team in the 1994 World Cup. The prospect became a national obsession, forcing them to face repetitive and predictable questioning almost every day.

'I was not concerned about how far we were going to go,' Nikos Dabizas reflects. 'I thought that we had already achieved a big part of what we set out to do just by being there, but the ghost of 1994 hung over our heads. It was a really bad precedent so we were determined to continue performing like we had been during the qualifying stage. We didn't want to lose the credibility we had established. That's why we went into that first game really aggressively. We were happy to be the focus of interest of the entire continent.'

Takis Fyssas stresses, 'We were determined not to be a laughing stock, like in 1994,' and remembers Zagorakis coining a key catchphrase: 'Watch it, you assholes. Stay tight. We don't want to make fools of ourselves.' Zagorakis laughs at the memory: 'I wasn't wrong to say it. I really meant it. You can go from hero to zero in no time. Even now I still say it when we play.' Demis Nikolaidis argues that, 'It wasn't said in a defeatist way. He just wanted to keep us on our toes.'

According to Giorgos Karagounis, they made a positive out of a potential negative: 'We only wanted to enjoy taking part in the tournament, that's all. We had already achieved out first goal. Our target was to score the first goal and win a game in a big tournament, which was something Greece had never been able to do. 1994 was still on our minds so we didn't want to suffer heavy defeats. Things weren't working out for us during the last few training sessions, so we thought we were not in such great condition. However, it may have been the sense of fear and awareness of all the above that helped us start the first game in an ideal fashion.'

According to Michalis Kapsis, the belief of players like Karagounis, that the team would be able to get past the group stage, was instrumental in shaping the squad's character: 'When we got to Portugal, all I wanted was for the team to have a decent performance, and not be a laughing stock. I did not want to come back to Greece forever associated with a huge failure. I am not overly optimistic and I've always been low-key, unlike Karagounis who believed that we would win the trophy. A team, in order to function properly needs all of that. It's good to have those over-optimistic guys who can help you transcend your own fears.'

Stelios Giannakopoulos succinctly expressed similar thoughts during a press conference on 8 June, just four days before the opening match: 'We are not here to see the sights and those who do not take us seriously will be wrong. I am not saying that we shall win the trophy or that our head is in the clouds, but we will not quit without a fight. We will approach each game with the importance it deserves and whatever happens, happens.'

The Greek approach was distinctive. Game plans were drawn up through analysis of televised matches, rather than by empowering scouts to study opponents and collect intelligence. It was simple, but effective, as Giannis Topalidis explains: 'Our strategy for that first game, because they would press us in order to win the ball and attack against a disrupted defence, was that we should use long balls to prevent them from gaining possession. And that stressed them out.

'We didn't have scouts until 2004. We didn't have time to go everywhere, so we sent people, just to say we did, and worked from our videos. We mostly sent scouts to protect ourselves from the media, so they didn't accuse us of failing to study our opponents. We also wanted them to give us the names of players at set pieces, in case we weren't able to read them off the screen. Of course, if we knew anyone who lived or worked in football in the country whose team we were up against, we would contact them to gather intelligence.'

Jorge Andrade, Portugal's central defender, insisted, 'We knew the Greek team well because we had played against them some months earlier. We had not been able to beat them, despite the fact that they had ten men for most of that match. After the draw, our fans thought that Greece would be the weakest of our opponents but Luiz Felipe Scolari knew they were a tough team, difficult to subdue. He insisted on emphasising their quality and power. On the eve of the game, he passed by our rooms and put a paper listing information about the Greek players under all our doors. In addition, he had written us a note in order to motivate us and make us concentrate for such an important match.'

Andrade is an important witness to football history. His interview, for this book, undermines the assumption, shared by most Greek fans and observers that the blame for Portugal underestimating Greece lay with Scolari. Andrade's account leads us to the conclusion that Figo and the more celebrated players were guilty of complacency.

There is another possibility, of course, that the Portuguese never really underestimated Greece. When I asked Otto Rehhagel to pick the game he considered the most important, he replied without thinking: 'The first game against Portugal. It was Greece's and my first final stage game. I knew the whole planet would be watching it. It is the significance of that victory that makes me pick this one. It was a very substantial success. It was when the rocket was launched.'

That typically colourful phrase was an appropriate way to describe what had happened, for him as well as the players. On the eve of the game, Rehhagel in interviews with the German press, did not hide that he was anxious and impatient for his first game in a big tournament. The team's performance and victory was liberating for both himself and his boys.

'It's like a dream come true. Who could have imagined that we would beat the organising country's team in the opening game?' Stelios Giannakopoulos said after the game to uefa.com. Stelios Venetidis added: 'We felt so liberated after the game against Portugal. It felt like an avalanche that flattens everything in its way. It created the impetus that we needed.'

Even during that moment of exhilaration, Rehhagel maintained an even tone: 'Greece has always had good individuals but now it also has a good, well-organised team. They all work together towards a common goal. Tonight we shall rest but we are already focused on the next game against Spain.' It was only when he spoke later that evening, to the German magazine *Der Spiegel*, that he was more effusive.

'It is one of the greatest successes of my career,' he said. 'It reminded me of the victory against Monaco in Lisbon, when we also were the underdogs.' He was referring to Werder Bremen's win in the 1992 UEFA Cup Winners'

Cup Final, and neatly bringing together two strands of fate. That trophy was won in the Estádio da Luz, where he would also be crowned European champion.

He played a cagey game, even with his fellow countrymen. In nine years managing Greece he never shared his strategy in public, and took pains to ensure his instructions to his players stayed in-house. So, when journalist Ralf Douri asked what his plan had been, his reply was politically precise and unrevealing: 'I had all the plans in my head but I've already forgotten them because I am already preparing for the next match.'

Figo, stunned, would not admit that the result had been fair but he recognised that the Greek plan worked: 'We tried to respond to the first goal but we kept losing second balls and, by running to regain possession we relinquished control of midfield. The second goal effectively decided the game. After that the Greeks sat back to defend and they protected their victory very well. We did not expect to lose that match.'

Jozef Venglos, former Czech national team manager and president of the UEFA Technical Assistance Committee, wrote in his official report of the 2-1 win: 'Following Karagounis' goal, Greece dictated the tempo of the game. They played very well, with Zagorakis as the playmaker. The two central defenders were exceptional and Greece showed that they know how to counter-attack very well. The Portuguese found themselves under a lot of pressure and, even though Figo played well, he did not have much support.'

Giorgos Karagounis, who gave Greece such a fateful early lead, preferred to deflect praise to the entire team: 'The game really went our way. We were aggressive from the start. We had another opportunity after the first goal. Playing away suited us. We knew how to defend and the fact that they played with a single forward suited us because we didn't need to mess with our three midfielders. We had two central defenders with Dellas playing a bit further back and with three midfielders we had a very solid presence. We scored early too, so the Portuguese became more anxious and that led to a deserved victory.'

Antonis Nikopolidis gave credit where it was due: 'Karagounis' goal really boosted our confidence. The Portuguese became really careless and rushed and we were experienced enough to exploit that. We could feel that they were not doing well. We gambled on their stress and it turned out to be the easiest match we played, along with the last one. In comparison to what we had to go through with the Spanish, the Russians and the Czechs, that game went by like a breeze for us because of their carelessness.'

Kostas Katsouranis suggested surprise was an important ally: 'We were in it to win that first game and they were not expecting that. We were very strong mentally so we won most challenges. There was no real secret to how we played, we just had a clear head and an awareness that everyone would be watching. It was our first time taking part in a big event so we had taken it very seriously. The Portuguese considered us a minor obstacle. They were not expecting us to be so aggressive or that we would take advantage of their errors and score.

'Rehhagel said, "There will be millions of people watching you on TV. This is your chance," because he was going to start me in the game. When he said things like that he wasn't saying them to encourage you but to tell you that that's how things were. During our one-on-one talks he wouldn't give me instructions. It was up to you whether to humiliate yourself or move ever upwards.

'This is why I believe that the character of the players of my generation, our attitude, played such a great role. Older players, if they had been told something like that, they could have asked him not to use them. That used to happen in the past.'

Rehhagel had a similar conversation with Giourkas Seitaridis about Ronaldo. Ten years after the event, the manager revealed: 'They asked Ronaldo if he knew of any Greek players and he said no. We heard that so I told Seitaridis, "Today we read that he doesn't know who you are, who any of us are. But tonight, after the game, he will know who you are." That helped the player. I said, "You are as fast as him. No one has heard of you but you can run past Ronaldo."'

Takis Fyssas, who had been playing for Benfica since 2003, was Rehhagel's accomplice, in tweaking his team-mates' egos: 'I lived in Lisbon for six months before Euro 2004 and I used to tell my team-mates in the national team, "Guys, no one rates us." I had told my Portuguese international team-mates in Benfica that whoever wins gets the other's shirt. They had accepted, laughing, and I realised that they didn't rate us at all.

'They gave off this vibe of "first they ignore you, then they laugh at you, then they fight you, then you win" that has been attributed to Gandhi. That really was the case with us. In the first instance they would ignore us. Then they scoffed at the idea that they would lose. Then they thought that we were good and defended well, so they would fight us, and in the end they would lose. I would tell the guys every single day before the match that the Portuguese underestimated us.'

Fyssas's 31st birthday was on 12 June. The hotel had prepared a cake in the shape of his shirt with his number and the colours of the national team and the Portuguese waiters, despite their bitter disappointment, stood there smiling to sing 'Happy Birthday' to him. The hotel manager recalls, 'That night they had champagne for the first time. They emptied all their mini-bars, also for the first time. They were not big drinkers.' But there would be much to celebrate.

- - - - - - - - - -

Portugal 1 Greece 2
Tactical Analysis by Athanasios Terzis.

In the opening match of Euro 2004, Rehhagel deployed a 4-3-3 formation, which countered the shape that Scolari chose for the Portuguese team. In defence, Dellas was

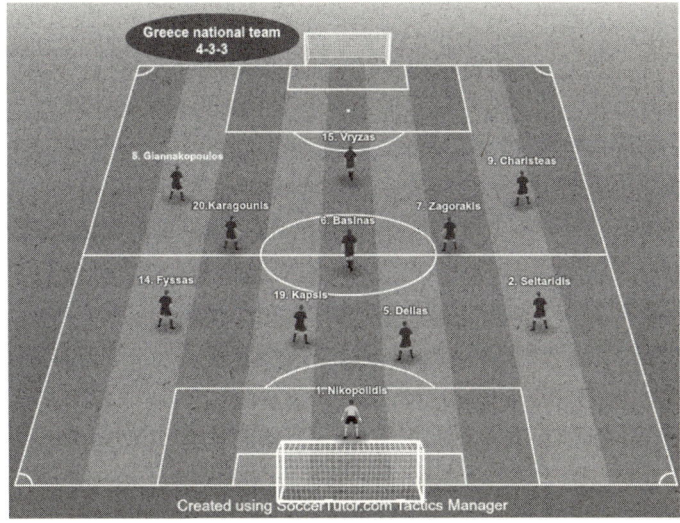

Greece formation

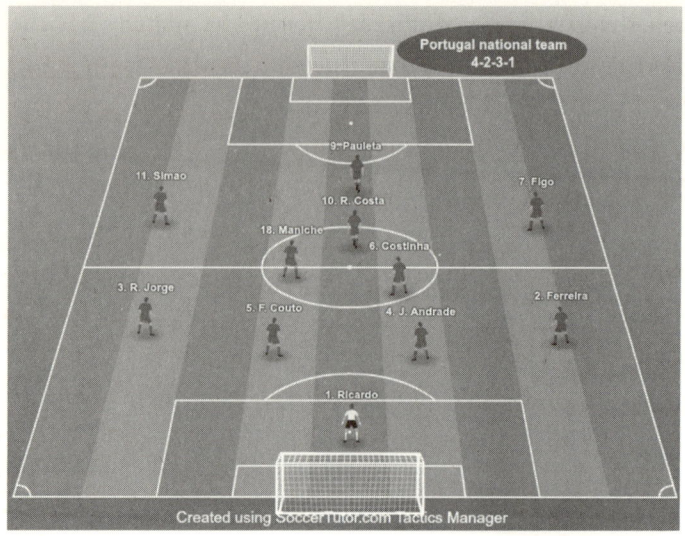

Portugal formation

once again the sweeper, while Kapsis, as a centre-half, would man-mark Pauleta, the sole Portuguese striker. In midfield, Basinas was the central midfielder, with Zagorakis on the right and Karagounis on the left.

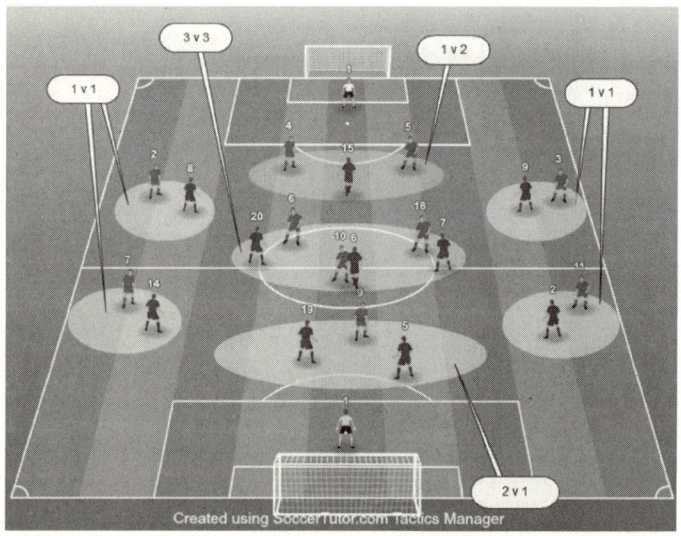

Portugal vs Greece, the matchups

Scolari went with a 4-2-3-1 formation which often changed to 4-3-3. Costinha was the defensive midfielder, Rui Costa the attacking midfielder, and Maniche was in the centre. Figo was the right wide midfielder, with Simao on the left and Pauleta as the striker.

The two formations were well matched positionally. Rehhagel, as was his habit, maintained an extra player at the back, which resulted in 2 vs 1 in defensive situations. There was an equal match-up of players in the middle of the park, with 3 vs 3, while in the centre of the Portuguese defence they had an extra player, which created a 2 vs 1 against the Greek striker. On the wings it was 1 vs 1.

The Greek defenders marked their designated men, with Kapsis shadowing Pauleta, Seitaridis on Simao and Fyssas watching Figo. Dellas acted as sweeper and provided additional support in defence. In midfield, the Greek trio focused on man-to-man marking within their area of responsibility. Thus Basinas watched Rui Costa, while Zagorakis and Karagounis marked either Maniche or Costinha as Maniche moved freely to the right or left and Costinha adjusted accordingly to maintain the balance of his team.

Right from kick-off, while everyone expected Portugal to have the upper hand, Greece surprised with their aggression. Vryzas, in particular, had a wonderful first half. Just two minutes into the game, he crossed low towards the penalty spot but Charisteas failed to connect. A minute later, the ball was again in the area from Seitaridis' long throw-in, but goalkeeper Ricardo cleared the ball before it reached Giannakopoulos. In the seventh minute, Karagounis won the ball after a mistake by Ferreira and

Karagounis goal

scored past Ricardo, with a shot from just outside the penalty area.

Greece continued to be threatening at 1-0 up, seeking to advance mainly through long passes to Vryzas and quick support by Charisteas and Giannakopoulos, but also through situations of rapid attacking transition. In the next few minutes, after passes by Vrizas, both Charisteas and Fyssas had shots off target.

The Portuguese were unable to find their rhythm. Whenever Figo sought to isolate Fyssas, there was help from Karagounis, Basinas or Giannakopoulos, who helped hold up the attack. As the Portuguese captain realised that he could not threaten from the wing, he began to converge towards the centre and to operate as an attacking midfielder, often towards the left wing, in order to escape Fyssas' marking. This produced a 4 vs 3 advantage in favour of the Portuguese. Greece's response came through Vryzas retreating more often, in order to control Costinha and restore the numerical balance as Zagorakis was now concentrating on Figo. When Figo was about to receive the ball, Dellas would immediately move to pressure him. The Greek defender played a decisive role in the match, restricting any of the Portuguese players who managed to free themselves from their personal marker.

Vryzas drops back to create balance

The Portuguese plan, besides taking advantage of the numerical advantage in midfield (4 vs 3), also intended to exploit empty space along the flanks. In many cases, Simao and Figo would converge towards the centre in order to free up space on the wings, as Seitaridis and Fyssas followed them. The space created was intended to be exploited by either the full-backs or midfielders Maniche and Rui Costa. However, both Giannakopoulos and Charisteas showed great application in their defensive duties, checking the advances of the Portuguese full-backs. When the

Portuguese midfielders attempted to take advantage of this, Dellas would always cover the gap and either intercepted the passes, or directly pressed the receiver to deny him space and time on the ball.

Dellas moves to cover

The Greek sweeper played a very important role in defensive transitions. When Greece were in possession, in most cases, Figo would not follow Fyssas. As a result, when the ball was lost, the Portuguese captain was left unmarked. However, Dellas' positioning on the pitch (he was always next to him) and timely interventions either allowed him to intercept the ball or pressure Figo if he gained possession.

Portugal's first major chance came in the 27th minute when Rui Costa's header from the penalty spot missed Nikopolidis' goal. Three minutes earlier, Charisteas had threatened the Portuguese goal in exactly the same way from Giannakopoulos' corner.

Created using SoccerTutor.com Tactics Manager

Deco moves behind Zagorakis

Scolari started the second half with two substitutions. In place of Rui Costa and Simao, he put on Deco and Ronaldo, without changing the formation. Rehhagel also made a change with Katsouranis replacing Karagounis. Katsouranis took a central midfield position as Basinas moved to the left side of midfield.

Despite the changes, the Portuguese were not able to threaten, and the fact that Dellas was covering gaps in defence allowed the Greek defenders to stay close to their personal opponents. This eventually led to Seitaridis winning the ball when Andrade tried passing to Ronaldo. Seitaridis passed to Charisteas and continued his run, leaving the Portuguese striker behind. Charisteas passed back to Seitaridis inside the penalty area at the right time and Ronaldo tackled him from behind and brought him down. Referee Collina gave the penalty, and Basinas scored in the 51st minute, putting more pressure on Portugal.

After the second goal, Portugal became more offensive. Their formation morphed into something closer to 4-3-3, with Costinha as defensive midfielder, Deco as attacking midfielder on the left and Maniche as attacking midfielder on the right. In addition, Figo continued to play a free role and move between the centre and the right wing. This forced Greece to change their marking, with Zagorakis staying close to Deco, Basinas watching Maniche and Katsouranis on Costinha.

The home team attempted to move the ball on the left towards Ronaldo, playing opposite Seitaridis. However, the effectiveness of the Greek defender, combined with the support provided by Zagorakis and Katsouranis, did not allow him to create any dangerous moments for goalkeeper Nikopolidis. At the same time, Deco began to break forward and demand the ball behind Zagorakis in order to avoid his marking. Greece's response involved Dellas taking over from Zagorakis when needed in order to counter Deco's advance.

Although after the second goal Greece could not keep possession and continue attacking, they were not seriously threatened by Portugal. In the 65th minute, Scolari put on Nuno Gomes in place of Costinha, turning the formation into a more versatile 4-4-2 as Figo would often move alongside Deco and Maniche. In response, in the 67th minute, Rehhagel brought on Nikolaidis for Giannakopoulos.

The addition of another striker confused Greece for a few minutes, as Dellas, who took over marking Gomes, continued covering other possible gaps, leaving the Portuguese striker unattended at times. Greece eventually countered this by putting Katsouranis on Gomes, with the

Change to 5-4-1 formation

formation turning to 5-4-1. With this move, all defenders were assigned individuals to mark, while Dellas was still free to assist when needed.

In the 74th minute Lakis replaced Charisteas. As time passed, the Portuguese were putting more pressure on Greece by getting the ball closer to Nikopolidis' area. The Greek defenders, however, positioned themselves and blocked their opponents' crosses and shots before they reached their targets. The main source of concern was Figo who, after Katsouranis' reassignment, had more space in the centre and as an attacking midfielder was causing problems.

However, the first real opportunity for Scolari's team in the second half came in the 82nd minute when Ronaldo attempted a shot only for the ball to be deflected by Seitaridis and end up just wide of Nikopolidis' post. The only reply the Portuguese managed to make was pulling a goal back one minute before the end of the game with a header by Ronaldo from a corner by Figo.

Based on the two teams' performances, Greece's win was not surprising, as Rehhagel's team created better chances than their opponents. Even when the Portuguese dominated possession in the second half, Greece controlled the game and did not allow them to create any noteworthy goalscoring opportunities.

Chapter Sixteen

Coping with Pressure

THE DREAM was alive. It was taking shape, becoming bigger, more vivid and convincing. Since it was not the time for false modesty, Demis Nikolaidis was unafraid of making the most relevant comparison, in a packed press conference on the eve of Greece's second match, against Spain in Porto on 16 June.

'The 1992 Danish team is a great example for us,' he said, reviving memories of the most unlikely of European champions, a side given only a week's notice to prepare for the tournament. 'They were able to do amazing things even though they were far from being the best squad. I don't think that that team was better than our team today.'

The Spanish had beaten Russia with the only goal of the game, scored by Juan Carlos Valerón, in their opening fixture, yet the result troubled Ináki Saez, their coach. Under pressure from a demanding media, he was concerned about the tightness of the group, and the prospect of several teams tying for qualification.

There were nerves on both sides. Antonis Nikopolidis, acknowledged as one of the coolest of the Greek players under pressure, lucidly remembers the anxiety he suffered on seeing the 20,000 Spanish fans whose red shirts dominated the stands in the newly built 28,000-seat Estádio do Bessa.

'That game was when we felt the most pressure,' he acknowledged. 'It was really hot and there were so many Spanish fans. I remember feeling afraid when I went out to warm up and I have not felt that way often in my career. I'm not one of those people who claim they're not afraid of anything. We are all human. It has happened two or three times in my career but it's something you get over with experience. But I felt that way with Spain. I didn't have any such issues in the rest of the tournament. All that red in the stands stressed me out but I soon got over it.'

That is a telling admission from a player of such stature. Nikopolidis, who would go on to win 90 caps between 1999 and 2008, never showed any overt sign of nerves or anxiety on the pitch. In fact, his calmness as a goalkeeper helped both his team-mates and Rehhagel feel more secure during the Greek team's matches.

'I wasn't like that at the beginning of my career,' he remembered. 'I had to work at it. Older players would tell you to be tense, to yell and even curse at your team-mates "to wake them up". I chose to create a different persona on the pitch. I told myself "be calm, think clearly, be specific in what you ask of your team-mates". I came up with that in my 30s, not in my 20s. It took time to appreciate that my team-mates required guidance with specific instructions, calmly, without stressing them.

'I had realised that you don't gain anything by yelling and cursing. I needed my team-mates to help me out. I had to win them over, so I would explain clearly what I needed. I gave them specific instructions, not generic stuff like "play better" or "wake up". That was helpful to me and also relieved some of their stress. So it was a gradual process, I didn't have that from the start.'

Kostas Katsouranis is similarly frank: 'We really suffered in the game against Spain. They were just outside our area constantly. And the coach helped with his substitutions, when he saw that they had moved an extra player to the left-hand side. That was the most important match and we managed not to lose despite not being at our best. We probably played worse than against Russia who beat us.'

Katsouranis offers an insight into the preparatory process. Rehhagel would reveal a piece of paper, with the starting 11 written on it, during his main pre-match speech. This was a deeply ingrained ritual, enacted at the team hotel before their departure for the stadium. The players then sat down for their own meeting.

According to Katsouranis, the manager's team talk 'lasted for about 40 minutes. It would start out in a general fashion: "There are 11 of us and 11 of them. You know where the goals are, you know how to take corners. You know you must keep the ball away from our defence," things like that. Then he would move on to discuss the players in order to let us know that we were better. He always said that we were close to our goal and that, if we won, it was in our hands. He would say that we shouldn't be afraid of any of the teams in our path.'

Nikopolidis adds: 'During those speeches, the manager would bolster our psychology but the players' meeting after that would also play an important role. We would sit down and Zagorakis and Dellas would usually start things off. The magical thing was that we all agreed to what was being suggested. Our plan for the Euro, was that, if we're doing OK until the 70th minute, we will win it. We don't change anything until then. Even if we're down one goal, we will keep trying. After 70 minutes, we will take it upon ourselves to start pushing forward more, take more risks. We knew that the manager would agree.

'So we would look at the time and, if we were still at 0-0 we were encouraged that we had achieved our primary target. Now we could win it. That's what happened with Spain too. Even though we were losing, the game proceeded without us taking any risks. After 60 minutes, we felt we were in control of the match so we created an opportunity and equalised. Zagorakis would say, "If we do well until the 70th minute, we will win." So there you go.'

Far from being bothered by his footballers developing the game plan, Rehhagel encouraged it. He had trust in their experience and belief in their character. Besides, he always knew what was going on within the team by keeping in touch with those players he believed were pivotal in developing his strategy on the pitch. Angelos Charisteas was among them:

'Karagounis, Zagorakis, myself, Dellas, and later Katsouranis had some influence with Rehhagel. Dellas had always been his favourite. He would call me over even if Topalidis wasn't there and say, "Ask Dellas or Zagorakis, what do they think about the game?" I would go back and tell him what they thought. Over time we realised that we shouldn't tell him everything in order to avoid being a negative influence.

'He made mistakes too, in that his initial assessment wouldn't work out, so we would change our play in the last

20 minutes to better adjust to the match because we knew he trusted us to do that. If someone wasn't doing well, we would rally to help them because we knew that we would need them. That's how you build a great team. You can build empires if you get past problems in this fashion. That sense of camaraderie was the result of that run of 17 to 18 games when we had remained undefeated.'

At 24 years old, Charisteas was coming off a stellar season with Werder Bremen, who had won the Bundesliga and the German Cup. His goal against Spain set him up for a tournament that proved to be the springboard for a very successful club career in which he scored 74 goals in 330 games stretched over 16 seasons.

'That really had been my year,' he remembered. 'I had played 28 times with Werder Bremen during the past season and we had won the Double. My confidence had sky-rocketed. I had travelled on a private plane with the German national team to meet with the Greek team for pre-tournament training so I felt great.

'I thought that everything was possible. Fyssas always said that he was impressed by my confidence. I wanted to break into the scene and there were many others who wanted that at the time. It was our moment and we took advantage of it because we had intelligent players who would not let that chance pass them by.'

Michalis Kapsis remembers the intensity of emotion that defined that 1-1 draw in Porto: 'The second half against Spain was the toughest time we had. As I had been responsible for the goal they had been able to score, I felt really stressed. When we equalised, I ran to Tsiartas who had made the assist and said "Vasilis, thank you so much." I felt so liberated.'

Greece had more bookings, five, in that match than in the rest of their games in the group stage. As Rehhagel explained during the post-game press conference, 'We had stressed to the players how passionate they had to be in this match. That is why we had so many bookings.' He had asked his players to be more aggressive in their challenges because he believed I was the only way to counter Spain's superior passing.

The bond between manager and players was growing firmer by the day. Theo Zagorakis, who rose to the responsibility of captaincy, reflected: 'During half-time, the coach was able to prevent us from feeling discouraged. He convinced us that there was still time to get something out of the match.'

Ináki Saez, who had been complimentary about Greece's performance, assumed part of the responsibility for his team's failure to win by admitting that his strategy had been at fault. 'We were held to a draw because we had decided to go after a 2-0 or even 3-0 win in that match,' he said, in the following day's debrief. 'Before the game started, we had estimated that there was a possibility for a three-way tie in the group, so we continued to play more openly because we were after more goals.'

Saez in effect agreed with the official report, drawn up by the UEFA Technical Assistance Committee. By winning the opening match, Greece had upset the plans of both the Portuguese and the Spanish. It upset the balance of the group and forced rival managers to rethink their initial calculations regarding the potential development of the tournament. Thanks to that opening victory over Portugal, Greece played with the minds of their opponents. That gave them the ultimate advantage.

Often, in football, the most significant compliments come from the opposition. Fernando Morientes, a world class striker who won the Champions League three times with Real Madrid, had scored the opening goal against the Greeks in Porto. He instinctively recognised their quality and today, with the benefit of hindsight, is happy to lead the praise for a team that so many underestimated:

'I remembered the match in Zaragoza, during qualification for the finals, very well,' he said. 'That was when we found out that Greece is a very tough team to beat, but I would never have thought that they would do so well in Portugal. I soon came to realise, after the first two games with Portugal and ourselves, that they were a favourite to win. They would always score but not concede goals. That's a great recipe.

'Things became very difficult for us from the start because Greece performed so well in the opening game. No one believed that they would get to the final and win the trophy but, game by game, they proved to be a very stable team, very convincing, with great footballers. In the end, they deserved to be champions.'

- - - - - - - - - - -

Greece 1 Spain 1
Tactical Analysis by Athanasios Terzis

The two teams knew each other well due to the fact that they had met in the qualifying group, where they had each won one game against the other. Rehhagel adapted his formation to counter that of the Spaniards, employing 5-4-1 with Kapsis and Katsouranis as centre-halves and Dellas as sweeper. Seitaridis and Fyssas were the wing-backs, while Karagounis and Zagorakis were the central midfielders and

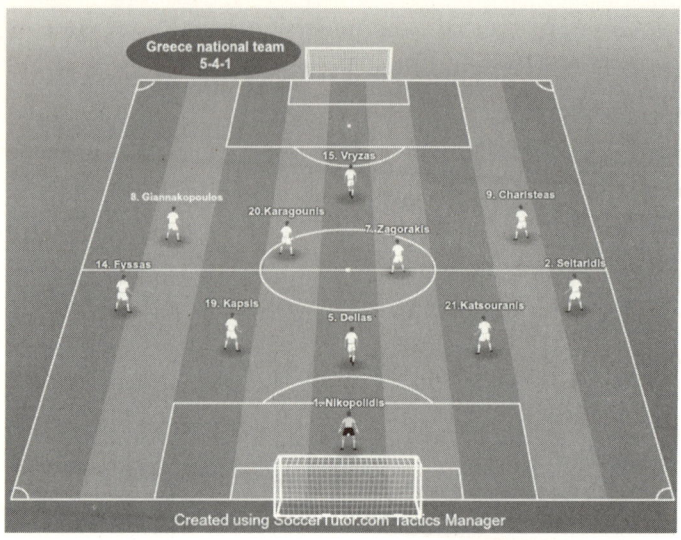

Greece formation

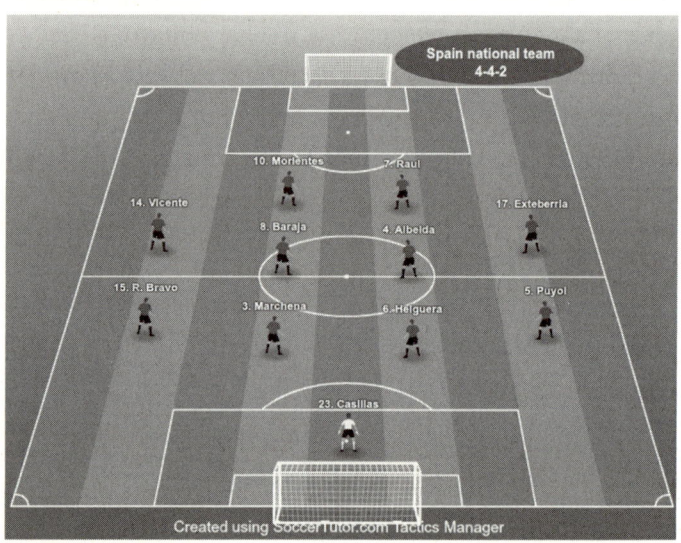

Spain formation

Giannakopoulos and Charisteas were on the the wings. Vryzas was the lone striker.

Iñaki Sáez chose to employ a 4-4-2 formation, with Helguera and Marchena as his central defenders, Puyol

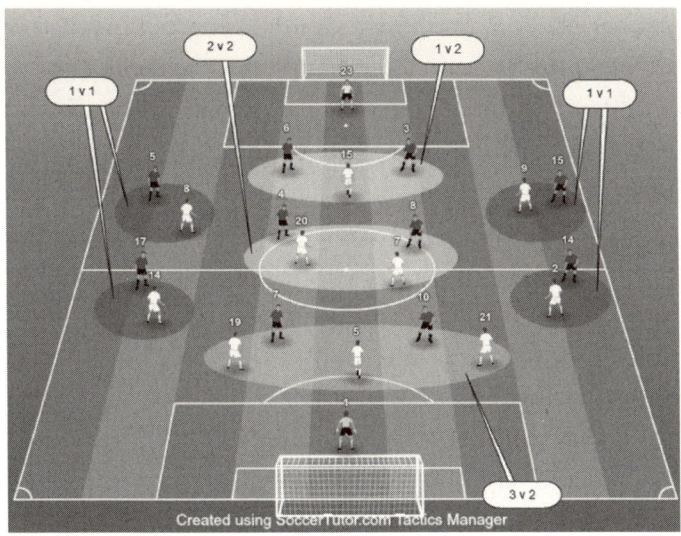

Greece vs Spain: the matchups

on the right and Raul Bravo on the left. Albelda and Baraja were the central midfielders, Etxeberria was on the right, with Vicente on the left. Raul and Morientes were the two forwards.

Greece retained the numerical advantage in the centre of its defence with 3 vs 2. There was a balance of 2 vs 2 in midfield, while the Spaniards had an additional player in their defence which created a 1 vs 2 situation in favour of the defenders. There were 1 vs 1 ratios on the wings.

Greece once again relied on man-to-man marking, with Katsouranis on Raul, Kapsis on Morientes, and Seitaridis and Fyssas on Vincente and Etxeberria respectively. In midfield, Zagorakis was on Baraja, who had a more creative role, while Karagounis was on Albelda, who was the defensive midfielder. When the two Spaniards changed sides, Zagorakis and Karagounis would follow them. Midfielders Giannakopoulos and Charisteas had been tasked with checking the advances of full-backs Puyol and

Raul Bravo. Vryzas, the Greek attacker, would mark any central defender trying to advance with the ball.

Right from the outset, Spain sought to maintain possession and to get the ball into the Greek penalty area. Greece were vigilant in midfield, looking for a chance to counter-attack. In the first quarter of the match, Saez's team kept the ball and attempted to take advantage of Bravo and Puyol's runs in wide positions. Both Charisteas and Giannakopoulos consistently performed their defensive duties and left little room for the Spanish full-backs. The Spanish winger Vincente would try to draw Seitaridis away from his area of responsibility, to free up space for the two strikers.

From the 20th minute onwards, Raul began to drop deep to avoid being marked and help develop the play. Spain had the initiative, but they were not especially threatening. Their first good moment came in the 23rd minute when from a free kick by Vicente, Helguera connected with the ball

Available space near the side line

Available space wide

Moving the ball to the free player

but sent it wide. Five minutes later, Spain unexpectedly scored. Kapsis intercepted a pass towards Morientes, but attempted a weak pass to Dellas. Raul won the ball and fed Morientes who finished cleanly, past Nikopolidis. Greece's response came six minutes later when Vryzas tried an overhead shot from the penalty spot, but the ball was blocked by Marchena.

Greece were unable to retain possession. Their principal aim was to quickly move the ball forward using long balls towards Vryzas and Charisteas. This tactic was not very successful, as Spain maintained pressure and won most of the second balls.

Spain kept possession and moved the ball easily in midfield. This was facilitated by the fact that Seitaridis often did not follow Vicente when he pulled back for fear of leaving too much free space on his side. However, Vicente operating as a central midfielder created numerical superiority for the Spanish (3 vs 2 in the middle), which

Charisteas goal

they exploited with their passing. Towards the end of the first half, Greece managed to keep the ball a little better and threatened through set pieces without any great success. Spain started the second half with Joaquin taking the place of Etxeberria. Greece had a good chance almost immediately, a long shot by Zagorakis flying just wide of the post. Although Greece were behind, they failed to impose themselves. Rehhagel recognised the team's inability to create situations that could lead to a goal, and sent on Nikolaidis and Tsiartas in place of Giannakopoulos and Karagounis. Not long after, Zagorakis hit another powerful shot that was blocked by Casillas. Spain countered when Raul headed just over the bar when substitute Joaquín picked him out unmarked at the far post.

Greece continued to probe in their usual way. In the 63rd minute, Dellas headed the ball on to the roof of the net from Tsiartas' corner. A minute later, Saez sent on Valerón, aiming to further strengthen his midfield. The change was accompanied by a change of formation to

4-3-3 with an attacking midfielder. When it seemed that Greece would only score from a set piece, Tsiartas had a moment of inspiration, seeing that the Spanish defenders were poorly positioned.

Tsiartas received the ball on the right of midfield. Charisteas had pulled back, dragging Helguera with him. At the same time, Nikolaidis had dropped back into a central midfield position and the Spanish right full-back, Puyol, followed him. This created an overload for Greece as well as free space on the right of the defence. Charisteas moved to Helguera's blind side and Tsiartas picked him out with a crossfield pass which the Greek striker controlled instantly before sending a shot under Casillas.

From then on, Greece focused on defence, while Spain sought to regain the lead. After the change of formation, Greece continued man-marking in midfield with Tsiartas on Albelda, Zagorakis on Baraja and Katsouranis next to Valerón. As time passed, Spain increased the pressure on the Greek defence with their slick passing. Their first good chance after the equaliser came when Joaquin's cross-shot went just wide of the post in the 70th minute. Helguera missed a good opportunity to put his team in the lead three minutes later, when he headed a corner straight into the hands of Nikopolidis.

Dellas' contribution was decisive in the remaining minutes. He had to intervene frequently, either by marking free players, covering the gaps on the sides of the defence, or blocking crosses into the area. In the 77th minute, Valerón's shot from the penalty spot was blocked, and a minute later, Joaquin, after a solo attempt, had a shot cleared by the Greek defence. In the 79th minute, Saez made his third substitution with Fernando Torres taking the place of Raul. Rehhagel sent on Venetidis in place of Fyssas in the 86th minute. Several corners won by Spain in the last few minutes were unexploited and Greece gained a valuable draw that put them in a strong position to qualify.

Chapter Seventeen

A New Pressure

EVERYONE LOVES an underdog. Greece, regarded as favourites for the first time, now had to deal with the pressures of being top dog. They had to deal with a different dynamic, which changed in the build-up to their final match in the group stage, against Russia in Estádio Algarve in Faro on 20 June. Since their opponents had already been eliminated, the Greek public leapt, en masse, to a dangerous assumption.

Victory seemed inevitable to those unversed in the ways of high-level sport. Expectation of success turned into a demand that the players continue to make the nation proud. Qualification for the quarter-finals would send the fans out into the streets to celebrate, and Otto Rehhagel had a new aspect of management on which to concentrate. He was concerned, because his experience of Russian teams had bred respect for their resilience.

'We were all very optimistic about the match against Russia but Rehhagel was cautious,' remembered his assistant, Giannis Topalidis. 'He kept saying, "I have faced Russian teams many times and they all proved difficult.

They were always technically very good." He came back to that after the match. "Didn't I say so? The Russians are always dangerous. They have great players." He thought really highly of them. He was the only one feeling unsure about that game. I would say to him "What, Russia???"'

When a team grows together, in the image of their manager, instincts are honed. Stelios Venetidis sensed Rehhagel's unease: 'He was really unsure in the match against Russia. It was difficult to work out what would happen in the event of defeat. Some of us, like Georgiadis and Dabizas, had already made the calculations and knew that we would qualify even if we lost 2-1. So we would tell the others that we had to be careful to contain it to that. The manager did not know these things.

'During that match it showed that we couldn't justify being called the favourites. It felt like the exact opposite of the game against Portugal. It was like "this is something big, something impossible". Russia, on the other hand, seemed liberated because they didn't have anything to prove, unlike us. There was a half-hour where we didn't know left from right. It was awkward.

'He tried to calm us down during half-time. We were all distraught because we were two goals down. He thought that 2-1 wasn't enough for us to qualify. We were telling him that it was, if we didn't let it get worse. Georgiadis even told him that in German. He hadn't realised that. Our confusion was also apparent during the substitutions. The players on the pitch would yell at the substitutes to be quicker while the guys on the bench would say, "Relax. We're still good." This went on until the last minute.'

Rehhagel appeared deceptively calm and visibly relieved during the post-match press conference. 'I had told my players that the match against Russia would prove difficult,' he insisted. 'Whoever the next opponent is, it will be a good prospect for us. All we have to do is enjoy the fact that we are in the quarter-finals.' He was more strident, and personal, with the German press: 'You said that Rehhagel is only good in Bremen but I have proved by now that I can make it everywhere.'

Theo Zagorakis admitted that the team was initially shocked by the quality of the Russians, but he was revealingly reluctant to dwell too much on the game. 'We have fulfilled our promises,' he stressed. 'We have taken Greece to a point where we are the talk of the entire planet, not just Europe.'

It wasn't an easy process: 'There was this one time in the 90th minute when there were five Russian players trying to score against us. I won't forget that easily. We didn't know if we had qualified. We didn't want to know. We didn't know if we had to play offensively or defensively. Karagounis came on to the pitch at the end screaming "we're in". We were so stressed, we kept asking if it was true.'

Nikos Dabizas looks back with a distinctive perspective: 'I have come to believe, as a coach myself, that it was clearly a matter of stamina. We had come out of two really demanding games in the space of five days. We had really suffered with Spain and were not able to replenish our energy in three days, while Russia made so many changes to their line-up. After the first 60–70 minutes when they started getting tired, things evened out. I remember talking to Dellas and he was telling me how exhausted he was. The Russians played looser because of their changes. We were exhausted. There had been no real tactical differentiation so I attribute that defeat to our tiredness.'

Kostas Katsouranis, in time-honoured fashion, chose to dwell on the positives: 'We felt very confident both because we had made it to the last stage and because of our victory over the Portuguese, who had a good team. Even while we were losing to Russia we still believed. We had faith.

An older Greek team would have lost 5-0, but we were able to turn it around and do what was needed. Rehhagel made an early substitution, replacing Basinas with Tsiartas after an error. We still didn't know we would qualify at the time.'

Dmitri Bulykin, the Russian striker, who was building an impressive reputation at Dynamo Moscow at the time, was impressed by Greece's defensive durability: 'During our meeting before the game, we said they were a very well-organised and disciplined side. We knew it would be our last game, and wanted to excel in order to thank our fans. Our defeats to Spain and Portugal motivated us, because our ego wouldn't let us leave without at least one victory.

'We scored two goals very quickly. The Greek team was not expecting that but once again proved that they are fighters. Their defence helped them win the trophy. That opened doors to some of the top clubs in Europe for many Greek footballers. Many children who watched the tournament on TV grew up wanting to be involved with football professionally, so your national team reached another level. They had a great decade after that. Many teams started to trust Greek defenders because they realised their potential.'

That was in the future. In tournament football there is no time to sit back, and contemplate what might be ...

Greece 1 Russia 2
Tactical Analysis by Athanasios Terzis

Otto Rehhagel went into the match against Russia with his usual 5-4-1 formation. Kapsis and Katsouranis were centre-halves and Dellas acted as sweeper. Seitaridis and Venetidis played as full-backs, while Basinas and Zagorakis were the central midfielders. Papadopoulos was on the left side of midfield with Charisteas on the right. Zisis Vryzas was once again the lone the striker.

Georgi Yartsev, the Russian coach, trusted a 4-4-2 formation. Malafeev was the goalkeeper. The four defenders consisted of Evseev on the left, Anyukov on the right and Bugayev and Sharonov in the middle. Radimov was the defensive midfielder, with Gusev on the right, Karyaka on the left, and Alenichev as the attacking midfielder. Bulykin and Kirichenko were the two strikers.

Greece retained numerical advantage in defence with 5 vs 2. In midfield, Russia had similar supremacy with 4

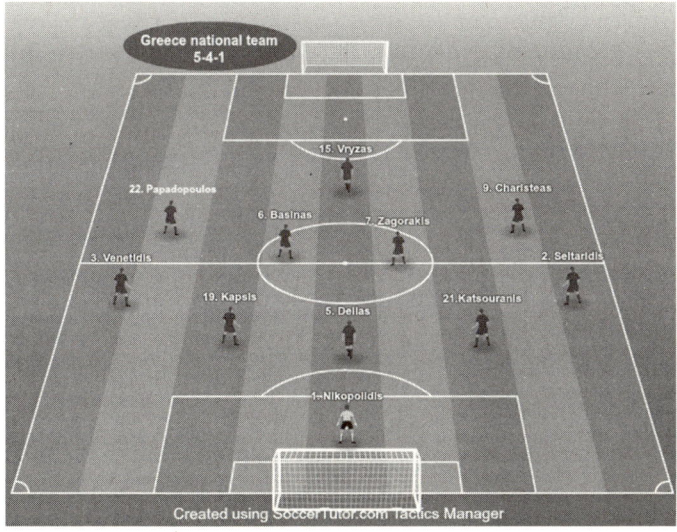

Greece vs Russia

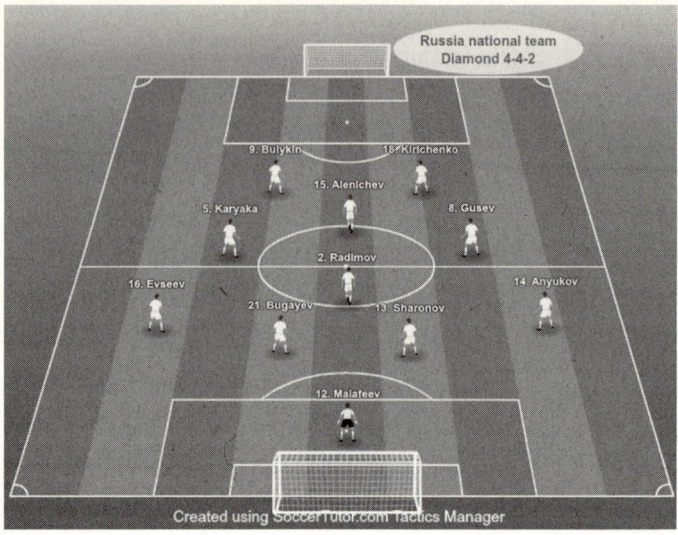

Russia line up

vs 2. Russia's defence had a 2 vs 1 advantage over Greece in the middle. In wide positions the ratio was 1 vs 1. The formation of the Russian team had the potential to create problems for Greece due to the clear numerical advantage in midfield.

In order to overcome this, full-backs Seitaridis and Venetidis had to move forward, close to Karyaka and Gusev respectively. This, however, would result in additional free space for the two Russian strikers.

Defensively, Katsouranis marked Kirichenko and Kapsis was on Bulykin. In midfield, Zagorakis marked Alenichev and Basinas was on Radimov. Papadopoulos, on the left, was checking Anyukov's runs down the wing and Charisteas would keep an eye on Evseev. Vryzas was positioned between Sharonov and Bugayev, taking on whoever had possession of the ball. The positioning of full-backs Seitaridis and Venetidis opposite the Russian central midfielders was more fluid.

Greece had a major setback within two minutes, as Kirichenko, after a long goal kick by Malafeev and a backwards header by Alenichev, won the ball and found himself in front of Nikopolidis. He scored easily, forcing Rehhagel's team to press their opponents in search of an equaliser. The Greek attacks were mainly aimed towards Seitaridis, who was making runs on the right flank, which led to successful one-on-one duels with Karyaka and Evseev. Noticing this, Yartsev changed the formation to a straight 4-4-2, with Alenichev pulling back next to Radimov and Karyaka going wide so as to counter Seitaridis. Gusev did the same on the other side. It was by now obvious that Russia were defensively focused, while trying to threaten mainly via counter-attacks.

During the tournament, many observers claimed that Otto Rehhagel's philosophy was to adapt his team to the formation of the opponent. However, perhaps because of Russia's early goal, Yartsev was the one who adapted to

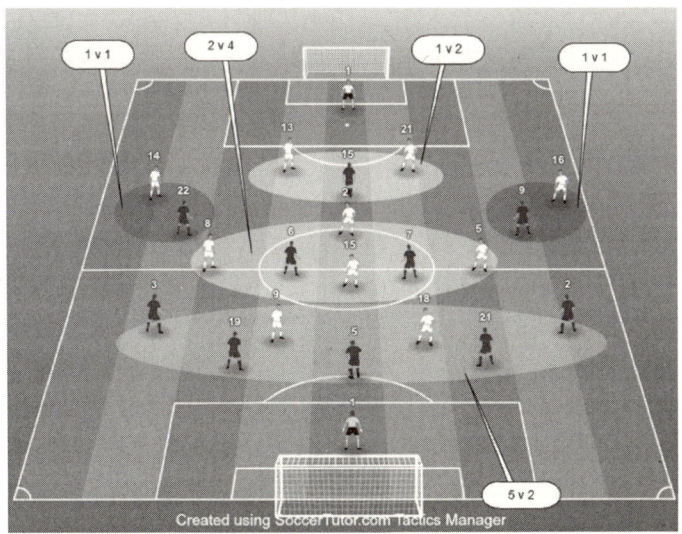

Greece vs Russia: the matchups

the formation used by Greece. The change in formation led to 1 vs 1 situations on the wings, while in defence there was numerical superiority of 3 vs 2 in Greece's favour. In midfield, the ratio was 2 vs 2. In the Russian defence the 1 vs 2 relationship did not change.

Despite Seitaridis' efforts, Greece did not threaten Malafeev's goal. A weak shot by Vryzas which went wide in the eighth minute was their best moment. To make things worse, Gusev's corner kick in the 17th minute picked out Bulykin unmarked at the heart of the Greek defence and his header led to a second goal for Russia. A minute later, Basinas fired in a free kick from outside the area, which Malafeev saved. Greece tried to react. They passed the ball more effectively, taking advantage of the 3 vs 2 advantage in the Russian defence and had a chance in the 20th minute with a cross-shot by Katsouranis but the ball was deflected for a corner.

In the 23rd minute after successive defensive errors by Greece, Bulykin shot narrowly over the bar from just outside the six-yard box. Rehhagel's team responded two minutes later, when a cross by Venetidis found Charisteas, whose shot went wide. In the 27th minute, the Russians threatened again from a set piece, but Bulykin's header hit the post. The Greek coach, wishing to strengthen his team's attack, sent on Tsiartas in place of Basinas three minutes before the end of the first half. A minute later, Charisteas crossed from a wide area, and Papadopoulos headed the ball towards Vryzas. He controlled past Sharonov, turned, and from a difficult angle successfully shot past Malafeev. Greece had pulled a goal back.

The second half started with Yartsev making two changes, with Bulykin making way for Sychev and Karyaka

Russia formation defensive phase

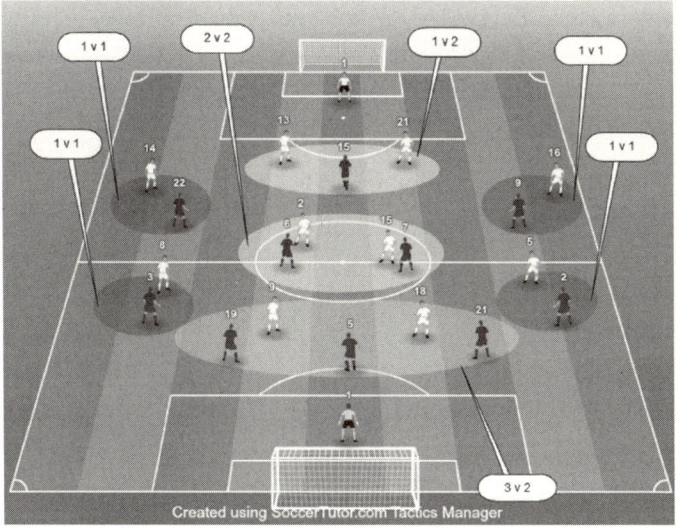

The matchups after Russia change

for Semshov. Greece tried to push forward more and get the ball into their opponents' area. This resulted in shots from Tsiartas and Zagorakis and a header by Charisteas that failed to find the target. The Russians had their moment

Vryzas goal

with a shot by Sychev, which was saved by Nikopolidis. From the 65th minute, the game became more open, with both teams showing a lack of coherence and no tactical changes. Greece had the upper hand but the Russians were always dangerous. Venetidis' shot in the 73rd minute went wide and Nikopolidis blocked a shot by Kirichenko two minutes later. In the 76th minute, Tsiartas crossed the ball to Nikolaidis, behind the Russian defence. The Greek forward controlled with his chest but Malafeev kicked the ball away before he managed to shoot. A free kick by Tsiartas, a minute later, was also saved by the Russian goalkeeper. With Tsiartas spraying passes around and Venetidis making more runs down the left flank, Greece increased the pressure while Russia started to make more errors. But the equaliser would not come. In the 83rd minute, after a corner kick by Tsiartas, Katsouranis' header was blocked. Russia missed a late chance when, following a cross from the right, Kirichenko, Sychev and Gusev saw the ball pass in front of them without being able to head it into Nikopolidis' net. In the 89th minute, Rehhagel sent on Fyssas in place of Venetidis but the 2-1 score remained unchanged.

Greece lost against a Russian team with nothing to play for. They had used Rehhagel's tactics against him. Direct play led to the first goal. A fast transition from defence to attack and a set play led to Russia's second goal. However, Portugal's 1-0 victory over Spain meant Greece and Spain tied in second place in the group. Greece went through to the next round on superior goals scored, having netted four times to Spain's two.

Chapter Eighteen

Breakthrough

WELCOME TO the big time. This generation of Greek footballers had never taken part in the final stage of a major tournament before Euro 2004. Now, nine short days into the competition, both they and their coach had to get used to a completely new situation. They knew achievement of limited initial targets, like scoring a goal and winning a game, meant nothing.

The quarter-final against France on 25 June, at the Estádio Jose Alvalade in Lisbon, was a major turning point for the Greek team. Their performance against the 1998 world champions and 2000 Euro winners was enough to convince themselves and their manager that they were capable of the biggest upset in the history of international football. The consequences of understandable caution were immediate. The EPO, who had booked a charter flight for the team's return to Greece for 21 June in anticipation of disappointment, suddenly needed to find a hotel in the Portuguese capital. Other teams had the foresight to book in advance, as a contingency plan for qualification for the knockout stage.

Greece were the exception. Their federation failed to find accommodation in the aftermath of the Russia match, and were reliant on the tournament organisers. The best they could do was the hotel Tivolli, which was unsuited to catering for a football team and its delegation. The oldest five-star hotel in Lisbon might have once housed the Dalai Lama and Fidel Castro, but the players were allocated random rooms on various floors, among other guests, including France supporters.

According to Antonio Leitao, manager of the hotel restaurant, the Tivolli was so unprepared that the administration 'had to purchase a new refrigerator for the team's sports drinks'. The restaurant itself, Beatriz Costa, proved a source of irritation for Rehhagel because it was on the ground floor and hordes of Greek supporters would spend hours in front of its large windows trying to catch the eye of the footballers. The German asked for additional security measures in order to maintain one of the fundamental elements of the team's success, isolation. Americo Nunes, chief porter of the hotel, recalls him repeating, politely but firmly, 'My boys, my boys. Do not bother my boys.'

Managing a team through a major tournament involves negotiating a minefield of different problems, each of which has the potential to cause damage. Problems with the hotel were placed into perspective on arrival in Lisbon when Rehhagel was confronted by a fundamental challenge of man-management. Vasilis Tsiartas expressed his disappointment at not having been included in the starting 11 during the group stage.

Tsiartas explained the background the following year, in an interview with *Sport Day*: 'I didn't play in the first game. I came on as a substitute in the second game and helped achieve the draw with Spain. In the third game, again as a substitute, I helped the team score again. So, on the way to Lisbon, I asked to talk to him. I asked if he had something against me. He said, "I don't negotiate with anybody."

'I said, "I'm not here to negotiate but to ask if there were any complaints about my performance." He then replied, "I use you when I think the time is right. That is mainly when the opponent is tired." That's when I said, "So is that why you put me on in the 35th minute against the Russians? Because they were tired?" He didn't say anything so I told my wife "that's it, let's go".'

Giannis Topalidis believed that Tsiartas, who had asked Rehhagel to talk with his wife as translator, was being unfair: 'Rehhagel sang his praises as a player. It was just that sometimes a game would have certain defensive demands which required qualities that he didn't possess. Other than that, I remember that the coach would not stop recommending him to Cologne.'

As horizons broaden, attitudes change. The Rehhagel of the qualifying stage, who dropped anyone who caused problems for him, would have decided to drop Tsiartas or marginalise him. The Rehhagel of Portugal, however, decided to keep him in the squad. If he did 'penalise' him, it was by not making a third substitution during the final, thereby depriving him of the joy of participating.

'The manager showed how flexible he was with the whole Tsiartas situation,' reflected Nikos Dabizas. 'It was a typical example of what he was like as a person. As uncompromising as he was, and he proved that by dropping players or never calling them up, I think that he did the smart thing and went beyond his ego to compromise with a player that had a complaint. If he had let his ego and selfishness get the better of him, he would have let him go. He went with the more difficult option and that was what made the difference in all his decisions.

'Given that it hadn't happened in public, he was able to filter and manage the situation in the best possible fashion, without directly impacting the team in a negative way. That's what any charismatic and special person who can let go of their ego and make a decision based on the good of the team would have done. It is not easy to come across people who can be so firm in their beliefs and yet able to display flexibility at the same time. Being true to your principles is one thing, being dogmatic another.'

'He was not unfair, for a manager,' insisted Takis Fyysas. 'I believe that Tsiartas made a big enough contribution to the team to have played in the final, but Rehhagel was not like that.' His view is informed by a subsequent spell as Rehhagel's technical director. Fyssas was able to appreciate that the German was more than able to manage the personalities with which he had populated the national team:

'If it hadn't been for Rehhagel cherry-picking those whose attitude suited him from the start, we wouldn't have gotten anywhere. I knew Nikolaidis since our time together in the youth team. He was the star of the team. I couldn't ever imagine the starting line-up without him. During Euro 2004, however, it was a different Nikolaidis. He would come on as a substitute and still run all over the pitch like a madman.

'He had the same attitude. He didn't complain because he wasn't in the starting 11. He still gave it his all. That is why I claim that we were a group of players out to prove people were wrong not to take us seriously. We were good footballers. Yes there were two stars, Nikolaidis and Tsiartas who were generally more widely respected, but they were not in the starting 11. And they went with it. Despite the fact that Tsiartas complained, he was still there for the team.'

As Rehhagel's employer, Vasilis Gagatsis had a vested interest in such a cohesive approach. He recalls: 'That was the toughest relationship Rehhagel had to deal with. He considered Tsiartas' complaint an insult but he still kept him in the team. "He came and asked why he didn't play, as if I have to explain myself," he would say to me. But he decided to keep him.'

Stelios Venetidis saw things through the prism of the dressing room: 'Tsiartas complained, but the coach did not want to lose him. He had the well-being of the team at heart so he had to manage the situation. It is something a manager has to do because the team is like a family. He has to use psychology and try to change the player's attitude. It is human for the player to have a huge ego. It is something the manager has to acknowledge and still have love for the player. If he cannot set that aside, he will be in constant conflict with his players.'

Demis Nikolaidis had the courage to make concessions. He explained: 'That entire scenario should be an example for all of us. It would help us come to certain conclusions regarding the elements necessary for a team of people to succeed. We reached a point where we would kill ourselves for each other. I love those people for what they were able to achieve. I had been a starting player all my life but I wasn't in Portugal. My mood was so good there that, when I thought about it, I realised I had taken on a different role. I provided support and encouraged the team. It wasn't easy but I was still able to enjoy the process despite being a substitute, which I had never been in previously. Ever since then I've said that we wouldn't have won if I had played more.'

Antonis Nikopolidis recognised the cultural difficulties: 'I still say how much I admire Rehhagel for being able to keep 23 Greeks together for 40 days without giving them a reason to fight among themselves. He was able to do that without being controlling, but by fostering respect for each other, for the process and the operation of the team. That wasn't how we did things in Greece. He realised very early on that he would have to invest in the psychological make-up of the players, because he had just come to a country that wasn't particularly rich in footballing talent. Yes, he was lucky in that he came across a good generation of players, but he was the one who picked them.'

The second major issue faced by Rehhagel before the game against France was one he created himself. On the eve of the quarter-final he invited Gagatsis to sit with him and demanded to be informed precisely when he would receive his bonus for qualifying for the knockout stage, as stipulated by his contract with the EPO. The president was taken aback:

'He and Topalidis were waiting for me in a room on the ground floor of the hotel. Tsiartas, Nikopolidis and Papalanis were just outside, watching. "What about the bonus?" "What bonus?" "We won the group stage." "Yes, but we are moving on. Do we have to talk about this right now?" I reacted. He insisted and that hurt me. It was very strange. To me it was like he believed he had accomplished his mission. It gave me the impression that he was not entering the knockout stage with ambition. I went to my room and lost it.

'Papalanis went up to Topalidis and says, "What are you doing? Why did you do that to him?" Topalidis called the next day and invited me to training, which I hadn't planned on attending, because Rehhagel wanted to see me. He said, "I apologise. I was wrong." I appreciated his directness. He wasn't calculating or insincere but that was the most difficult moment between us.'

Managers, despite their aura of authority, are generally as insecure as their players. Rehhagel had always regarded maintaining a good working relationship with any president he was working for as being of paramount importance. He was at his most successful when he felt he was trusted and free to do things his own way. This, conspicuously, was not what had happened during his nine-month stint with Bayern Munich, after which he was let go.

His ideal boss had been Jurgen Friedrich, president of the board of Kaiserslautern FC. With his support, Rehhagel went on to win the Bundesliga with the team he had helped promote the previous summer. Rehhagel and Friedrich had been friends since their days as footballers, so he instantly felt reinforced and secure from the start. 'That show of support felt like the right kind of psychological support after the intrigue with Bayern,' Rehhagel subsequently told his biographer, according to whom Gagatsis had taken Friedrich's place. The manager felt they communicated on the same level.

Takis Fyssas, again, speaks from personal experience: 'What he did about the bonus wasn't due to a lack of ambition or faith in what the team could do,' he insists.

'It was a very German thing to claim what he believed he was entitled to. As his technical director I always saw him claim what he knew was his.'

Gagatsis was aware of the imperfections of the system. 'There were never any major difficulties between us,' he insists. 'He was always accommodating during a time when we would often fall behind in our payments. He was a very positive person.' Giorgos Papalanis, the old hand, cuts to the chase: 'When Rehhagel asked for his bonus, before the game against France, the EPO simply did not have the money.'

On the day of the game Rehhagel had his usual meeting with the players in order to discuss strategy and reveal the starting 11. It seemed significant that this should be the first time he had acknowledged the possibility of defeat while the team was in Portugal. When he said, 'It's one thing to lose 1-0 or 2-0 and another to lose 3-0 or 4-0,' Giorgos Karagounis was the first to react.

'I was sitting in the front,' he recalled. 'It wasn't that I didn't have respect for France. It was that I always went out to win, no matter who the opponent was. So I said, "Why talk about losing? Who did we lose to? Why would we lose to them? Let's go out and play!" It was the first time he ever brought up the possibility of defeat or going home having conceded many goals. I felt that he didn't believe that we could turn things around in such an event. We were already very driven. He didn't have to encourage us more. I thought that he didn't believe we could do it against the best player in the world or against a team that seemed invincible.'

Giannis Topalidis saw both sides of a shiny coin: 'Karagounis was a world class personality. I met him when he joined the national team and took a liking to him. Rehhagel said all that, but he also said something really important, that the French hadn't lost in a while, so statistically, it was a matter of time before they did. They were like a ripe fruit ready to fall from the tree if we gave it a good push.'

Once again, Nikos Dabizas provides an impressive summary of the situation: 'I remember him saying that how you lose is important. Defeat is a fact of life but how it comes about matters. France were a juggernaut, so he wanted us to realise that we shouldn't be complacent because we'd come this far. We should retain our dignity. During a moment of calm, he tried to present the negative scenario to us, which was realistic at the time. It wasn't like he brought it up during the match, when it would have been very difficult to turn things around if we were down 2-0 after 20 minutes.

'We were still very fired up, so it wasn't like he brought us down. The way I took it was that he was trying to tell us to remain dignified and in control even if the result wasn't in our favour. I didn't think he was being defeatist. He may have been thinking that that was as far as we could get and being a realist, he wanted to talk about it. I didn't believe we would get past France either. I don't blame anyone who thought that before that match.'

Angelos Charisteas reflects: 'Otto's greatest gift was that he would help you lose your nervousness. He had a lot of means at his disposal. I spent much time talking to him because I spoke his language. He would tell us that what we had achieved was huge but he knew how selfish we were. He conveyed to me that we would win. It wasn't that he believed we would lose. He simply did not want to add to our stress.'

Fyssas felt reassured by the manager's pragmatism: 'I didn't take it wrongly myself. I thought that it was normal for him to mention the possibility of defeat against a team like Zidane's France. It got a reaction out of some of the guys, Karagounis first and foremost, but it was the good kind of reaction. Seeing your team-mates being annoyed at the mere mention of losing, you think that you may be able to do it again after we had come this far. So we went in and played a hell of a game.'

Antonis Nikopolidis felt the force: 'His last words were "even if we lose and have to go home, let's do it with our heads high". He wanted us to fight and leave with our dignity. I don't know if the translation was precise but he wanted us to fall like Greeks, if we did. I was not aware of the situation with his bonus but he did not look like he had given up. He simply realised that we had a tough game ahead of us against a very important team, so he wanted us to give it our best.'

Rehhagel went on to outline his strategy. He relied on familiar virtues to neutralise key French players. Topalidis explains: 'Once we got past the group stage, we knew we would be up against either England or France. Otto went to see England play Croatia and I went to see France play Switzerland. We then met back at the hotel to compare notes. Rehhagel rated France very highly. I told him that we needed to neutralise Henry and Zidane, which of course he was already aware of. We managed to restrict Henry with Seitaridis, who, in a way, was a great player and should have had a bigger career. As for Zidane, we tried to neutralise him by using our entire midfield. We didn't want him left to his own devices, so we had everyone mark him. That was the initial plan that we counted on, but the attitude and performance of the entire team played a role as well.'

Stelios Venetidis was conflicted, but retained his faith: 'I detected fear in the way he talked about our opponent, like we had exceeded our abilities. It didn't seem like he was able to encourage us and build our confidence. It felt forced, where before it had always felt very natural. It felt to me like he didn't believe in it, like he no longer had the passion. I think it all came down to the fact that he doubted the effectiveness of his plan. He had set aside Seitaridis to man-mark Henry. He knew that Henry would often converge inwards, which threw the formation out of alignment.

'He wasn't able to make it work with the players that he had in mind, so he suddenly came up with that 1-2-2-2-2-1 formation. Dellas and Nikolaidis would be the only free players, while everyone else would mark man-to-man. We said that that wouldn't work, that someone had to cover the right side at the back, so we left the meeting talking about that all the way to the bus. We talked things over among ourselves, trying to make the plan work tactically on the pitch but on the bench as well. We talked it over for so long that in the end, any fear we may have had about the match evaporated.'

Kostas Katsouranis worked through the changes, and the challenge, in his mind, 'We had all been assigned players to mark in the game against France. We had enough freedom to adjust to random developments during the game. But we couldn't do as we pleased. We had to follow the coach's instructions. He didn't mind us changing men in midfield, as long as everyone was covered. When he told Zagorakis to mark Pires and Pires went left, Zagorakis would play as a right-back. That's also what happened with Seitaridis and Henry.

'Henry wouldn't play right. He kept going from left to right, so Seitaridis no longer played as a right-back. He was a centre-half. Rehhagel wasn't bothered by anyone changing positions, as long as you still marked your man. He saw that we were implementing his instructions. We had our forward worrying the two central defenders at the front and Dellas as our free man at the back, which really helped us. He gave the players the freedom to play. He thought that offensively we were good so we would find each other. Attitude was key. We all believed we would be very competitive.'

Traianos Dellas explains the offensive plan: 'While you're defending you play in your third of the pitch. When the opponent comes up high, that creates the opportunity to exploit the free space behind them, which is what we counted on. Looking back, I would kick the ball long even when there were no opponents near me. Our play was very direct and that makes it harder for the opponent's manager to plan for. No matter your defensive plan, the central defender will transfer the ball to his forwards directly. You cannot block the long ball. You have to win the second ball in order to be able to counter a side that plays like that. We also counted on winning second balls as well.

'Vryzas or Charisteas would jump for a header and everyone converged to win the ball. If that didn't work, we would pull back and try again. Rehhagel's approach was empirical, not theoretical. His logic was so simple that it seemed almost naïve to us. He would say something like, "Where is the ball going to go from a corner kick? Towards the goal post. You know that so clear it away."

Everything was so predictable during training. We started to joke among ourselves. Then again, everything would work perfectly during the match.'

Nikos Dabizas insists: 'No, we didn't lose our trust in the manager when he showed us his plan for the match against France. That paled into insignificance based on our achievements until then. Our psychology was great after those games and that counted in his favour. Yes, we did start looking for solutions among ourselves after the meeting, but that's what teams are about. His rationale to have Seitaridis shadow Henry no matter which side he played, was a bit rigid but it made sense because Henry was in top form at the time.

'However, focusing on that single aspect of the opponent's game would derail our overall approach. It didn't make positional sense to us, so we attempted to find a solution. We did not lose our confidence in him, however. If you do something like that in a championship you may pay for it later, but in a tournament it's all about how you manage things in the moment. It doesn't matter that the coach misguidedly decided to focus on Henry, in the end we were able to manage it well.'

This was a mature team in action. As Theo Zagorakis explains: 'We discussed changing positions on the bus. Katsouranis wanted to play further right, marking Pires. I said, "I will play right but don't tell Otto." Otto of course realised what we were doing so Topalidis comes up to me ten minutes into the game and says, "Coach isn't happy." I said, "Don't worry Giannis, tell him we're doing fine, there's no reason to change things now." And he did. He had confidence in the team he had put together and he knew we wouldn't let him down.'

Traianos Dellas adds: 'Topalidis would always grab me, Zagorakis, Karagounis and Charisteas, as well as Nikopolidis, before each game, to keep us up to date on what we would be doing. One player from each side of the pitch: that's how trust works. We knew the coach had confidence and trust in us so we chose to use that, and expand on certain things for the benefit of the team. He picked us. It wasn't mere luck that he found us. He picked the more dependable among us for his team.'

There were tensions, inevitably. They flared at half-time against the French, when Michalis Kapsis, who had injured his back in a challenge with David Trezeguet in the 11th minute, said he might be unable to continue because of the intense pain he was still experiencing. Rehhagel had been concerned about his condition throughout the first half: now, under time pressure, he kept asking the team doctor and Kapsis himself, if he was in a position to continue.

'Kapsis is a sensitive guy so he needed more support,' argues Stelios Venetidis. 'It seemed like the manager had seen that and he attacked him to let off some steam. We didn't expect that. It was as if all the pressure he felt suddenly unleashed itself because he thought Kapsis was jeopardising his plan.' He is backed up by Kostas Katsouranis: 'He did seem angry during some matches but he would rarely explode. It was just that one time against France, when he yelled at Kapsis because he assumed that his plan wouldn't work without him.'

Giannis Topalidis concedes: 'He was very stressed when he talked to Kapsis during half-time, but didn't intend to be mean. Rehhagel never let himself get carried away with his players. If he got a bit harsh on occasion, I made sure to smooth his words out in translation.' Yet Rehhagel's behaviour upset the players, who were close to Kapsis.

Kapsis himself never felt he was being attacked or insulted. 'I would like to point out that I do not recall such an episode between myself and Rehhagel,' he insists. 'I remember everyone on the bench being anxious when I fell to the ground and my back started to hurt, and that the situation over whether I would be able to continue got a bit intense. However, I do not recall him pressuring me to continue. He may have been stressed earlier but he didn't say anything that bothered me except to ask me if I was ready.'

It was an untimely shock, since Rehhagel had never been unduly harsh. He consistently took care to express his anxiety towards the bench to avoid upsetting the players on the pitch. As Venetidis says: 'He let off steam by turning and talking towards the bench. Not many managers do that nowadays but he used to do that a lot, in order to avoid unloading on the starting players. He did not want to add to their stress.'

As soon as Rehhagel left the dressing room, the players rallied around Kapsis. Another incident took place which highlighted the unprecedented level of unity achieved by the Greek players. Nikos Dabizas, one of the best-known Greek defenders and the one who would be taking Kapsis' place if he failed to emerge for the second half due to his injury, decided to put his ego aside for the good of the team.

'I knew I would be subbing for him if he didn't continue but I still stepped in and tried to talk to him because Rehhagel's anxiety and irritation had gotten to him,' Dabizas explains. 'That was what was magic about that team. We all complemented and were able to support each other in various ways. The only time when I felt that "We" meant more than "I" was with that team, despite the fact that there were some very strong personalities among us. The toughest thing to achieve in a team is for the players to subsume their egos. It was the result of the atmosphere of credibility, authenticity, effectiveness and reciprocity that prevailed within the team. It's not like it happened overnight. It took two years for us to reach that level of unity.'

Kapsis appreciated the significance of the moment: 'Dabizas' behaviour is telling. For 25 days during preparation we all hung out with each other and the mood was always great. There were no frictions. That atmosphere persisted in Portugal, due to the good results we were able to achieve. If we had lost three times in a row, we may have ended up hating each other. There were some isolated instances where people may have had issues but that's a healthy thing to see in a team.

'The secret of our success was unity. I don't know if it was something that we did ourselves, or that Rehhagel or Zagorakis were able to achieve, but we stayed good friends for the duration. We cared about and supported each other. Even the players on the bench were part of it, which is a very difficult thing to have happen. That may have had to do with our decision to split the bonus evenly, but it was also the fact that everyone wanted to maintain that sense of balance and sense of well-being. No one wanted to spoil things for the team.'

Giannis Topalidis contends: 'What we were able to achieve in that game had nothing to do with luck. Rehhagel and I were wondering what to do about the second half because they were going to really come down on us hard.

We had thought of using Charisteas in order to be more threatening. Nikolaidis was a great player but he wasn't in top condition. He could be very threatening while his strength lasted but, due to his injury, that did not last long. The coach had a lot of respect for him because it was really hard to play against him when he was in peak condition. So we decided to go with Charisteas, who scored five minutes after coming on. That move really worked for us.'

Theo Zagorakis gives the captain's overview: 'The French had been really blasé towards us, but I remember Makelele tackling me really hard at some point by stepping on my shin. That was what made me realise that we had started to irritate them. Before that it was clear that they hadn't been taking us seriously. We had been told that they had made rather dismissive statements about us in the press, that they would have considered it a failure if they won by less than 2-0.'

The winning goal was a by-product of the Greek team's continuity. 'During training, I would practise crossing to Charisteas,' Zagorakis remembers. 'It wasn't something that the coach had us do but he wouldn't tell us to stop either. That was something I had been doing since I was a kid. I would stay and practise after hours. That moment with Lizarazu was simply ideal, everything went perfectly for us. I flicked the ball and everything went really smoothly. Katsouranis really helped there because he was able to draw away the defenders and leave space for Charisteas, who went up with confidence and powered that header home.'

The UEFA Technical Assistance Committee's report on the game contained some fundamental facts: 'Despite having prevailed in their group, France were not on great form and the Greeks were able to knock the holders out.

They stifled their attempts at recovering their usual shape and feeding the ball to their forwards. The French were not able to find solutions to the man-to-man marking and the close coverage that their forwards and other key players were under in all areas of the pitch. Despite having 55% ball possession, they were only able to shoot on target four times from seven shots, compared to five out of five shots on target for the Greeks, one of which led to the winning goal. Santini made some structural changes, which failed to trouble the Greeks.'

The day before the match, Michel Platini, who at the time sat on the UEFA Executive Committee, had explained to Vasilis Gagatsis that Greece would be able to defeat France if they could last for 20 minutes without conceding a goal. Platini's experience told him what Rehhagel had emphasised during the team meeting, that France would be complacent, ripe for defeat if Greece would only push hard enough.

Gagatsis recalls Platini telling him 'this is a dangerous match for France. If you do not concede an early goal, they will not go through. These players are completely satiated. They have won both the World Cup and the European Championship. They have won everything with their clubs also. So much money has crossed their hands that the green of the pitch tomorrow will only remind them of the green waters of the Maldives, where they will be going on holiday.'

Arsene Wenger, quoted in June 2006 in the book *Thierry Henry: The Biography: The Amazing Life of the Greatest Footballer on Earth*, agreed: 'France had some great footballers but the fact that they remained undefeated during the qualifying stage blinded them to any issues within the team. The same happened during the group stage, when they were able to secure seven points. That was what ended up being a trap for both the manager and the players. They believed that their condition would improve because they saw the team continue to win. France, however, did not have the right balance, and they eventually became aware of that fact when they faced Greece.'

Jacques Santini, the French coach, acknowleged: 'When you run out of free space, you need to take full advantage of your skill and we just didn't do that. Technically, we left much to be desired and we ran out of ideas in the last minutes of the match, even though that was something we had previously discussed. Our passing game was not good enough to open up the opponent's defence.'

Time offers perspective. In 2012, Marcel Desailly, who was captain of France at Euro 2004 but did not play against Greece, provided the following explanation in an interview with the French website *sport.fr*: 'We couldn't play in that match, we were paralysed. It is often difficult to perform against a team that is supposed, in theory, to be inferior. No matter if you face Brazil or Greece. You will still have the same meal, prepare in the same way and do everything as you would normally. Subconsciously however, you will not be up to your usual standard on the pitch. It is similar to what happens when you play for a large club and you have to face a smaller team for the domestic cup.'

The French press, predictably, had a lot to say in the days following the game. They focused on the troubled relationship between the Arsenal players and those surrounding Zidane, and explored communication issues between the older and younger players. They also condemned Santini's inability to lead and inspire. Such inquests are part and parcel of the international game, but they overlook a pivotal fact – there are two teams on the pitch.

Giorgos Karagounis, for one, sensed the magnitude of his team's achievement: 'The victory against France was the greatest ever achieved by a Greek side at any level. That's when we won the Euros. The victory over Portugal gave us the impetus, but that was a landmark game for us. We took some initiatives without disobeying the manager's instructions. Zagorakis moved to the right because Seitaridis would play up front and I closed in from the left in order to help mark Zidane. We ended the first half with four shots on target against none from France.

'They could have recovered during half-time. They still had time to rethink their approach. We performed very well both tactically and in terms of teamwork. When we scored the goal we had four players in their area: Lakis, myself, Katsouranis and Charisteas. Perhaps it happened because we wanted to prove ourselves against such an important opponent. What I kept saying, which was what Rehhagel and others said, was that, yes, we have already achieved something great and we will still be heroes if Zidane's France knocks us out, but when would we ever get to this stage again? Maybe never.

'It happened again in 2012, but at the time, I couldn't ever imagine finding myself in the knockout stage again. So I would say, yes, France is an amazing team but now is our chance to do everything we can, even if we lose. It helped that some of us had played abroad and had trained with the French players. We had become accustomed to important matches and facing great players.'

This wasn't the first game where Rehhagel's man-to-man strategy proved effective. But this was about the quality of its execution, and the circumstances in which it was carried out. The fact that it worked against France caused huge ripples in the football world. UEFA's official technical report from the tournament specifically addressed the issue of man-to-man marking and its impact on contemporary football following Greece's successful implementation of the tactic:

'One of the fundamental questions posed by Euro 2004 was whether the success of the Greek national team will encourage managers to support the revival of man-to-man marking. It has to be said from the start that the system demanded the infusion of several other elements in order to work. Based on Otto Rehhagel's plan, it also took enormous discipline, total focus and fighting spirit besides very concrete and precise tactical instructions. It is therefore to Rehhagel's credit that he had instilled those elements, along with other motives which fuelled the team's competitive flames as they got closer to achieving their first international success.

'What Rehhagel implemented was a mixed system based on man-marking the opponent's forwards and other key players. The Greeks would monitor and cover even those players that were not man-marked until the attacks were over. When the Greeks were under attack, their instructions were to stay on their man and not hand them over when they left their individual zone of responsibility. Given that the system was not new, the question is how it worked so effectively. While the system itself was not new, it was new to the generation of players that comprised Greece's opponents at Euro 2004.

'Some of them not only failed to find solutions but they also adopted tactics that made the Greeks' lives easier. Moreover, their opponents found it difficult to block Greece's counter-attacks because the Greeks' tactic of sticking to their player allowed them to move in areas from which they could run offensively practically unopposed whenever they got hold of the ball. This tactic often blind-sided their opponents.

'One disadvantage of man-to-man marking is that it lets the opponent dictate your side's formation. For example, the defenders have to go where the forwards take them. In general, however, their opponents' reaction was fairly static, which made the Greeks' job easier. One way to counteract man-to-man marking is increased mobility when attacking but this element was absent from most of their opponents. Deployment from the wings and penetrating from the central axis can also cause trouble, but Nedved's injury in the semi-final and Figo and Ronaldo's more static play allowed the Greeks to maintain their tactics and composure.

'Other possible solutions could have included one-two passes to neutralise defenders, or keeping the ball and only passing when near another attacker in order to draw the defenders away, thereby allowing the receiver of the pass space to manoeuvre, but those were again not used extensively by other teams. As Rehhagel undoubtedly knew very well, those counter-measures were a lost art, no longer widely taught. As a result, the Greeks were able to succeed by simply recycling a lost art and using it to maximum effect.'

25 June was a sleepless night in Greece. It was a night of pride, and euphoria. Greek President Kostis Stefanopoulos suggested he had 'not seen such crowds in the streets

since the transition to democracy in 1974'. Those crowds, duplicated and even enhanced after subsequent wins over the Czech Republic and Portugal, reminded him of the day the military dictatorship that ruled Greece for seven years collapsed and democracy was re-established in the country.

The 7,000 Greek fans, chanting joyously at the Jose Alvalade stadium soon had other priorities. Their main concern was to find a way to cancel or change their return journey and secure tickets for the semi-final, due to be held on 1 July at the Estádio do Dragao in Porto. The EPO was under constant harassment by Greeks who either wanted to extend their stay in Portugal or were trying to find last-minute tickets. They wanted to be able to witness the most important moment in Greek sports history.

It worked in the team's favour that social media was not advanced at the time. Facebook had launched in early 2004 but was not yet the media colossus it has become. That reduced the distraction of constant reporting of the impact their success had made in their home country. Rather than being engulfed by the implications, they were able to remain focused and hungry for an even greater achievement, getting to the final.

'The absence of social media and the fact that the internet was not yet omnipresent was good for us because we had no idea of how big this whole thing was getting back in Greece,' Kostas Katsouranis comments. 'That helped us to remain focused on our job. We had our mind on the target, on the game. It was all about training and messing around back at the hotel.'

Giorgos Karagounis reflects: 'We could access the internet on a computer in the reception area. We would go on there just to get an idea whenever we had a bit of free time, but that happened rarely and never for long. We did not stay well informed. We were barely aware of maybe 15% of what had been happening in Greece. It was that and watching a Greek National Television news report for Greek expatriates, which we watched whenever we happened to be in our rooms. That is what kept us grounded. We were less stressed because we did not feel the pressure to live up to expectations. Being isolated was good for us.'

They weren't living in a vacuum, though. They were unable to ignore the evidence of their own eyes. The scenes in the stands at every game hit home. 'We started to see more and more Greek fans with every game and that was when we realised that we were accomplishing something,' recalls Theo Zagorakis. 'It was particularly palpable in the games against the French and the Czechs. We would feel that we were doing something for our country when we saw all those people. They looked like they believed more than we did, so what was going on in the stands affected us during the matches. It was a practical demonstration of the theory that the crowd is like a twelfth player.'

- - - - - - - - - -

Greece 1 France 0
Tactical Analysis by Athanasios Terzis

This critical match was intriguing, tactically. Otto Rehhagel had to choose the optimal set-up to enable Greece to take whatever chances they created against the 1998 World Cup winners and 2000 European champions. He went with a 5-4-1 formation, with Kapsis and Seitaridis as centre-halves and Dellas as sweeper, as usual. On the right, playing as a wing-back was Zagorakis, with Fyssas on the opposite wing. Basinas and Katsouranis were the central

Greece line up vs France

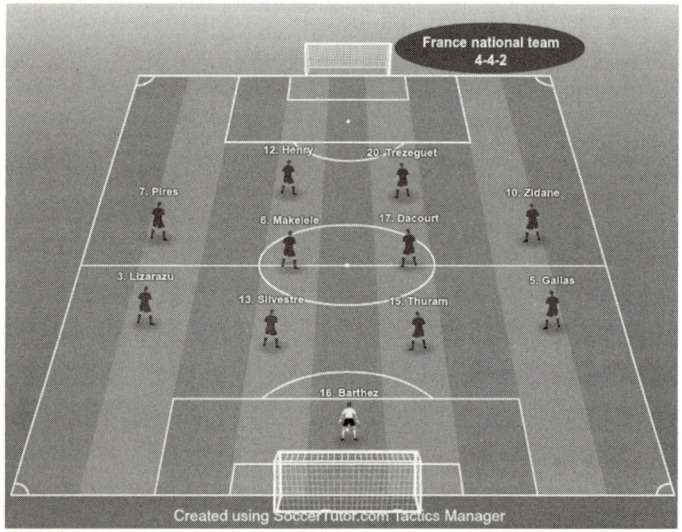

France line up 1

midfielders. Karagounis was on the left and Charisteas on the right of midfield. Nikolaidis was the lone striker.

The French coach Jacques Santini fielded a 4-4-2 formation with Barthez in goal, Gallas on the right, Lizarazu

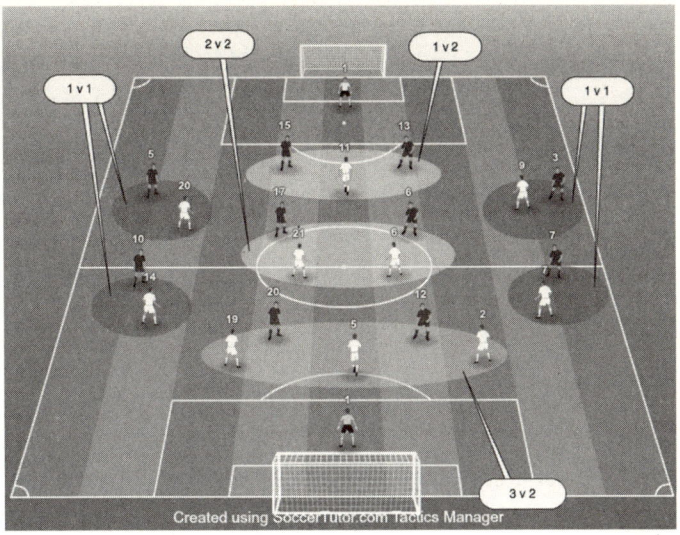

France vs Greece: The matchups

on the left, and Thuram and Silvestre in the centre of defence. In midfield, Makelele and Dacourt were the central midfielders, with Zidane on the right and Pires on the left. The two strikers were Trezeguet and Henry. Greece retained the numerical advantage in defence, with a 3 vs 2 ratio. In midfield, it was 2 vs 2. The French defence had a 2 vs 1 advantage in the centre, while on the flanks it was 1 vs 1.

Rehhagel tasked Kapsis with marking Trezeguet and asked Seitaridis to oversee Henry. His choice was based on the profile of the Greek defender, whose size and physical attributes (strength, speed, explosiveness) matched those of the French striker. In midfield, Basinas' main responsibility was to restrict Makelele, while Katsouranis and Fyssas had been instructed to mark Zidane. Zagorakis on the right undertook to restrict Pires. Charisteas and Karagounis would be marking the opposite full-backs, Lizarazu and Gallas respectively, while Nikolaidis stood between the two central defenders with the task of closing down whichever of them was in possession of the ball.

Greece started the match with a solid defensive display but also with the intention to threaten in attack. The main tactic was to get long balls to Charisteas in areas where the Greek striker would have to face either Lizarazu or Silvestre, over whom he had a significant height advantage. Nikolaidis ran in behind the French defence in order to receive the ball every time there was the possibility of Charisteas winning a header. The second Greek tactic was to get the ball to the wing-backs Fyssas and Zagorakis, who would advance at every opportunity and get crosses into the French penalty area.

When defending, Greece's efforts to counter Zidane, who, like Portugal's Figo, had the freedom to move either from side to side or up and down, were of great interest. In order for a player to always stay close to him and avoid creating room on the side of the defence, Rehhagel had

Zidane near the sideline

instructed both Fyssas and Katsouranis to mark him. This approach also influenced Karagounis' tactical play. Specifically, when Zidane moved up the wing, within Fyssas' area of responsibility, the Greek wing-back would be the one to mark him. When this happened, Katsouranis supervised Dacourt, while Karagounis focused his attention on restricting Gallas.

Zidane centrally

When Zidane was attacking centrally, Katsouranis would be the one who had the responsibility of marking him. Karagounis would then converge centrally to stay close to Dacourt, ensuring that there were no free French players in midfield. Fyssas would then be left without a direct opponent, which allowed him to sometimes move up higher to restrict Gallas while Karagounis was otherwise occupied.

For this tactical approach to be effective, communication between the three players involved was essential. When Zidane was positioned centrally, Karagounis had to either scan the area or to have been told by Katsouranis to focus on marking Dacourt. Otherwise he would focus his attention on Gallas.

Greece were the first to appear threatening, when Fyssas crossed for Charisteas who could not get his head to the ball. A few minutes later, Nikolaidis shot from outside the area but the ball ended up in the hands of Barthez. In the 15th minute, after a Karagounis wide free kick, Katsouranis met the ball but Barthez managed to save. The French made their first dangerous foray into Nikopolidis' area in the 24th minute, when Lizarazu crossed from the left and Henry headed the ball just over. The attacking runs by France's left full-back were the biggest problem for Greece at this time. However, Charisteas, following instructions from Rehhagel, focused more on his defensive duties and restricted him.

The French players would sometimes change positions, with Pires going right and Zidane left. This tactic did not particularly appear to concern Greece, as Fyssas took over marking Pires and Zagorakis went on to Zidane. Katsouranis' shot in the 27th minute was saved by Barthez and ten minutes later a long-range volley by Fyssas forced Barthez to concede a fruitless corner. The first half ended with Greece having been able to restrict the French stars and show dangerous attacking intent.

The second half started without any changes by the two teams. However, the French seemed determined to exert more pressure on Nikopolidis, the Greek goalkeeper. On 48 minutes, Henry turned and shot under pressure but the ball went wide. Five minutes later, Lizarazu made a run into the penalty area, but Kapsis was able to stop him with a challenge before he became dangerous. Four minutes after that, the other wing-back, Gallas, entered the area only to be stopped from shooting by Zagorakis.

The French threatened mainly through individual efforts, while the Greek players were unable to keep possession and slow down the pace of the game. Another problem was that the ball was not reaching Demis Nikolaidis, Greece's lone forward. Rehhagel realised this and on the hour replaced Nikolaidis with Lakis, moving Charisteas to the top of the Greek attack, so that he could contest balls in the air, while adding to the marking of Lizarazu by placing Lakis on the right. Three minutes later Basinas passed to Zagorakis on the right, the Greek captain cleverly flicked the ball over Lizarazu and crossed to Charisteas, who was at the heart of the French defence while Katsouranis darted towards the near post. Katsouranis' move drew away Thuram, leaving Charisteas completely free. The ball was accurately delivered to the Greek striker, whose textbook header left Barthez no chance.

Charisteas goal

After the goal things became easier for Greece. The French put more emphasis on attacking, constantly trying to pick out Zidane, who was tightly marked. This tactic led to several errors by France, while Henry, Trezeguet, Zidane and Pires were too slow to fall back to defend. This was exploited by Greece who kept the ball and lowered the tempo of the game. In the 71st minute, Santini sent on Wiltord and Saha in place of Trezeguet and Dacourt, maintaining the 4-4-2 formation. France now had a right-sided wide midfielder in Wiltord, which allowed Zidane to play as a central midfielder. Saha took his place next to Henry to lead the French attack. Greece remained unchanged, with Kapsis taking over marking Saha, Katsouranis shadowing Zidane and Fyssas marking Wiltord.

Santini's changes gave his team new impetus, at least for a while. Saha went past Kapsis from the left and entered the area but his shot was weak and easily dealt with by Nikopolidis. Henry's effort a minute later ended similarly.

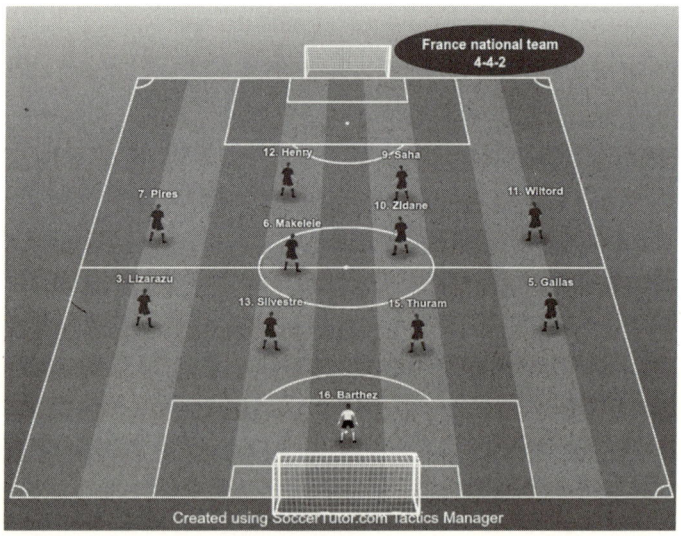

France line up after the changes

On 78 minutes Santini sent on Rothen in place of Pires. At this point Greece needed to keep the ball and lower the French tempo. Karagounis did this by shielding the ball and winning fouls, which gave his team-mates much-needed breathers. Rehhagel pulled off Basinas and sent on Tsiartas in the 84th minute. The French had their last very good chance on 87 minutes, when Gallas picked out Henry whose header went just wide. The end of the match saw the Greeks celebrating qualification to the next round and the defending champions returning home prematurely.

Chapter Nineteen

A Golden Silver Goal

FOOTBALL IS a passion, the world's favourite sport, but it is also a business. As Paolo Rossi, the forward who inspired Italy to win the 1982 World Cup, infamously observed: 'I cannot feed my child on glory.' In that spirit, the Greek players had a dangerous distraction two days before the semi-final against the Czech Republic.

Money, and particularly promised bonuses, had been an ongoing issue since the draw against Spain in Porto had opened up the way to the knockout phase. Already discomforted by the need to move hotels, because their base for the previous fortnight was fully booked, the squad asked to meet with federation president Vasilis Gagatsis.

Given that the Greek government and the EPO had agreed to cover the bonus for the team's qualification for the knockout stage on a 50/50 basis, the players were under the impression that the deal covered their achievement in making the last four. They raised the stakes by asking for one million euros each in the event they reached the final.

The meeting, after dinner, was stressful. Gagatsis, who began by insisting the EPO simply did not have that sort of money, remembers: 'It was a very tense conversation and we had words. "You are being unreasonable because you do not see the EPO's position," I told them. "You don't care where the money comes from as long as you get it." The response was explosive.

'That caused Angelos Basinas' outburst, during which he threw plates and cutlery around,' Gagatsis recalls. 'I found that offensive, so I got up to leave and said that, henceforth, I would only speak to the captains [Zagorakis, Karagounis, and Basinas] about the issue. Basinas later told me that he had not meant to offend me, and that it happened in the heat of the moment. As for Rehhagel, he was never involved in matters outside his remit or that he didn't believe concerned him. He did, however, demand that any issue that affected the team be resolved in any way possible.'

In the end, the issue went to the very top. Kostas Karamanlis, then prime minister of Greece, addressed the players on the eve of the final: 'Regardless of what may happen tomorrow you are the real winners as far as we are concerned, so you can ask anything you want from us.' The squad then reiterated their demand for a bonus of one million euros each to the then Minister of Culture, Fani Petralia.

The State awarded them 157,000 euros each. The shortfall had to be covered by the EPO, who came close to the initial figure due to the 22 million euros they received from UEFA as champions. The federation topped up the government's contribution with 600,000 euros for each player, in addition to the agreed 100,000 euros for qualifying for the knockout stage. Otto Rehhagel's bonus also came close to one million euros.

Gagatsis' belief that both the State and the EPO should prove to the players that they acknowledged the importance of their efforts led him to a very clever decision. Before the final he announced to the players that they would receive the bonus win or lose. 'That was a very smart move by Gagatsis. It helped them retain their good spirits and enthusiasm before the final,' observes Giorgos Papalanis.

Financial considerations aside, preparations had been thorough. 'We started getting ready for the semi-final immediately after the victory against France,' recalls Giannis Topalidis, Rehhagel's assistant. 'We went, with the president of the EPO, to the Dragao stadium to see the Czech Republic play Denmark. The Czech Republic scored their first goal in the 49th minute and we thought that Denmark had been the better side until then, which meant something to us. The Czechs' 3-0 win did not discourage us. We didn't believe that the score reflected their performance, despite the praise heaped upon them by the media.

'We had to think about what to do. Being a manager is about cunning too, not just training and tactics, particularly at national team level. That had always been Rehhagel's view, that training is important and defining at an early stage, when the footballers are still young. Not when we are talking about experienced professionals. Our strategy would be to block their key players. We decided that we should neutralise Koller, Nedved and Rosicky. We initially considered assigning Dellas to Koller and use someone else as a central defender. Man-to-man wasn't really Dellas' thing however, so we would lose that element we had relied on so far.

'We considered Kapsis and someone else but decided on Kapsis in the end. When we told him he was to mark

Koller, he simply said, "If that's what you want." Despite the 20cm height differential between them he marked him really well. But his marking was a more complex affair because we had instructed Dellas to challenge Koller during crosses from wide areas in order for him to head the ball away. Kapsis wouldn't be able to beat Koller in the air. We were lucky with Nedved even if his injury was not really a defining element. Ronaldo also missed the Euro 2016 Final due to an injury, but Portugal still managed to win the trophy.'

Kapsis vividly recalls not receiving any specific instructions: 'They didn't ask me to do anything special. That was the great thing about my relationship with Rehhagel. He had confidence in me and I respected him because we never had to talk about things. I knew what to do on the pitch and he knew what to expect from me. He never had to coach me or explain what I had to do because he had trust in me.

'It was the same with Koller. He didn't have to tell me about it the day before the match. He just announced it during the team meeting when he revealed the starting line-up. I had imagined that he would use someone taller against Koller: I expected to be assigned to mark Baros. It went well, however. I made a choice and I was vindicated. It was my idea to defend like I did by running to head the ball first, before he challenged me. I could have missed the ball and been exposed but I decided to make a decision and it never failed during the match.

'The coach's slogan during the team meetings was "protect and conserve what we have gained". He had the gift of knowing when to hold the stick and when to use the carrot. He could tell when he needed to boost our confidence or keep us grounded and after the match against France, he needed to keep us grounded. "Don't lose it," he told us. "We didn't do anything fantastic. Don't miss this opportunity because you will never have another like it again. Suddenly everyone is interested in you and that means the opportunity to play abroad, money, and contracts. Now is the time to prove that nothing so far has happened by accident."'

Stelios Venetidis had sensed a mood swing: 'The Czechs were deemed the favourites. We were watching the matches, so were aware of the fact that France had been on the way down, whereas the Czech Republic were a much better team. We were also a bit lucky in that match, but everything plays its part when you try to do something this important. It was obvious that we were not as good as them and you could tell, during the team meeting, that while the manager thought of them as a really strong opponent, he did not seem as afraid as before the game with France. It is possible that fear disappeared after the victory over France, and he started believing that we could go all the way.'

It would be a test of nerve, trust and durability. Topalidis offers an insight into the thought processes of the Greek management team, as the semi-final entered extra time: 'Otto said, "What should we do? Should we use Nikolaidis?" I replied, "Why not use Tsiartas? We are aiming for a set piece, a silver goal." He thought about it and we ended up using him. We could have done so and lost but in the end it worked for us.

'During extra time, the Czechs were practically paralysed with fear. On the other hand, we used Tsiartas because we wanted to go for it. That's why we didn't use a defender. We had good players to choose from and we owed that to Rehhagel because he had picked all of them. That was Kapsis' first time in the national team, Dellas as well. When we called him up he said, "They will criticise you, don't call me up now," yet he turned out to be a key player. Nikolaidis returned to the team because of Rehhagel. Nikopolidis, Vryzas, Katsouranis, Seitaridis and Basinas all became starting players in the team because of Rehhagel.'

That silver goal by Traianos Dellas, at the end of the first half of extra time, has entered the folklore of Greek football. Theo Zagorakis can recall it as if it was scored yesterday: 'Tsiartas put the ball through the eye of a needle and it reached two of our players. The Czechs lost their concentration, whereas we were always focused during set pieces. Katsouranis, Basinas and myself had drilled similar situations in our area countless times. We owed that to Rehhagel. The Czechs hadn't been able to eliminate us during the 90 minutes, so they tried to conserve energy. As a result, we took the initiative and created many opportunities during extra time, which forced them to fall back. They didn't make any changes because they thought they were doing well and they paid for it. It was a crazy match.'

Vasilis Tsiartas gave his version in an interview in 2005: 'Before the goal, I had taken a free kick and the ball hit Dellas on the shoulder so it didn't go towards the goal with sufficient power. At that stage I had said, "I want you to go towards the penalty spot and I will find you." I talked to him again later, before the goal, and he was aware that he had to stand by the near post because that's how we did it in training. I would always ask him, as I did all the taller guys who came up front, to go there.

'After the goal, Dellas shouted "You are a magician." Before making the decision for me to enter the game, Rehhagel had been arguing with Topalidis for ten minutes. He wanted to use Nikolaidis while Topalidis insisted on getting me on. They spent another ten minutes not talking to each other until they ended up putting me on.'

Dellas' goal is the first thing that comes to Michalis Kapsis' mind every time he hears the words 'Euro 2004': 'That goal has stayed with me. It is what I remember most of all about the tournament because that was the moment I thought that we could win the cup. Even after France, I had been keeping those thoughts to myself. But after Dellas' goal I said to myself, "It's just a match, so why not?"

'And I thought that being first is not the same as being second. It would not be the same thing today if we had just been the finalists. The title matters. For this match against the Czechs, I have heard it all: that God slept, that the universe wanted it that way ... everything. It is true that we felt real pressure in this match. Together with the second half of the match against Spain and the first 25 minutes against Russia, these were our toughest moments.'

Traianos Dellas, the man of the moment, says today: 'I was worried when he took off Vryzas who was very active and put on Tsiartas. It turned out that Rehhagel obviously counted on set pieces. A footballer can never understand, while playing, what the coach is thinking or what the coach wants to do. As a player lacking the mind of a coach and therefore being unable to analyse his decisions, I may have been hasty in judging his decisions. At the same time as a coach myself now, I realise that doing something to help your team can have the opposite effect. You can never be sure.'

Rehhagel had nothing but praise for Dellas even before the team reached the semi-finals. He used his favourite outlet, the German press, to justify his decision to use three defenders against France, telling Peter Hess of the *Frankfurter Allgemeine Zeitung*: 'If I had Nowotny and Lucio [German and Brazilian international defenders playing for Bayer Leverkusen at the time] I could always have four defenders lined up at any time. When I have two defenders that run 100 metres in 15 seconds, I cannot do that. So I brought my own colossus from Rhodes, who led us to success.'

Dellas had told me during an interview published on the day of the Russia match: 'There is no secret to my performance. Otto Rehhagel's faith in me was the key. I wasn't playing in any games with Roma when he called me up. He believed in me and said so right from the start. He was the first manager who ever told me that I was his first choice. I felt obligated to prove, first to myself and then to Rehhagel, that it had been a mistake for Roma not to use me. So we developed a relationship of mutual trust and respect. He has the same relationship with all the players, which is why he has not faced any internal issues with the team. Instead, he is able to inspire and guide us.'

In the opinion of Giorgos Karagounis, it was the Greek players' psychological condition, boosted by the landmark victory against Zidane's France, that played the most important role in the semi-final. He reasoned: 'After our victory over France, my attitude concerning the next game was a bit "provincial". I was like, who cares about the Czechs? Despite the fact that they had four wins in four games. Despite the fact that they were second favourites for the tournament and had played better than everyone.

'They had a well-rounded team with players like Nedved, Rosicky, and Poborsky, but since we had been able to eliminate France, the world champions and Euro winners, I believed we would be able to beat the Czech Republic too, somehow. It is important to approach a match in that mood. We were very confident. Many have been left with the impression that we faced several difficulties during that game but despite having viewed it a number of times, I don't see that. Even though the Czechs had two great opportunities and kept pressing us at the start, the game was even after that.

'We didn't feel as pressured as when we faced Spain or France for a while there. Yes they did have a good 20 minutes, but the game could have gone either way. It was us that had more chances in extra time. I wouldn't say that they underestimated us; they came in strongly and created chances for themselves, but I believe they had had more exposure than they needed. They were a good team, not a great one. I had seen the 3-0 win against Denmark and it had been magical, but the fact that they were coming from that series of four victories with their minds at ease counted in our favour. They had some great players on the pitch, like Smicer who replaced Nedved, but still.'

Kostas Katsouranis was reassured by the vibe of the entire country that summer: 'We were not worried. We believed it was under control, that it was going our way. There is no luck in football. It wasn't that Rehhagel was lucky. Everything went our way in the Euros but we fought hard for it, we challenged our fortune. We had the entire country supporting us so it wasn't just Rehhagel's aura. We had been able to unite the Greek people and that gave us wings. I remember that me and Fyssas would say the same thing before every match:

"Enough. Let's go home, we have weddings to go back to."
[Both players would be getting married in July 2004.] The
match against Spain had been the turning point, because it
had been touch and go. After France it was like, "There are
only two games left.'"

According to Antonis Nikopolidis, not only did the
Czech Republic have the best team but they were also the
only opponent to take Greece seriously enough to study
and adjust their game. 'They were so well-organised that
we found it difficult to create scoring opportunities against
them. Tall players, and great at set pieces. They hadn't
conceded a goal from a set piece in three years. While
we knew we could score against France from a free kick
or corner, with the Czechs we didn't have the sense that
it would work because they were able to neutralise our
weapons. That was an issue because we felt that we could
hold out against them but we couldn't find our way to
the net.'

UEFA's technical report had the following, slightly
florid, perspective: 'Except for the Russians, who were the
only team to beat them, everybody was rated favourite
to beat the Greeks. The Czechs were no exception. They
certainly carried the weight of the game, dominating two-
to-one in terms of goal attempts and corners and enjoying a
slight edge in possession. But, like Greece's other opponents
– except the Russians who prised the Greek can open with
an early goal – they found it unusual to dominate rather
than counter-punch.

'History will ask academic questions about what might
have happened had Pavel Nedved not been forced to
withdraw before half-time after trying in vain to continue
despite a knee injury. It would be an exaggeration to claim

that the Czech ship had been de-masted, but the mainsail had certainly been torn. Vladimir Smicer, his replacement, added width on the left but no single substitute could match Pavel Nedved for pace, change of tempo, finishing and the explosive sprinting that would potentially inflict most damage on the Greek *modus operandi* of picking up opponents in zones and man-marking until the move broke down.

'With Nedved stirring attacking cocktails with Jan Koller and Milan Baros, Tomas Rosicky and Karel Poborsky had been assigned more defensive roles than they habitually played in club football. Nedved's departure obliged them to contribute more in an attack where target man Koller was allowed to chest the ball down or nod it on, but rarely allowed to turn. Even though they struggled to cope with individual marking and lack of space, the Czechs created chances and clipped both bar and post against a Greek team that overtly prioritised not conceding a goal.

'Unusually for a match that goes into extra time, only three changes were made, with Karel Bruckner contributing only the enforced substitution of Pavel Nedved. Otto Rehhagel made a straight midfield change of Stylianos Giannakopoulos for Angelos Basinas and, as extra time kicked off, sent on Vasileios Tsiartas, whose technique allowed the Greeks to retain more possession, though he found it difficult to match the high-pressure game of Zisis Vryzas. But it was Vasileios Tsiartas who scripted the dramatic denouement after 55 of the 60 seconds of added time at the end of the first period of extra time. His corner from the right was perfectly delivered for Traianos Dellas to produce the near-post header that took the Greeks into the final. It was the last ever silver goal to be scored and it had a golden hue, as the timing gave the crestfallen Czechs no time to reply. They were the only semi-finalists to have won all four of the previous games and had made an outstanding contribution to the tournament. But they were not alone in finding the Greeks a tough bone to chew.'

The silver goal had already been abolished by the FIFA International Board in February 2004. The silver goal officially ceased to exist after 1 July that year but FIFA and UEFA decided to repeal the regulation only after 4 July, following the Euro 2004 Final. This was 'for purposes of coherency, given that the tournament started on 12 June when the regulation was still in effect'. Dellas' goal, the only goal he ever scored for the Greek national team, is the only silver goal to be scored at national team level.

'We are disappointed by the result but only that,' Czech manager Karel Bruckner said immediately after the match. 'I told the guys that I am really proud of them. Nedved told them they were the best national team he ever played in. I must congratulate the Greeks for their clever tactical approach and wish them luck in the final. We played well in the second half, but they were more effective than us. In the three years and 30 games I have counted as manager of the team that was the only goal we conceded from a corner.'

It took courage to speak in those terms, given the scale of his disappointment and the ramifications of the defeat. He admitted that he had been planning on using forward Marek Heinz before Dellas' goal derailed his plans. Bruckner has never spoken about the match since. He even politely refused to take part in this book, as did most of the former Czech internationals.

Rehhagel retained his focus, despite a very special meeting at the hotel, just before the semi-final. 'Papalanis contacted me to say that Beckenbauer had met with the coach,' Vasilis Gagatsis reveals. 'Rehhagel had not mentioned anything about that. Later, at Lisbon airport on the way back to Athens he said, "Beckenbauer came to see me. You know what he wants." I had not included a release clause in the contract we had drawn up that lasted until 2006. I was afraid he would say "my country is calling, you understand", but instead all he said was: "Do not believe anything you hear. Whatever happens I will be the one to tell you."'

Rehhagel had his heart's desire within reach. Not only was the German FA offering him the job he had been set on since at least 2001, but he had turned their perception of him around. He had again become popular, relevant and commercial in the consciousness of German football. He had proved his theory that 'relevant is he who wins'. It was especially sweet that it was Beckenbauer who came to see him, to discuss him taking over the German national team.

Beckenbauer had been one of those responsible for firing him from Bayern Munich after nine months. Rehhagel took it hard, accusing him, in conversations with close associates, of 'stealing' his chance to lift the UEFA Cup in 1996 by letting him go just five days before the two-legged final against Bordeaux. Beckenbauer took charge himself, overseeing a 5-1 win on aggregate.

Gagatsis realised Rehhagel had been offered a very attractive financial package. 'They would give him ten million euros for two years, with five million coming from the German FA and five million from sponsors,' he explained. 'Plus, he didn't have to play in the qualifying stage. He would be the German national team manager for the 2006 World Cup, to be held in his own country. We only offered him 600,000 euros a year. When we went out to eat about a month later, after he had made his decision to stay known to me, I asked, "It's so much money, why didn't you go?" He replied, "You pay me 600,000 and I eat half a steak. Even if I got paid ten million, I would still be eating half a steak."'

Giannis Topalidis admits: 'We were supposed to leave after the Euros because that had been the ultimate goal. The Euros was tougher than a World Cup, if one factors in how difficult our group had been in Portugal as opposed to groups in the World Cup. He had asked me what to do before the final and I had said "Go". I was also thinking that he would be taking me with him to Germany. I mean, we won the Euros, what else is there to do in Greece? I never regretted it though. We had a great time here all these years.'

According to him Rehhagel turned down the German offer 'because he did not want to work with certain people in the German FA. They had deprived him of a trophy by firing him from Bayern Munich just before the UEFA Cup Final. He wouldn't have been able to move past that.' Whatever the merits of that view, it is certain that Rehhagel made his decision to stay in Greece in conjunction with his wife, Beate.

'He always consulted with his wife,' Gagatsis reflects. 'She was well versed in football and would join us for the away games. I remember him saying, "I don't understand why in Greece you say that it is a bad thing to consult with the person I live with. Why are you contemptuous of that?" He had a different mentality. They had been through a lot together and he really loved her. He trusted her blindly. And in our world who could he trust? Managers are quite insecure because of the nature of their role. If you asked your wife about things and she was right ten times out of ten, wouldn't you trust her?'

By contrast, Topalidis believes that both the German and Greek media exaggerated her role in Rehhagel's career: 'Beate has been at his side since the beginning. Yes, she is his wife and they always talked things over, but she never had the amount of influence that she was made out to have. I have spent a lot of time with them. She did have opinions about football but she never took part in the actual decision-making process when it came to football. Rehhagel has a very strong personality. I would never argue with him when I saw that there was a difference of opinion. Beate was similar in that but much calmer. Otto would always talk about how smart she was.'

- - - - - - - - - - -

Greece 1 Czech Republic 0 (aet)
Tactical Analysis by Athanasios Terzis

For the Euro 2004 semi-final Rehhagel chose once again to counter the perceived strengths of his team's opponents. He used a 5-4-1 formation. As with France, he chose Kapsis and Seitaridis as centre-halves. Traianos Dellas was sweeper, while on the right this time was Katsouranis. On the left of the defence was Fyssas. Zagorakis and Basinas were the central midfielders. Karagounis was on the left side of midfield, and Charisteas on the right. Vryzas was the lone striker once again.

Czech coach Karel Bruckner went with a 4-4-2 formation with Cech in goal, Grygera on the right, Jankulovski on the left, while Ujfalusi and Bolf were the central defenders. Galasek and Rosicky were in central midfield, on the right

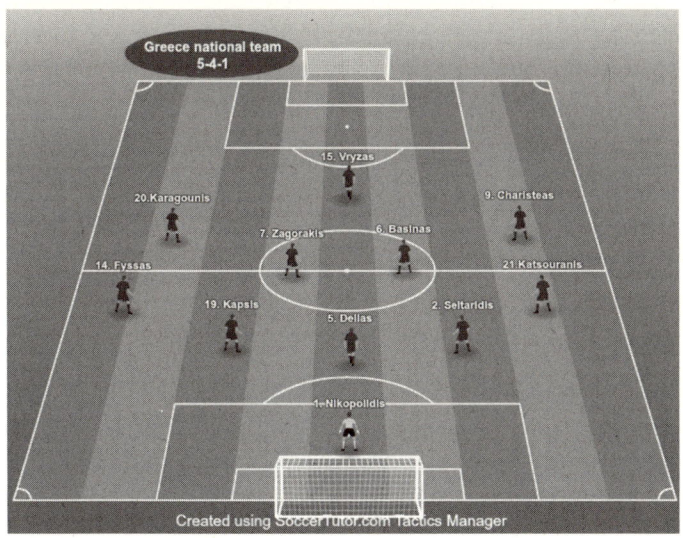

Greece vs Czech Republic

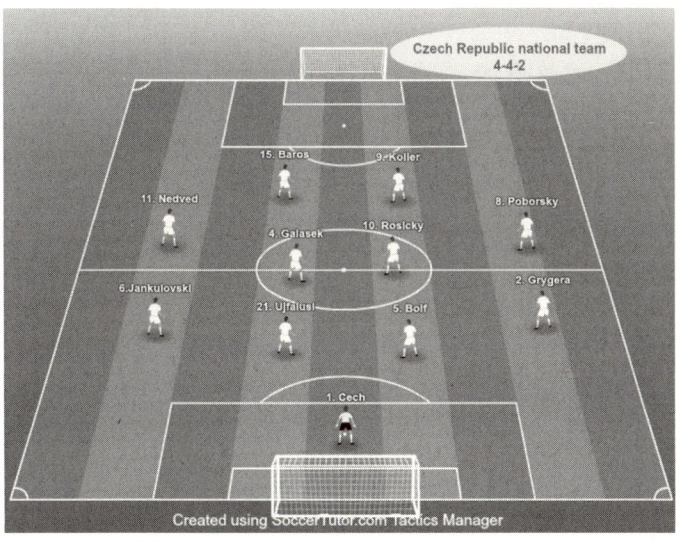

Czech Republic line up

there was Poborsky and Nedved was on the left. Koller and Baros were the two strikers.

As usual, Greece had an extra player in defence, where there was a 3 vs 2 advantage for Greece. In midfield, there was an even 2 vs 2 balance. In the centre of the Czech defence they had a 2 vs 1 advantage, while on the wings the match-up was 1 vs 1.

Greece used man-to-man marking again, with Rehhagel using Seitaridis as a centre-half, as he thought he would match Baros' attributes, while Kapsis had to cope with the much taller Koller. Katsouranis marked Nedved on the right, even though Nedved operated more like a central midfielder. Fyssas, on the left, would mark Poborsky. In the middle of the park, Zagorakis would be on Rosicky and Basinas on Galasek. Karagounis, on the left, would be checking Grygera's advances and Charisteas those of Jankulovski on the right. Vryzas would close down whichever of the defenders happened to be on the ball.

The Czech Republic started the match with the aim of imposing their own tempo by pressing hard, maintaining good movement of the ball and high mobility from the players. This resulted in Rosicky's long-range strike against the post in the second minute, while in the fifth minute, Jankulovski shot from an angle but Nikopolidis parried for a corner. The Greek defence was kept busy by Koller, as every time the Czechs crossed to him, Kapsis would seek to intercept from the front, while Dellas would provide support from behind in case Kapsis lost the duel. Defending set plays, Dellas would be the one who undertook to supervise Koller.

In midfield, Basinas' tactical position was flexible, as Galasek had mostly defensive duties and stayed close to the central defenders, which allowed Basinas to drop back and support either Zagorakis or Katsouranis. After the first 15 minutes, Greece were able to find their rhythm

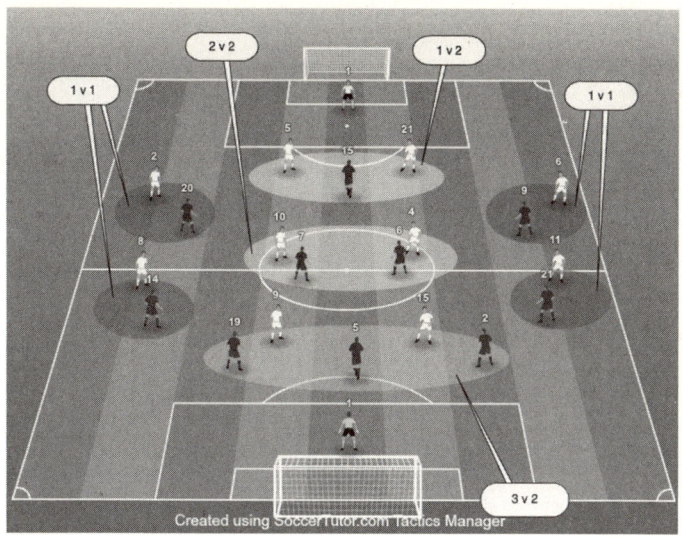

Greece vs Czech Republic: The matchups

and started passing and keeping possession of the ball. Karagounis was instrumental in this, because he managed to retain possession under the pressure of Grygera and gave his team-mates time to come to his assistance. At the same time, he often made moves towards the centre, either to shoot or pass, or to free himself from Grygera, who would not follow him outside his area of responsibility. Kostas Katsouranis was also excellent at the start of the match, both in his defensive and offensive duties, as he won all his duels against Czech captain Nedved. The team's principal attacking tactic was to quickly get the ball forward with long passes to either Vryzas or Charisteas, who either sought to head the ball to a team-mate or to keep possession while waiting for support.

When the Greek players won second balls in areas behind the Czech midfielders, they were quite fluid, aiming to either pass to Karagounis or to Katsouranis and Fyssas, who would make runs up the wings trying to

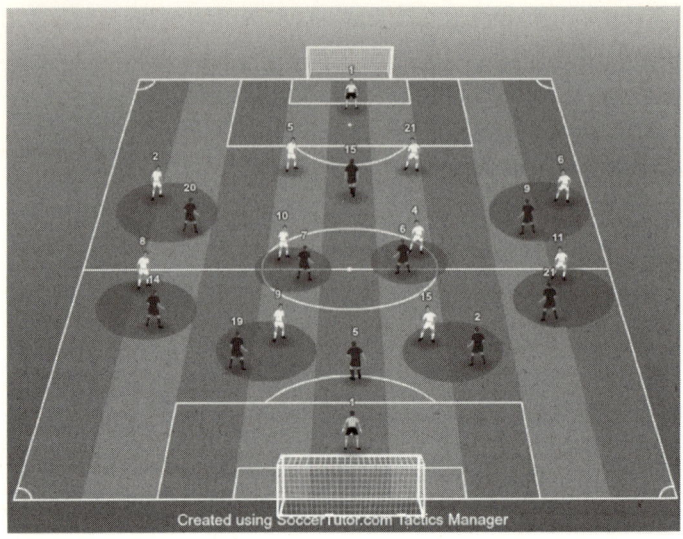

Greece vs Czech Republic: pairs of players man to man

cross for either Vryzas or Charisteas in the penalty area. After such a team move on 29 minutes, the ball reached Fyssas on the left, who managed a low cross but neither Vryzas, Charisteas or Katsouranis were able to connect with the ball.

As Greece began to retain possession, the Czechs chose to defend in the middle third of the pitch, affording them some space. This tactic was risky for the Greek team, as during transitions from attack to defence, there was the possibility for their players to lose the men they needed to mark, which could potentially be exploited by the Czechs. That was exactly what happened in the 33rd minute, when during a transition, Rosicky found himself alone on the right. Dellas moved to close him down, but the Czech player managed to cross. Katsouranis stood between Jankulovski and Nedved and as the ball headed to the Czech midfielder, Katsouranis moved to block a possible shot. Nedved was not able to connect, under pressure, but the ball ended up with Jankulovski, who shot but Nikopolidis was able to parry for a corner.

In the 40th minute, Vladimir Smicer replaced Nedved, who had been injured. The first half ended without further incident, as Greece had been able to neutralise the Czechs' threats with both Kapsis and Seitaridis winning most of their personal duels. Katsouranis and Fyssas had all but neutralised Nedved and Poborsky, while Zagorakis and Basinas had been very mobile in midfield. Under these circumstances, Dellas did not have much to do at the back, as the Czechs had not been sufficiently threatening.

The second half started without any changes for the two teams, and there were no tactical variations. The first 15 minutes passed with the teams sharing possession; the Czechs were unable to threaten the Greek defence. On 60 minutes, a shot by Rosicky from outside the area went wide. The statistics showed that, up to the point, the Czechs had 11 shots to the Greeks' three, but only shots from Rosicky and Jankulovski in the first half had threatened.

Greece were trying to score mainly through set pieces. On 64 minutes, after a wide free kick and an unsuccessful attempt to clear by Cech, Fyssas headed the ball just wide. On 67 minutes, from a Karagounis free kick, Vryzas headed the ball into the Czech goalkeeper's hands. Five minutes later, Rehhagel introduced Giannakopoulos for Basinas, who had made a very important contribution throughout the game and especially in the first minutes of the second half. The Greek midfielder played a role similar to that of Dellas. He was there to provide support if one of the other midfielders lost their man.

Giannakopoulos' entrance led to Karagounis moving to the centre, while the substitute went to the left. This illustrated that Rehhagel was looking for something more offensively. In the 76th minute, Vryzas headed over from a corner by Giannakopoulos. Four minutes later, the Czechs missed their best chance when Koller found himself unmarked in front of goal but shot wide. The Czechs stepped up their pressure in the last ten minutes of normal time and threatened again, especially when Baros wriggled through the Greek defence only to shoot wide just before the end of normal time.

Rehhagel began extra time by sending on Tsiartas in place of Vryzas. Charisteas moved to spearhead the attack, Giannakopoulos moved to the right and Tsiartas was on the left wing. On 93 minutes, from a goal kick by Nikopolidis, Charisteas won a header and Giannakopoulos found space behind the Czech defence. The Greece midfielder headed at goal as Cech came towards him,

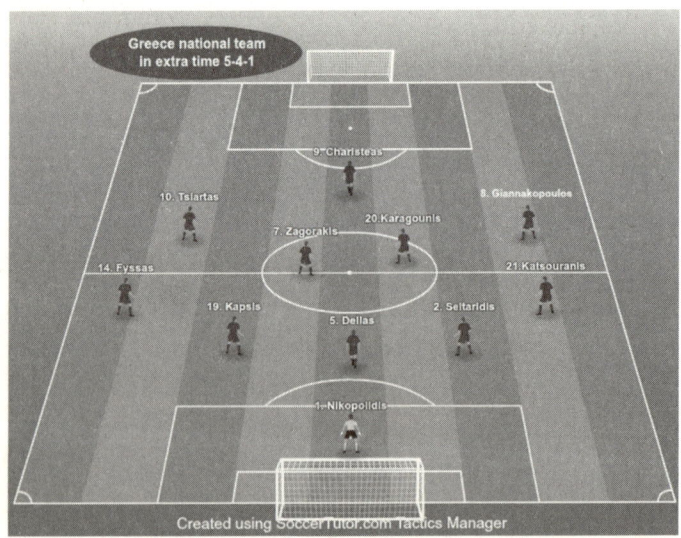

Greece vs Czech Republic extra time

but the goalkeeper denied the best Greek opportunity up to that point.

Greece continued to be more threatening and in the 102nd minute came close again, as Dellas directed a header from a Tsiartas free kick at Cech. The match was decided when Greece won a corner at the end of the first half of extra time. Tsiartas swung it towards the near post, where Katsouranis and Dellas were waiting. Katsouranis missed, but the ball was headed in by Dellas, sealing a historic silver goal win for Greece.

Dellas goal

Chapter Twenty

For All Eternity

BY THE time the squad returned to Lisbon on 2 July, the city had been christened 'the capital of Greece' by a euphoric Greek media. It was flash-mob football, confirmation of the wonderful madness that can overtake a nation at a major tournament. The interest was overpowering.

Around 7,000 Greek fans attended the win against France. In excess of 10,000 were at the breathless semi-final against the Czech Republic. An estimated 15,000 flooded Lisbon in the build-up to the final, when the preoccupation with securing a ticket reached epidemic proportions. The maths, as so often on the big sporting occasion, was not promising.

The EPO receceived an official allocation of 12,000 tickets, 2,000 of which were made available through a specially erected kiosk in Lisbon. They sold out in four hours; the kiosk was then destroyed by frustrated fans. The federation sourced another 1,000 tickets and Vasilis Gagatsis, its president, even secured another 30 from ticket touts. That still left more than 2,000 Greek supporters, resigned to watching the final in the fan zones surrounding Estádio da Luz.

Greek expectation was, however, nothing compared to Portuguese hysteria. Hundreds of fans camped, night and day, outside the Sporting Lisbon training ground, where the home squad was based, just to grab a glimpse of their heroes. The country seemed trapped between a nervous breakdown and a continuous party. The bigger cities were in a permanent state of carnival.

The scenes on the day of the final were unprecedented. Thousands lined the route taken by Portugal's team bus on the way to the stadium; it took over an hour to negotiate a 20-minute journey. The Greek players had a similar experience the day after the final, when the bus was mobbed on the way from the airport to the Panathinaiko Stadio in Athens, but they didn't feel the full weight of expectation beforehand.

Portugal's yearning for their first major football title, made even more special by it being won on home soil, played into Greek hands. An overwhelming air of premature celebration undoubtedly helped Rehhagel's team to gain the upper hand over Scolari's. The Portuguese players were carried away by the atmosphere and lost their concentration. Instead of focusing on their opponent and their game plan, they concentrated on the celebrations that would follow their seemingly inevitable victory.

Jorge Andrade, the former Portugal defender, admits: 'Our path to the final was a difficult one. We had to beat Spain, England, Holland. What was taking place all around us was extraordinary. There were thousands of people milling around the bus, even following us on horseback! Those are images I will never forget. However, now, I think that we should have been sheltered from what was taking place around us because the final called for us to be more grounded and focused, which I do not feel we were able to achieve.'

The Greek footballers, meanwhile, spent their time much more quietly. They were isolated in the Pestana Palace, a five-star hotel on top of the Alto de Santo hill originally built as a palace in 1904. It has a view of King Christ, the 110-metre statue that was inspired by the Cristo do Corcovado statue in Rio de Janeiro. Bill Clinton and Madonna have been patrons of the hotel; the Italian team loved its splendour during their stay earlier in the tournament.

'The last hotel we stayed in was a palace,' recalls Giorgos Papalanis. 'Me and Topalidis had been to see it before the Euros and they had been very dismissive and told us that the Italian team would be staying there. I had then told the manager that I would remember that. Whenever I ran into him before the final he would apologise profusely.'

What went through the Greek players' minds as they were preparing for the biggest match of their lives? Giorgos Karagounis, who would not play because of the number of yellow cards he had accumulated, remembers: 'We thought that conditions favoured the Portuguese. We were playing at their home again. They had played their last game on Wednesday, we played on Thursday. Moreover, we had finished around 1am because of extra time and had ended up going to bed after 2.30am with all the celebrations. We had to travel to Lisbon the next day while they were already there, and we had only one day left to rest before the game on Sunday. It wasn't easy, but it seemed like we were on such a high following the victory against France that we couldn't help but win the trophy. That's how we felt at the time despite the fact that we would be playing against Portugal again and it would be difficult to beat them a second time.'

Karagounis goes on to explain why the Greek players were able to go out on the pitch free of any anxiety. 'The coach would always bring us face-to-face with our responsibilities. We were stressed because we really wanted that trophy and the possibility of coming second weighed on our minds, but we were experienced players, so we did not let the feeling of pressure get to us. The manager gave a good speech during the team meeting. After the game with France even he was more relaxed and less hesitant. That victory had made everyone believe. That's why to my mind, there was a pre-France and post-France stage to the tournament, as far as we were concerned. That doesn't mean that I didn't respect our opponents, of course.'

As with every previous game, Rehhagel paid a lot of attention to his players' psychological and mental preparation. Before he went into the team meeting, the manager followed his favourite stress-release habit. Papalanis reveals: 'On the day of the match, just before the meeting, I would bring him 40 of his favourite pastries. That was the only time he broke his dietary rules.'

Stelios Venetidis recalls Rehhagel's speech during the team meeting, when he also unveiled the starting 11 against Portugal: 'His speech went as usual, "We have all been through this together and we have reached the top." What he also did was to dismiss second place. "Whoever comes first takes away the trophy and leaves nothing for the finalist. Years from now, only the winner will be remembered. No one remembers the finalist, only those who win." After enumerating several examples, he went on to remind us that we had already beaten the Portuguese. He was trying to be direct and understood through his expressions and movement, despite the fact that he spoke in German.'

Kostas Katsouranis felt manager and players were on the same wavelength, mentally and psychologically. They were ready to give their all because they were aware that this was a once-in-a-lifetime chance: 'I remember him describing what would happen if we lost. He was very vivid. He told us: "We have struggled to reach the ultimate point. It isn't like you don't care about losing. There will be frustration, disappointment and tears and that is natural when you reach this stage. That does not negate what we have achieved. We will return as heroes and as such we will be welcomed by the entire nation." The team was very confident. When we went out on the pitch, we looked at the trophy and believed that we would take it home.

'We wanted to come out happy. We did not want to allow the Portuguese to play to the best of their ability. We wanted to give our best, even if we lost, but no more than 1-0. We did not want to go back after a heavy defeat because that's how the Greeks are. They would negate the rest of our performance in the tournament on the strength of the last result. All we wanted was to play like we had been playing throughout the knockout stage, to not concede any goals and risk everything in the last ten minutes in order to win. We may not have been as good as our opponents but we were not scared of them. We were expecting them to perform well.'

Scolari's final preparations, outlined to his players on a video screen were thorough, but had an edge of concern. 'I want you to really experience the friendship that you feel for each other,' he told the group. 'I want you to participate in this spirit. Think that the nation is grateful for your appearance so far, but they still want you to win the trophy.' That covered the philosophical aspects of reaching the final; practical problems were more pressing.

Scolari was well aware of the possibility that his team could concede a goal from a corner: 'Bear in mind that set pieces are the most difficult situations we will have to deal with in this match,' he urged his players. 'If there is a corner in our area, Seitaridis will be here, so I want Miguel and Pauleta to mark here. You will stay close, do you understand that? Don't think that this is extreme.'

The Brazilian coach's tone was urgent; he was animated as he used the screen to show where he wanted his players to go:

'Let's say there's a foul in their area. If the wall is right on the edge of the area, I want you to take the kick Cristiano, to surprise them. You will tell Figo to pass the ball but then you will run and shoot yourself. The outcome of this match may depend on a single detail, so we have to own that detail. We have to die for Portugal.'

By analysing specific plays, he was doing the exact opposite of what Rehhagel was doing at the same instant. As Giannis Topalidis tells it, the German told his team: 'The match calls for specific answers and reactions. It is up to you to decide which that will be.' The plan was clear: having made his players aware of their responsibilities, he then had the trust and confidence to let them play.

'We did not make any changes to our strategy for the final,' Topalidis explained. 'Scolari made the mistake of playing with one forward. All the teams that used two forwards created problems for us, like they had done during the final part of the first match in the tournament. We did not concede goals easily. As they started pressing and going for a goal right from the beginning, they became frustrated very early. They did not try to control the game, they simply pressed on. They had not studied our style because we were the underdogs. Things could have ended badly for us if they had used more forwards, but, as it was, they found themselves behind.'

Videos of Scolari's speeches, included in a Portuguese TV documentary about the performance of the team at Euro 2004, clearly show that the Brazilian manager had studied the Greek team carefully and had attempted to prepare his players accordingly. According to Jorge Andrade, the mistake they made was that 'we did not make sufficient changes to our game plan compared to the opening game. Even though by now we knew that they were a tough team, we held on to the same structure, playing with a single forward, while the Greeks had two or three central defenders which gave them the advantage. They played like we expected. They kept a tight defence and waited for an opportunity to score a goal.'

Before they went on the pitch, Scolari and his players embraced and offered a prayer to God. That was something that Rehhagel never did. 'Seeing anyone cross themselves before a match really annoyed him,' Angelos Charisteas recalls. 'He would say, "What are you doing? Do you expect that God will come down here and help you?" He was a fearless man. He would tell us: "I've lived through war and bombings. I was in the trenches and saw parents being killed." He had had some tough experiences ...'

During half-time, Scolari updated his instructions: 'When we are in possession of the ball, I want you Cristiano, to move along the central axis between Seitaridis, the right-back and the centre-half. I want Seitaridis to follow you so that he frees up space for Nuno Valente. It is what Miguel has been doing well on the right wing. Paulo Ferreira has 45 minutes at his disposal in order to do this. When Deco or Maniche have the ball, I want Figo to move inwards, between Fyssas and Kapsis and pass towards the right-back, who will have gone wide.

'Our only chance is to play from the wings with either Nuno Valente or Paulo Ferreira. Deco, there are always two players behind Katsouranis who marks you, which means that you do not have space, so I want you to move to the side. That's when you, Costinha, have to move up to take advantage of the space left by Deco. Figo and Deco, if we win a free kick on the side of the area and they only use a two-person wall, I want you to signal that you will be crossing to the far post. Shoot on goal instead because the keeper will be expecting a cross and will therefore be away from the corner you will be aiming for. And watch the set pieces, guys, they are very well drilled.'

Scolari's search for solutions testified to the problems they had experienced during the first half, against a team that defended very tightly, with all ten players if needed. Rehhagel was responding to the occasion, according to Traianos Dellas: 'It all had to do with individual instructions he gave us. He gave you a lot of freedom about what you were supposed to be doing, but he tried hard to convey what he did not want you to do. He told me, "I don't want you to keep the ball indefinitely. I want you to find someone to pass it to." But he was flexible and let me decide because he was well aware of the fact that I can dribble, hold the ball and pass. He didn't tell Charisteas to mark the opponent's defender because Charisteas would do that anyway.'

Nikos Dabizas agrees: 'It was inevitable, due to the manager's philosophy and the nature of our opponents, that defensive play would be integrated into everything we did, which meant that the players' positional identities would be quite fluid. Midfielders would turn into full-backs and would then have to really exert themselves to cover their original responsibilities as well. It sounds paradoxical and disproportional, which was only natural because when you pay so much attention to the defensive dimension you end up affecting the strengths and characteristics of midfielders and forwards. However, it would be unfair to say that the defenders were more important than the forwards in our style of play. Our defensive performance was exceptional not only because our defenders were so good, which they were, but also because they counted on the additional support provided by the rest of the team. Our team spirit came to the fore in order to establish balance between us and our opponents.'

During half-time, Rehhagel boosted his team's confidence and helped them maintain their calm and focus: 'We don't have to change anything,' he told them. 'They cannot break us down. We are disrupting their rhythm. We will bide our time and find our chance to score a goal which will give us the trophy.'

Giorgos Karagounis, who had been watching the game from the stands, highlights Scolari's pivotal mistake of not using a second forward: 'I cheered when I saw that he replaced Pauleta with Nuno Gomes. Right when he's got Ronaldo and Figo playing from the wings and crossing into our area, while all of us are essentially playing defence and not counter-attacking, he chooses to remain with a single forward. All that when he had really caused trouble for us by playing with two forwards at the end of the opening match. It worked out for him against England but not against us.

'What he did worked in our favour because anyone who used two forwards against us proved tough for us to handle. France ended up playing with four forwards. Everything has to go your way in order to win a European Championship, even your opposing manager's strategy. Scolari may have operated selfishly in order to prove his plan, but if a manager operates like that he loses. Winning is what ultimately matters. If he had won the Euros because he had come to amend his plan no one would remember that, would they? They would only remember that he was European champion.'

Similar thoughts were going through Antonis Nikopolidis' mind during the game: 'Scolari sought to break us down and watch out for counter-attacks and set pieces. He did not succeed in solving those three problems. The main thing was that we were in their heads. They thought that they could not score against us. Their executions were mediocre or even downright bad. They would come to an appropriate distance from our goal but then fail to shoot on target. They were not focused on scoring.

'On the other hand, we had one major problem, which anyone who had spent time watching us would have realised immediately. If you used two forwards against us, you threw us off because we'd have to change our entire formation around. During the final, while it was just Pauleta up front, we were calm and collected. When

I saw Nuno Gomes warming up, I thought that would be an issue, what with Figo and Ronaldo crossing from the wings. But then I saw Nuno Gomes replacing Pauleta and I immediately took heart because they replaced a good forward with a mediocre one, who found it hard to find the net. If both of them had stayed on I don't know what would have happened, but Scolari did not reinforce his attack so that's when I thought that we'd be fine.'

According to Nikos Dabizas, Portugal paid for their manager's intransigence: 'Scolari paid for being dogmatic. He did not leave his ego behind. He wanted to prove that what happened in the opening game was a fluke. He was being dogmatic, not arrogant. All that played a role in what happened.'

The moment that scared Theo Zagorakis involved Figo's shot in the 89th minute, when the ball came off Fyssas' foot for a corner. 'I keep going back to that one, even more than Charisteas' goal and the celebrations afterwards. It was crazy the way Figo shot and the ball practically scratched the post because of Fyssas' foot. If they had been able to equalise there it would have been a completely different match.' His instinctive sigh, so many years later, tells you the incident still lives with him.

Everything seemed to have gone Greece's way. Even Jimmy Jump, who gained international infamy after invading the pitch to throw a Barcelona flag at Luis Figo during the final, unwittingly played a role. His incursion lasted two minutes and served to disrupt the Portuguese attack, thereby granting the Greek team some welcome respite. The then 28-year-old Catalan wanted to protest Figo's move from Barcelona to their arch-rivals Real Madrid four years earlier in 2000.

His real name is Jaume Marquet. This is what he told me in the summer of 2007, after he had disrupted the Champions League Final in Athens:

'My webpage crashed from all the messages and visits the next day. Many of those were from Greek fans who congratulated me on disrupting the Portuguese attack. I was not intending to do that though. I like Portugal and players like Deco and Ronaldo, but I really hated Figo for what he had done. He had been our captain and he left us for Real.'

It's safe to say Andrade is not a fan: 'Even Jimmy Jump invaded and caused interference at the last moment. Everything went wrong for us. The dominant feeling after the match was one of frustration. It was very strange to realise that for all the times we had been celebrating, we wouldn't be able to celebrate the one time it mattered. That's how it goes and I don't blame anyone for that. We all gave our best.'

Zagorakis was the last Greek player to touch the ball when he shot and missed Ricardo's goal by a significant margin. Two seconds later, the final's man of the match and the player of the tournament was on his knees with his hands pointed towards the sky because the German referee Markus Merk had just blown the final whistle.

The words of Martin Tyler, the commentator whose voice provided the soundtrack for the official Euro 2004 review highlights: 'I am telling you again and you better believe it. A team that started this tournament without ever having scored in the final stage of a tournament, a team that was 80/1 at the start of this tournament and 12/1 to win the final tonight is the 2004 European champion.'

Thirteen years later, Rehhagel had this to say to me: 'I was already an experienced manager so I could weigh the importance of an achievement. At the final whistle, when you saw me lift my fists in the air, I knew that we had just written a great chapter in the history of football. It was a success for all eternity, just as I had told my players before the match.'

- - - - - - - - - - -

Portugal 0 Greece 1
Tactical Analysis by Athanasios Terzis

For the Euro 2004 Final, Otto Rehhagel chose a 4-3-3 formation, to match the shape of the Portuguese team. Nikopolidis was the ever-present goalkeeper. Kapsis and Dellas were the central defenders, with Kapsis the man-to-man marker and Dellas as sweeper. On the right side of defence he selected Seitaridis with Fyssas on the left. Midfield consisted of Katsouranis as the central midfielder,

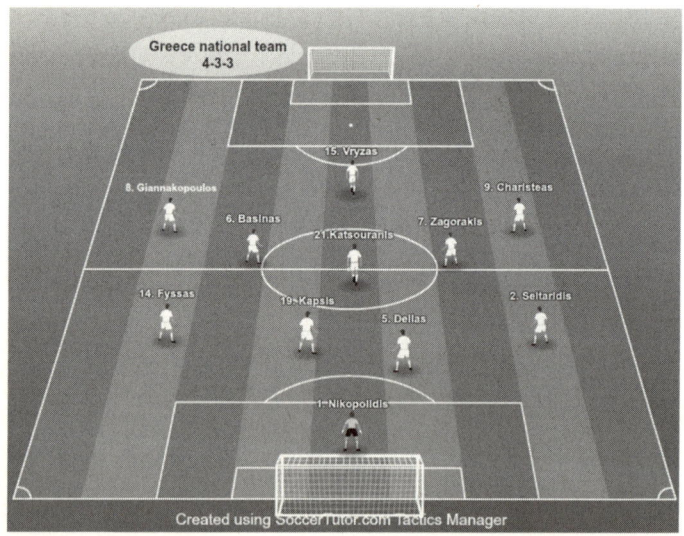

Greece formation

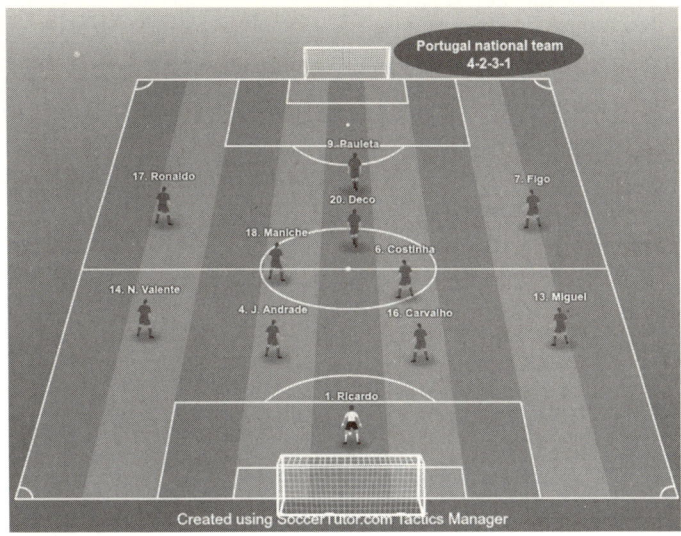

Portugal national team

with Basinas to his left and Zagorakis to the right of him. Charisteas was on the right wing and Giannakopoulos on the left. Vryzas spearheaded the attack.

Portugese coach Felipe Scolari chose a 4-2-3-1 formation which, as in the opening game between the two sides, often turned into 4-3-3. Ricardo was the goalkeeper, Costinha was the defensive midfielder, Maniche was the central midfielder and Deco the attacking midfielder. Ronaldo was to the left of the attack, Figo on the right and Pauleta in the middle.

Once again, there was numerical superiority for Greece in defence with 2 vs 1. In midfield there was a 3 vs 3 balance, while the Portuguese had an extra player in their defence, where there was a 1 vs 2 ratio. On the wings it was 1 vs 1 for both teams.

In the first half, Greece once again man-marked their opponents. Kapsis was on Pauleta, while Seitaridis and Fyssas had Ronaldo and Figo under their supervision.

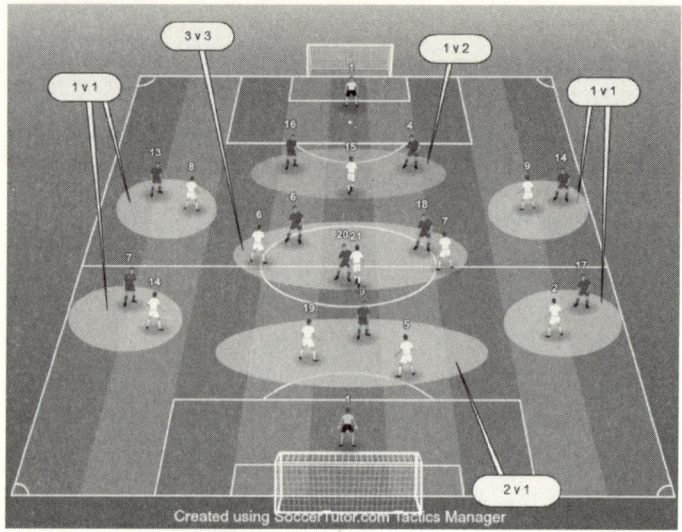

Greece vs Portugal: The matchups

In the middle, Zagorakis tracked Maniche and Basinas watched Costinha. Katsouranis shadowed Deco, who was in a more advanced position and had a freer attacking role. Charisteas and Giannakopoulos marked Valente and Miguel respectively. From very early in the match, the two Portuguese wingers attempted to draw Seitaridis and Fyssas away from their area of responsibility by converging towards the centre or dropping deep. Deco and Maniche tried to operate in the spaces created to the right and left of the defence, as they had in the opening match. However, their markers stayed tight and Dellas, who closed any gaps quickly, did not allow this tactic to threaten.

In another duplication of the opening game of the tournament between the teams, Figo often moved into a central midfield position in order to free himself from Fyssas' marking and to create an overload in the centre. Portugal sought to exploit this with combination play, in order to pass the ball to a free player. Greece's response

Basinas providing support

involved Vryzas pulling back near Costinha. This freed up Basinas and offset Figo's movement to the centre. As a result, Zagorakis would take over marking Figo and Basinas Maniche, leaving no unmarked Portuguese players in central midfield.

If one of the Portuguese players freed themselves up and received the ball, Dellas was there with key interceptions, immediately closing down whoever was on the ball. Often, Vryzas' deep position, coupled with the fact that Figo was mainly wide and under Fyssas' supervision, gave Basinas the opportunity to help Zagorakis and Katsouranis mark their men, as well as to intercept incoming passes. Basinas also concentrated on maintaining the balance in midfield when Katsouranis followed Deco away from his area of responsibility.

Greece maintained an effective defensive shape, but struggled to keep possession of the ball, as the Portuguese transitions from attack to defence were very quick. As a

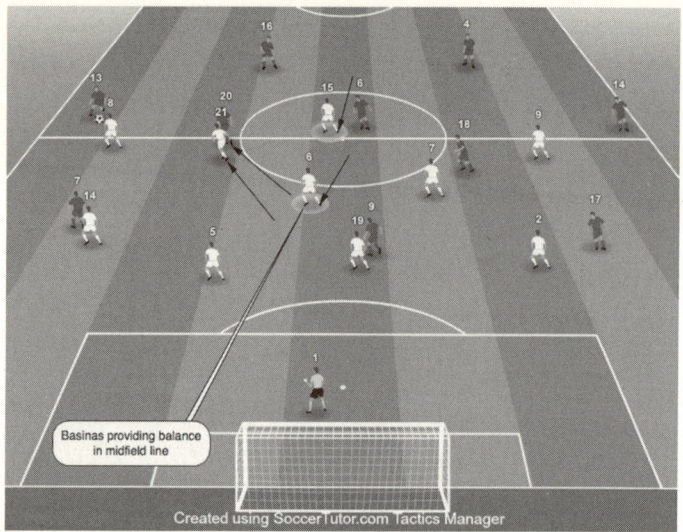

Basinas providing balance

Preventing the overload

result, they immediately regained possession and launched new attacks when the Greeks lost the ball. This led to an increase in tempo and did not suit Greece. However, effective defence did not allow Portugal to become particularly dangerous. A shot by Miguel on 13 minutes was pushed round for a corner by Nikopolidis. This was closely followed by Pauleta's shot into the hands of the Greek goalkeeper. These were the best opportunities for the Portuguese in the opening exchanges.

Moving on the blind side

In response, Rehhagel's team managed to worry the hosts in the 15th minute. Following Seitaridis' run on the right and an exchange of passes between Vryzas and Katsouranis, Charisteas faced the Portuguese goalkeeper but Ricardo, with a timely intervention, prevented the Greek striker from shooting. At times Portugal attempted to create numerical supremacy on the left wing with Figo and Ronaldo operating on the same side, but Dellas was always there to intervene.

In the 23rd minute, the ball reached Maniche after the Greek defence blocked the ball from a Figo corner and he hit a powerful shot just wide. The home team repeatedly

Maniche trying to exploit the free space

tried to take advantage of the available space behind the Greek defenders, especially on Seitaridis' side. More specifically, Pauleta often moved on Kapsis' blind side, while Maniche attempted to move into this space as a 'shadow' striker. But both Kapsis and Zagorakis reacted in time and intercepted the ball. Vigilance both in the middle and in defence did not allow any notable attempts by Portugal until the end of the first half.

Greece gradually increased their possession of the ball and, in the 42nd minute, Scolari took off Miguel due to injury and put Ferreira in his place. The second half started without further personnel or tactical changes. Greece seized the initiative briefly, but the Portuguese pressed effectively, and threatened to take advantage of any errors. The hosts were suited by the pace of play picking up again, but they continued to struggle against Greece's defensive execution.

The breakthrough came on 55 minutes. Basinas switched play from left to right with a long ball to Seitaridis.

The Greek defender took advantage of the available space and advanced with the ball, before Ronaldo tackled him and deflected his attempted cross for a corner. Basinas sent the ball into the heart of the Portuguese defence, where Charisteas was positioned. The Greek striker rose above Costinha and Carvalho and sent the ball into the net.

Charisteas goal

That lead would never be relinquished. The Portuguese tried to react immediately, but Ronaldo's shot was saved by Nikopolidis. On the hour Scolari gave his team a more attacking shape by sending on Rui Costa to replace Costinha. He changed the formation to 4-3-3 with Maniche becoming the defensive midfielder. Greece adapted their shape, with Basinas moving on to Costa, Zagorakis taking Maniche and Katsouranis remaining on Deco.

Rui Costa's introduction gave new impetus to the hosts. In the 63rd minute, Figo's shot from the right ended up in Nikopolidis' hands. The Portuguese took the game to

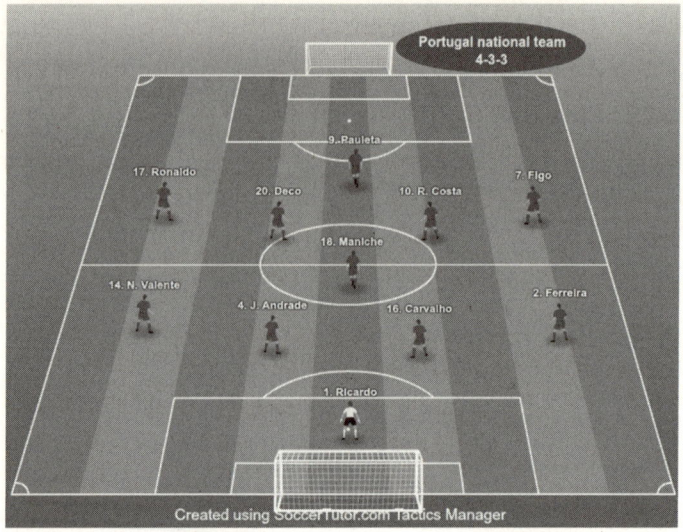

Portugal line up after the change

the Greek defence, where Dellas had to intervene several times, either by heading away crosses, filling in gaps, or shadowing any unmarked player who was on the ball. On 73 minutes, Nuno Gomes replaced Pauleta.

A minute later, Ronaldo found space moving between Seitaridis and Dellas and received the ball behind the Greek defence. He was alone with Nikopolidis, but his shot went wide. After the goal, Fyssas began to follow Figo everywhere. This tactical approach created space on the left of the Greek team, which Costa and Ferreira tried to exploit. Rehhagel replaced Giannakopoulos with Venetidis to shore up the left wing.

In the 79th minute, Ronaldo again found room between Seitaridis and Dellas and received the ball, but Dellas managed to deflect the shot for a corner. Papadopoulos came on to replace Vryzas a minute later, with Charisteas moving to the top of the attack and Papadopoulos to the right to check Valente's runs, as he had started advancing

Dellas moves to close down Figo as
Fyssas moves to put pressure on Ferreira

Created using SoccerTutor.com Tactics Manager

Dellas closes down the free player

more often. Almost immediately Carvalho had a dangerous shot from outside the penalty area which Nikopolidis pushed behind for a corner.

Greece defended in depth without retaining the ball, while Portugal maintained their attacking pressure. The final good chance for the hosts came in the last minute, when Figo received the ball inside the penalty area. The Portuguese captain managed to turn and shoot under pressure, but the ball deflected wide off Fyssas.

Referee Merk's final whistle led to Greece celebrating a victory that even the most optimistic of Greeks could never have imagined before the start of the tournament. Rehhagel's excellent tactical approach and correct reading of his opponents, coupled with the determination of the Greek players, led Greece to triumph in a major international football tournament for the first time in their history.

Chapter Twenty-One

Look Back In Wonder

EXPECTATION CAN play devilish games with the mind. The Portuguese, having survived opening-day nerves and dramas against England and Holland, were hot favourites to win the European title. Conventional wisdom prematurely crowned them champions, without recognising the potency of the Greeks' capacity to interfere with their opponents' psyche. They had become masters of injecting doubt, silencing crowds, and creating defensive webs that ensnared the unwise, or the unwary.

As the sun set over Lisbon on that fateful day, Deco, Luis Figo, Maniche and Ronaldo lit up the Portuguese midfield. Each one lively, each one producing moves from his impressive footballing repertoire. Artists always need protection, and behind the flamboyant four, Portugal's four-man zonal back line and the midfield 'libero' Costinha, were ready to offer reassurance.

The central midfield area was like a layered cake, with Costinha at the base, Maniche providing the substance and Deco the icing. Figo and Ronaldo, meanwhile, plied their trade down the flanks, and frequently changed sides in order to pose new problems for the Greek full-backs. The weakness was Pauleta, the lone striker, who operated at the apex of the attack. He was in desperate need of reinforcements that never arrived.

While the Portuguese looked for space, the Greeks, alternating from 1-3-3-3 in attack to 1-3-5-1 in defence, focused on man-to-man marking duties that owed much to Otto Rehhagel's heritage as a successful Bundesliga coach. This was a challenge from a bygone era. Deco found himself shadowed by his own security man, Konstantinos Katsouranis. Pauleta found it impossible to shake off his shadow, the tenacious Michalis Kapsis. Other Portuguese players were picked up in their zones and closely guarded until the danger had subsided.

In a first half full of frustration for the home crowd, including the departure of the injured Miguel after 43 minutes, Portugal dominated the ball, but not the opponent. They were restricted to long-range shots (one excellent effort by Miguel was deflected away by goalkeeper Antonis Nikopolidis) and set plays which rarely raised a Greek eyebrow. By contrast, Rehhagel's team, brilliantly led by Theodoros Zagorakis, flowed out of defence with assured possession play. On occasion, they threatened to break the deadlock; Katsouranis came close with a header four minutes from the break.

Often in football, as in life, the significance of defining moments is only recognised in hindsight, when the bigger picture, assessed in detail, offers greater sharpness and clarity. For Euro 2004 and for Greek football, such a moment took place at around 9pm on that balmy Sunday evening at the Estádio da Luz in Lisbon. 4 July was a form of Independence Day.

Destiny beckoned when, with effective group pressing, the Greeks regained the ball on the left of midfield. Angelos Basinas switched the play with a beautifully struck diagonal pass; Georgios Seitaridis, the right-back, raced on to the ball and forced a corner off Portugal's Cristiano Ronaldo. Basinas then re-entered the action by delivering, with his right foot, a superbly driven corner kick from the right-hand side. And then, with a 62,865 crowd transfixed and millions watching on TV, came the moment.

Angelos Charisteas, the big Greek No. 9, who had scored the winning goal against France in the quarter-final, met the silver ball with his head and struck gold. The ball flew into the empty, unprotected net. It was a freeze frame moment: Ricardo, the Portuguese goalkeeper, was caught on the wrong side of Zisis Vryzas, the Greek No. 15, who, in turn, was blocked from seeing the ball by Ricardo Carvalho and Costinha plus, of course, Charisteas.

Five players packed together in front of the goal, five players with their own roles in the drama, but only one man, or to be specific, one head mattered at that crucial moment. And it was Greek. The blue and white sea of supporters behind the goal exploded into a frenzy of joyous celebration. Otto's men had the lead, and, as they had shown before, the ability to keep what they had earned.

The Portuguese responded by laying siege to the Greek goal. Ronaldo and Deco were the first to indulge in target practice, to little effect. The flamboyant Rui Costa replaced Costinha in midfield in order to create a new impetus, but by this stage the Greeks were surging with confidence. They took their lead from Theo Zagorakis, their inspirational captain.

The man in the golden boots dazzled. In a flash of magic worthy of any major final, he accelerated down the right wing and outsmarted Jorge Andrade and Nuno Valente, flicking the ball over them to Kostas Katsouranis in the penalty box. Only a desperate block by Ricardo Carvalho prevented the Greeks from adding to their lead. The symbolism was irresistible: these were the skills, and this was the impact, everyone had expected Luis Figo to make.

While Zagorakis was showing everyone who was boss, Luis Felipe Scolari played his final card, bringing on Nuno Gomes as a direct replacement for Pauleta with 16 minutes remaining. Six attempts at goal, three corners and one penetrating Figo run later, the Portuguese found they had put everything in, and got nothing out. In another emblematic incident, it was left to the Greek captain, man of the match in the opening and final games of the tournament, to take the last shot, a right-footed half-volley which sped just wide.

Moments later, Zagorakis was on his knees, his arms held aloft in celebration of a famous victory. Cristiano Ronaldo, the icon of Portugal's new generation, wept uncontrollably. He was not alone. The Greek FA president Vasilis Gagatsis shed tears of joy. Eusebio, the local legend, carried the cup to the rostrum while Rehhagel and Scolari, victor and vanquished, hugged in a poignant, public display of mutual respect. Both were acutely aware of the minutely thin line between success and failure at the top level.

The Greek plan had worked to perfection. Rehhagel's coaching strategy had given hope and dreams to small countries with modest resources. For Portugal, talent-laden, passionate and wonderfully entertaining, only one thing was missing: composure in front of the goal. It simply wasn't their night. They dominated possession (58%) but couldn't alter the scoreline. Greece had heroes to cherish and a place in football folklore to celebrate.

Little things loomed large. Since Greek players tend to spend too much time and energy worrying about the referee, Rehhagel was at pains to stress the importance of the choice and attitude of officials. According to Gagatsis, this process began with the draw against England at Old Trafford in October 2001, when the manager and his squad were deeply dissatisfied with the performance of Dutch referee Dick Jol.

'We had a discussion with Theodoris Theodoridis, and we said that this should not happen again,' Gagatsis recalls. 'It was not just about refereeing. We could not continue to be belittled. Along with Rehhagel's recruitment, we had to start developing better relations with UEFA and FIFA. After the match in England, we brought the matter of refereeing to UEFA, to say that "we want to change, but they still do not treat us with respect. If it is to continue like this, tell us so that we stop trying to improve because it will be futile."

'We worked hard to gain everyone's respect, and eventually got to a point where referees came to show respect for us. We were vindicated in Euro 2004, when we saw that Pierluigi Collina would be refereeing the first match. We were sure we would be treated as equals. Before the game with Spain, Dellas, Karagounis and Basinas came to me with complaints about Michel, the referee. All of them had been wronged by the Slovak referee during a game with the youth team. "Do not worry, we'll talk after the match," I told them. I would always wait for them at the hotel. "You've been busy, huh?" they told me when they came back. "We are only trying to protect the team," I replied.'

Giorgos Karagounis, who won 139 caps between 1999 and 2014, recognised the significance of Collina taking charge of the opening match, against Portugal. 'The referee's attitude is always important,' he rationalised. 'When you are given fair chances against the host team, against France or the Czech Republic, the possibility of you performing better increases. If that doesn't happen, you are less likely to achieve such great goals.'

According to Theo Zagorakis, respect from referees was also an indirect by-product of Rehhagel's restless presence on the bench. It was, perhaps, inevitable that the Portuguese media would make mischief with the fact the final was controlled by Markus Merk, his German compatriot. Rehhagel was forced to deny that he was a patient of Merk, a dentist, and reminded the world he had been sent off by him during a Bundesliga match.

Nevertheless, Portugal defender Jorge Andrade argues: 'That was an important matter. We had to push to avoid a German referee in the final. He gave a lot of fouls and this favours the team that wants to play defensively. Scolari paid attention to detail and I wonder why he did not pay attention to the choice of referee. Perhaps it was that feeling of absolute confidence that we would succeed. I'm not saying that this was the reason we lost, but it was a detail we should have paid more attention to.'

So, what was the secret?

Andy Roxburgh interviewed Rehhagel for the UEFA technical report from the tournament. 'Is there anything in the regulations about the way you have to play?' the German coach asked his Scottish peer. 'I don't see a need to justify our style. It is designed to play to our strengths. If we spend time defending, it is because other teams who are technically superior push us back. But we are always ready to bounce forward again.

'Coaches cannot put the ball in the net, so we have to motivate players with knowledge and inter-personal skills. The biggest challenge of our lives is dealing with other people. We always have to control ourselves, keep learning, and carry on questioning ourselves. That is the secret.'

Chapter Twenty-Two

Team

IMMORTALITY ASSURED, the Greek players remained true to the rules they had shaped and chosen to follow, inspired by Otto Rehhagel's guidance. There was no room for egos and self-promotion when Theo Zagorakis received the trophy from Swedish UEFA president Lennart Johansson, turned towards his team-mates, and held it high above his head. Each player held the cup, one after the other, in perfect order. Their self-control suggested they had been ready for this moment all their lives.

Emotions broke and the magnitude of the achievement started to sink in when they ran out to celebrate with the supporters who had shared such an improbable journey. They made a lap of the stadium in order to thank their Portuguese hosts, who graciously applauded them, and 20 minutes later they were lost in the dressing room. The night of their lives would be long, and deliriously happy.

Such bonds do not break easily. Nearly ten years later, in December 2013, the legends of 2004 implemented a long-term plan to play charity matches in order to repay the love that had been showered on them by the Greek public.

315

Twenty of the original 23 gathered at the Toumba stadium in Thessaloniki, without their coaches, to face the great Romanian national team of Gheorghe Hagi.

Despite the absence of Rehhagel and his assistant Giannis Topalidis, the squad still obeyed their rules, both on and off the pitch. It was the same team with the same game plan, guided by the instincts of the past. You could still hear them joke about holding out until the 60th minute until Charisteas scored. He did so after an assist by Tsiartas, and the game ended in a 1-1 draw.

The mood has stayed the same, as the years roll on. They have the air of a group of childhood friends. Time contracts; within minutes, things are just like they used to be when they played together so long ago. Rehhagel is still the same way, according to Stelios Venetidis: 'The door opens and it's still the same guy. Even today, he comes in and talks as if we are still the same team, demanding to win with the same seriousness and passion. He cannot accept that he would ever go out expecting less than that.'

Old habits die hard. In June 2018, during a legends match against Spain, the Greeks found themselves trailing 2-0 at half-time. On their way off the pitch they were in no mood to joke or expound on their charitable activities. They dealt with frustration and nerves as efficiently as they had done in their prime, turning things around to win 5-3. These players still have the mentality of champions, although, as Giorgos Karagounis reflects, time has given them understandable perspective.

'The generations after us had it easier,' he acknowledges. 'They did not struggle growing up, which is why they would give up when the going got tough. You see it everywhere, not just football. I saw that when I returned to work for the national team as an executive. No one cared to ask me for information or advice. It's not a question of quality, everyone can play football nowadays. It's a question of mentality and attitude, which is always a big deal for Greek teams. We had great players but never on the level of a Messi, a Ronaldo or a Zidane, who could carry the game on their energy alone.

'That's what younger players do not understand. Because of that, we would lose sleep over a match against Malta. Those are the sorts of games that made the difference in the end. We would draw and be incensed about it but today's guys couldn't care less, even when they lose. They just carry on liking girls' photos on social media.

'For players of my generation, success was a one-way street. We went through many character-building experiences. When I was captain of the youth team, they wouldn't even let me play at Panathinaikos. That made me more determined to fight my way into the starting line-up. Other players would have given up but I always thought that you have to have the character and the ego to want to succeed and to prove yourself.'

Sociological research gives weight to Karagounis' observations. His generation, creators of the legend of Euro 2004, were brought up in the 1970s and 1980s, austere times that were challenging for the average Greek family. These players, and particularly those whose families lived in the provinces, grew up amidst great hardship. They saw football as a way to escape those conditions and make something of themselves.

This is in direct contrast to the generation that failed to qualify for Euro 2016 and the 2018 World Cup. Those national teams were populated by players who were born during a period of prosperity. Conditions in professional football had also eased. In the pre-2004 era, players found it hard to sign a good contract until their mid-twenties. This struggle bred a resilience and durability that is not shared by their more pampered successors, who tend to crack under pressure.

Karagounis adds, with revealing pride: 'We were the best team of the tournament. We never ended up in a penalty shoot-out. I would still have celebrated if we had, but we never did. We went through a group with Portugal, Spain and Russia, who were also supposed to be better than us. That was like a World Cup group. For both Portugal and Spain, it was like playing at home.

'We managed to also beat France and knock out the Czech Republic, the second favourites. Not only that, we beat Portugal again at the end. That wouldn't have been done by sheer luck. You need to have a great team, and ours was the best of the tournament. We very rarely allowed the opponents room to create chances, while scoring almost every time we had one. We won the trophy fair and square.'

The party at the Pestana Place Hotel was a free-for-all that lasted until the small hours. People jumped in the pools, emptied mini-bars and consumed countless bottles of Moet et Chandon champagne, but left an enduringly positive impression on hotel staff. Pedro Rosa, the bartender on duty that night, remembers: 'They apologised for the sadness they may have caused by winning against our team and they were all, including their families, very attentive and respectful towards our Portuguese guests.'

Rehhagel demanded discipline, but was flexible, in terms of his squad's diet. 'Our buffet had pizza, chips, anything we wanted,' explains Demis Nikolaidis. 'Rehhagel wanted to keep us happy and he was right in doing so. It was just a tournament. He wouldn't be coaching us for an entire year, so he didn't have to worry overmuch about our diet.'

Enrique Muro, sous chef of the restaurant Valle Flor, reveals the hidden drama of the team's last meal before the final: 'An hour before the scheduled meal we realised we were missing some basic ingredients. I left running for the supermarket which is about a mile away, to buy fresh pasta and some other items but everything was ready on time in the end.' One can only wonder what could have happened if the chef had acted, let's say, a bit more patriotically ...

The beauty of having a small support staff was the onus it placed on the squad's self-discipline. They travelled without the usual retinue, including a chef and a nutritionist, but ate sensibly, balancing carbohydrate and protein intake. According to Giorgos Karagounis, the Greeks made light of their lack of experience and infrastructure:

'Things would improve over time, but compared with teams like Sweden we were lagging behind in terms of know-how. We would train without cones. We did not have our own olive oil with us, but the Italians had brought tons. The Swedes had brought their own weights along, while we would jump in the car to go to a local gym downtown. We were behind because we didn't have the experience, not for lack of support.'

Since they did not have a goalkeeping coach, the Greek team's third goalkeeper trained with a physiotherapist, who doubled as a left-back during training to complete the reserves team. Topalidis, the assistant manager, would sometimes play as a right-back during training for the same reason. Adidas, the team's sponsors, ran a campaign that featured them sitting in a small stadium, like a bunch of friends relaxing after a five-a-side. The accompanying slogan 'Impossible is nothing' tied into the consistency of Rehhagel's message to his players.

'Otto would always tell us that everything is possible,' confirms Angelos Charisteas. 'He had been successful with all his teams. He would always mention the match Werder played against Maradona's Napoli in the UEFA Cup, which they won 5-1. He would tell us how they made it against Alemao, Giola, Careca, De Napoli and Maradona, without having any famous players in their line-up. That was a great feeling to convey to us.'

Cristiano Ronaldo of Portugal (R) sees his shot go wide during the opening match of Euro 2004 in Porto on 12 June 2004.

Spanish forward Raul feels the weight of Konstantinos Katsouranis' challenge.

Theo Zagorakis celebrates his side reaching the quarter-finals of Euro 2004 after the Group A match between Russia and Greece in Faro on 20 June.

Zinedine Zidane looks on as the Greek players celebrate their Euro 2004 quarter-final win over France in Lisbon on 25 June 2004.

A joyful Antonis Nikopolidis following the Euro 2004 quarter-final between France and Greece at the Jose Alvalade stadium on 25 June 2004 in Lisbon.

Greek fans carried away with their team's success.

Traianos Dellas of Greece (L) celebrates with Konstantinos Katsouranis after scoring the winning goal in the Euro 2004 semi-final against the Czech Republic at the Dragao stadium on 1 July 2004 in Porto.

Theodoros Zagorakis wraps a Greek flag around his head as he celebrates Greece's 1-0 win over France in the quarter-finals of the 2004 European Championship.

Player of the Tournament Theo Zagorakis lifts the trophy.

Greece celebrate with the trophy after winning the Euro 2004 Final against Portugal at the Estadio da Luz in Lisbon on 4 July 2004.

Greece captain Theodoros Zagorakis lifts the Euro 2004 trophy on 5 July 2004 at the Panathenaic stadium in Athens. Zagorakis, the player of the tournament, was honoured together with his team-mates by hundreds of thousands of Greeks in a homecoming celebration.

Coach Otto Rehhagel at the Panathenaic stadium in Athens on 5 July 2004.

Greek newspapers hailed the European football champions.

Chapter Twenty-Three

Credit Where It Is Due

IF YOU look closely at the video featuring the best players of Euro 2004, you will get a solitary glimpse of Theo Zagorakis, captain of the champions. He has the same prominence afforded the Portugese goalkeeper Ricardo, who failed to make the squad of the tournament. Why? Andy Roxburgh, the presenter, came clean. 'The video was made before the final,' he admitted. 'Greece was obviously a great surprise to all of us. Perhaps they even managed to surprise themselves.'

There were five Greek players in the select group of 23, chosen by a public vote and overseen by coaches on UEFA's technical committee. Nikopolidis, Seitaridis, Dellas, Charisteas and Zagorakis were recognised; Zagorakis was placed fifth in that year's Golden Ball vote, behind Shevchenko, the winner, Deco, Ronaldinho and Henry. He ranked above Nedved, Rooney, van Nistelrooy, Ibrahimovic, Cristiano Ronaldo, and many other stars of the time.

'Our team had players that never got above a seven in their performance, but we knew that if we all reached that, we would be successful,' Zagorakis reflected. 'At the Euros, we reached a nine, myself, Dellas, Nikopolides, Charisteas.' He was ambitious, but realistic.

'From the day of the match against Russia, up to and until the final, I would have my stuff ready to return to Athens every evening,' he admitted. 'After a while, I started doing it for luck. I never put myself through the process of believing that we would win the trophy. That's why I would tell the others to "stay close and not make fools of ourselves" which became a slogan among us. We remained with our feet planted firmly on the ground until the last whistle.'

Demis Nikolaidis stressed the importance of collective excellence, while naming Zagorakis, Dellas, Kapsis, Nikopolidis, Katsouranis, Seitaridis, and Charisteas as 'players who had the games of their life' in Portgual. Stelios Venetides praises Zagorakis as being 'responsible for a big part of that success, both on and off the pitch. He had an amazing, transcendent tournament and his behaviour in the changing rooms, his attitude, drove us. With Charisteas and Dellas, he provided more impetus, made a bigger contribution, both as players and men.'

For Kostas Katsouranis, the contributions of Nikopolidis, Dellas and Zagorakis were decisive: 'Everybody who played gave everything they had. Nikopolidis was the key player. Thanks to him we always started with a clean sheet defensively. He was in terrific mental and psychological condition; it was more than just being a good goalkeeper. He gave the team enormous confidence. Against Spain he had a great performance. Both the way he worked with his defenders, and the certainty he instilled in us that if something went by us he would get it, were great advantages.

'In terms of mentality and psychology, Dellas and Zagorakis were very influential. Zagorakis did not want to lose. Everyone listened to him and accepted what he said. They knew he cared about the team. I remember once, during training, that he had had an argument with Seitaridis. Zagorakis would be on your case even during training. Not listening to him was not an option. When I was in Zagorakis' position later, I realised he was right to shout. In the national team, it is not about just passing the time. Zagorakis may have been overpowering, but his heart was in the right place. When he shouted at you, even when he may have been wrong, you had to think about why he did it. He may have felt the need to jolt the team in order for us to wake up.'

Giorgos Karagounis doesn't see the point in enumerating the top players, because success was due to a team effort: 'It is difficult to mention names. Everyone had a part to play, even those who stayed on the bench. Those guys helped very much, even Katergiannakis, the goalkeeper, who would play as a right full-back during training with so much enthusiasm, when we were simply trying new moves. We loved to hang out with each other and it all came out on the pitch. In between matches, we would get together to chat about where we wanted to go, what we would do, how we would work. Certainly some players were more critical for the success of the team, but I do not want to name names.'

Everyone sees a defining achievement, in sport and in life, through the prism of their own experiences and attitudes. Angelos Charisteas is thoughtful, but forthright in rationing praise and responsibility: 'As players, we have the biggest share, because we embraced Otto, put aside our egos and decided to work as a team. If I had to speak in terms of percentages, I would give 45% to the players, 35% to Otto and the remaining 20% to the EPO and all those who worked to support us.

'Otto had his philosophy and it was us who followed it. We accepted him. If we hadn't, he would have left and the team would have stagnated. It is not a coincidence when all coaches tell you that they depend on the players. The EPO made a bold decision when they kept the journalists away from the team, at a time when the press was detrimental to the morale and inner workings of the team. We had come to see the journalists as snipers that were picking us off. We became isolated.

'Speaking for myself, I thrived on bad press; I saw it as a challenge so I would score goals to answer them. Not being under the immunity of a big Greek club helped me. However, criticism was often malicious, and it did not work that way for everyone. The EPO let us do our jobs and that was to the administration's credit, along with upgrading of services and overall care for the team. Good plane seats made me feel like a star. Even the socks: many footballers say, "The quality of your performance is only as good as the quality of your socks." We had the best clothes. They provided us with the best of everything.'

Nikos Dabizas cannot separate the coach from his players, since their unanimity of purpose was decisive: 'It's not easy to divide success into shares and percentages. I would say that 70–80% goes to the coach and footballers, and the rest, 20–30%, to the EPO. The EPO could not have influenced our course more. They decided to take a stand and start doing things for us, and they felt good doing them because they were receiving good feedback from the team. Gagatsis persisted even though, in the beginning, he had been under much pressure. He proceeded to take actions that may have been self-evident, the bare necessities, but the fact is that they did not exist for us before. It is also to his credit that he decided to not intervene in the process.'

Antonis Nikopolidis shares Dabizas' view, but affords the EPO president a bigger share of the credit: 'Players, coach and then the EPO, that's how I would see it. As far as the EPO is concerned, I take into account Gagatsis' relationship with us. I consider him a key player in shaping the spirit that existed within the national team. He solved problems and spent time listening to us in order to get a feel for the team. He put out a lot of fires. But the players and the coach were the vehicle. The relationship we had created between us, the players with the coach, was what drove the team. The coach was an entity with power and determination. The president and Zagorakis, who maintained balance, were helped by those around them. We all set our ego aside for the benefit of the group. We accepted that there were those who led, and we followed, each in his role, big or small.'

Traianos Dellas plays down the role of the federation, in relative terms, since Rehhagel's recruitment was a decision taken in isolation, rather than part of a strategic plan for the development of national football: '60% goes to the footballers, 30% to the coach and 10% to the EPO. The moves that brought success were not according to a plan. If the EPO had a five- or ten-year programme, as Belgium did, the percentages would be different. It was only in co-operation with the coach, that he isolated the team from all the hangers-on and the press. Gagatsis was barely willing to tolerate that. I would give him a larger percentage if what was done had been based on a plan. We had neither strategy nor tactics. We did not know where our course would take us. Rehhagel came and that was important because everything happens for a reason. Success was purely a matter of circumstance and chance. We are like that in football and as a people, but when we unite we are able to achieve many things.'

Stelios Venetidis perceives Gagatsis' support of Rehhagel as decisive: 'The very fact that they hired a foreign coach, whom the EPO then left to his own devices was crucial. They satisfied his request to isolate the team from courtiers and journalists, provided great conditions for the footballers and covered the coach's needs. That makes the EPO's contribution decisive. The fact they realised that they had to move into uncharted waters, and that they managed to escape the limitations of the Greek mentality, is much more than anyone could do in that particular country at that specific point in time. This, remember, was a time when the national team was so under-valued and under-appreciated.'

Giorgos Karagounis insists: 'The biggest share of the credit always belongs to those who play in the game, no matter if it is with the best or the most mediocre manager.' Yet Venetidis openly admits Rehhagel has been a primary influence in his subsequent managerial career: 'I was envious of his mentality, his flexibility, his sense of diplomacy. It is difficult to acquire them because they require a certain kind of personality. He was charismatic in managing people, emotionally intelligent.'

Giorgos Papalanis, the great survivor of the system, praises Giannis Topalidis, the assistant manager, and salutes the driving force supplied by the players, but has no doubt who deserves the greatest commendation: 'Rehhagel was a great coach. I admired him. His tactics will be taught in schools, just like his system of choosing football players.'

Topalidis deflects attention: 'Everyone helped, myself, the EPO and the office caretaker, but the players and Rehhagel were the protagonists. We worked with some of the world's top players, who were perceptive having picked up things from other coaches. However, they did not come up with the line-up, they did not decide which substitutions to make. They did not train the team. They did not study the opponent. It was Rehhagel who did all that. The players were always tactically disciplined. We provided the strategy, and because players want freedom on the pitch, Rehhagel gave it to them after setting the limits of that freedom. That's how we became champions.'

For Theo Zagorakis the deeper meaning of success lies in the realisation that it was accomplished because everyone involved gave their all: 'I give 100% to everyone. I cannot separate our contributions. If everyone had not done their jobs properly, and I include our supporters in this because what we gained from them was unbelievable, the miracle would not have happened. They all get full marks.'

Michalis Kapsis, who had the inside track as the team's press officer, shares Zagorakis' view: 'Without good administration, the right coach, patient caregivers, doctors, masseurs, agents and the media none of this would have happened. It is very important that everyone contributes to a team. Surely the coach has a big share of the responsibility in the way he built a real team, but perhaps a bigger share goes to the players who are the protagonists. As we are all responsible for the defeat, so do we all play a substantial part in winning.'

The final word on the coach goes to the boss, the head of the EPO at the time, Vasilis Gagatsis: 'There was no question of arrogance, no delusions of grandeur. Otto had a great deal of self-confidence from the beginning, but he always credited success to the players. In our first conversation he said, "We'll put everything in order." He promised nothing more. The moment he started enjoying his success was when we landed in Greece on the return from Portugal. He wanted to take part in the celebrations and was very excited. We put him in the co-driver's seat on the bus. He really wanted the full experience. It was his best moment. And yet, he stayed for only two days in Greece. He came to visit the prime minister and the president of the Republic, and then he left immediately.'

Chapter Twenty-Four

The King & I

MEN LIKE Otto Rehhagel do not mellow easily, but over time, the rougher edges become smoother. His perspective was best expressed when I met him in Crete for a charity match in June 2017. He was in his element, reconnecting with his team, and our conversation turned to his place in the history of Greek football. What did he think of his status as our greatest manager?

His reply bore out the words of Vasilis Gagatsis, at the end of the previous chapter. His humility was unforced, and impressive. 'All managers try to do the right thing,' he replied. 'I was fortunate to work with a wonderful generation of footballers. We all did the right thing and that's how we achieved that great a success.'

Earlier that year, in an interview with Martin Arn for the Swiss newspaper *Blick*, he had gone further: 'Our secret was that those guys were really good footballers. And no one knew it. Not even the press. They were all interested in France, Zidane and the more well-known players, and Portugal. Nobody knew anything about Greece. I told the players, "We have nothing to lose." And then we beat

France in the quarter-finals. In essence, we had already won the tournament because no one expected us to beat France. Of course, neither did I. No one becomes a European champion if they do not have a good team. And we had it, we had these players. The team was better than anyone thought.'

He describes his own contribution with a metaphor, his favourite way of making himself understood. 'I was lucky because I did what I always did, I was interested in people. I felt like arranging everything as it was in my mind. 95% of my footballers realised that I loved my players. Everyone had their place in the team. Let me give you an example. When a spaceship launches, no one at base can make mistakes, otherwise the spaceship will explode. That's why everyone's position is important. The Greeks are warm people with a wonderful history of civilisation. You can co-exist marvellously with them, but they want to enjoy life to the full.

'I always told my players, "You cannot drink a double espresso at 2.30am." And when I was to meet them in the morning, I would tell them, "9.30, German time, not Greek time." The Greek morning time was "we come when we want". Discipline and order were my priorities from the outset because you need discipline and order to play football. I remained a German, as always, but I also learned to respect and appreciate the Greek mentality.'

Ultimately, we reach a fundamental conclusion. Every part of the equation, the coach, his two associates, the players and the federation president, was inter-dependent. Without the strategy employed by Rehhagel and his trusted lieutenants Greece would have failed to qualify for Euro 2004. Without some of the players who helped him do so,

Greece didn't have great success in defending the trophy in 2008, or in the 2010 World Cup. Without Gagatsis being in charge of the federation, the EPO regressed, and began operating, poorly, with a pre-2001 mentality.

We were all touched, in our own way, by the events of 4 July 2004. It was, as the title of this book suggests, *The Miracle*. I have attempted to analyse, investigate, question, interpret, collate and compose all the information I have been given in 30 years of following the Greek national team. My hope is that these pages will form part of the heritage of a special group of people, fewer than 50, who left a huge footprint in football history. Their mentality, methods, principles and ideals made them champions.

Otto Rehhagel was holding the trophy outside the dressing room at the Estádio da Luz when he spoke of the moment as one when 'all Greeks were brothers, even for a little while'. Football stirs the soul, and I hope it will prompt us to reflect on, and learn from, our history. That's down to you, the reader. Researching this triumph does not make you a better journalist or a better professional, nor does it help you better understand football. It simply makes you a better person.

How to Manage a Team of B Players

OTTO REHHAGEL'S work became the focus of a study by UCL and Columbia University Business Psychology Professor Tomas Chamorro-Premuzic. He is also a member of the Harvard Entrepreneurial Finance Lab and Chief Talent Scientist for ManpowerGroup, one of *Fortune* magazine's 500 biggest multinational companies with over 29,000 employees, based in Milwaukee. In 2015, he published an article in the *Harvard Business Review*, entitled 'How to Manage a Team of B Players'. In the case of football that is taken to mean footballers 'of average quality compared to international standards', according to the study. He takes as his example of a team comprised of B players but had an A+ success, Rehhagel's Greece.

A great deal of scientific evidence suggests that the key determinants are psychological factors – in particular, the leader's ability to inspire trust, make competent decisions, and create a high-performing culture where the selfish agendas of the individual team members are eclipsed by the group's goal, so that each person functions like a different organ of the same organism. In the famous words of Vince Lombardi: 'Individual commitment to a group effort – that is what makes a team work, a company work, a society work, a civilization work.' This is true for all teams, of course, but if you're leading a team of B players (people who are just average in terms of competence, talent, or potential), your leadership matters even more. In fact, if you are leading a team of B players, you have to be an A-class leader; otherwise, your team will have no chance.

Although effective leaders can have a wide variety of styles, they do tend to share some common personality characteristics. First, they have better judgment than their counterparts, meaning they can make good decisions, learn from experience, and avoid repeating mistakes. Second, they have higher EQ, which enables them to stay calm under pressure, build close and meaningful relationships with their teams, and remain humble even in victory. Third, they are insanely driven and tend to have very high levels of ambition, remaining slightly dissatisfied with their success, this is why they stay hungry and continue to work hard, as opposed to becoming complacent.

In addition, there are four important tactics any leader can use to make their teams more effective. These key management elements have been found to work even with B players, and could transform a team of average individual contributors into an over-performing team. They are:

***Vision.** The first component needed to turn B players into an A team is vision, that is, a winning strategy that represents a meaningful – and attainable – mission for the team. It's true that all teams need a vision, even teams of A players.*

But with A players, you might be able to skate by with a hazy picture of the future, or a goal that shifts over time, or an endpoint that doesn't include a strategy of how to get there. If your players are not amazing, then you need to ensure that your goal is clearly defined and doesn't waver. It should be something that stretches them, but doesn't demoralize them by being unattainable. And it should include a plan of attack – milestones and tactics that will allow the team to figure out their next steps. When the strategy is right, success will be less dependent on the individual brilliance of the players (and you can always rely on the competition making a few mistakes).

Analytics. No matter how smart and experienced leaders are, they will make smarter and better decisions if they are armed with data. Data can cut through the biases and politics and create a culture of fairness and transparency. It can also highlight the key individual drivers of team performance, breaking down success into molecular factors that can be easily manipulated. Of course, intuition is still needed to translate any data-driven information into useful knowledge, and there are many problems data won't solve (see point 4). But a team with better monitoring systems for quantifying performance will always have an edge, and the power of feedback will always depend on the accuracy of the analytics (see point 3).

Feedback. Meta-analytic studies have shown that individual and team feedback improves performance by around 25%. This margin is substantial enough that it lets less skilled teams who get a lot of feedback outperform more skilled teams that aren't getting feedback. Why is feedback so important? Because it allows both individuals and teams to regulate their efforts – the essence of motivation is self-regulation, but self-regulation only works with accurate feedback. Of course, feedback is also essential for correcting mistakes and getting better, and leaders who fail to provide it risk coming across as indifferent and disinterested in the welfare and performance of the team. When you have a team of B players it is particularly important to be honest with them about their relative limitations. Instead of making them think that they are better than they actually are, tell them they will need to work hard to close the talent gap between them and their rivals because on skill and potential alone they would lose.

Morale. *Leaders own the job of creating engagement. Although individual engagement is critical, team morale is the key. You might have a team of B players, but when they share common values, drivers, and motives, and care about each other much like friends, they will raise their performance for each other. Thus any leader should focus a great deal on helping his/ her team members bond. If they fail to cohere, intragroup competition will trump any collective success, leading to intergroup failure. This may seem like common sense, but too many managers are so focused on managing processes and attending to the formal aspects of task performance that they forget to build an engaging culture. In addition, when leaders are interested mostly in their own career, and success is not defined in terms of their team's performance, they will tend to neglect and eventually alienate their teams.*

In short, good leaders can turn B players into an A team, by following the right strategy, gathering precise performance data, giving accurate feedback, and building and maintaining high morale. Since few leaders manage to achieve this even when they have a team of A players, there is much hope for those who do.

As Greece's soccer coach Otto Rehhagel explained when asked the secret to his team's success, he noted it was mostly about his relationship with the players: 'I cherish them. I hold them in the highest esteem. I know what makes these boys tick. I don't lead by committee. I take the responsibility for my choices.'

Vasilis Sambrakos comments: The only thing the author got wrong in terms of Rehhagel's practice was that Rehhagel never paid attention to statistics and feedback. He ignored them because he trusted his own judgement when analysing matches. 'UEFA would send us statistics but, from a point onwards, we stopped looking at them. We trusted our own analysis,' replied Topalidis when asked about the matter.

'During preparations for the game against France, he would try to convince us that we were better than Zidane,' says Giannis Goumas about the same issue. Even today, the players can recall Rehhagel's introduction before every match, including the final. 'There's 11 of them and 11 of us. They've got two legs and so do we. They've got a goalpost and so do we. We obviously can beat them.' With that exception, everything else Tomas Chamorro-Premuzic wrote about Rehhagel is spot on.

The Ultimate Application of the 'Controlled Offensive' Doctrine

Otto Rehhagel did not feel the need to convince anyone that Greece played creative football, and the numbers are on his side. During the opening game, Greece did not have high possession of the ball (38%), but given that they were 2-0 ahead by the 51st minute, it made sense for them to sit back. Greece had fewer shots overall (8 to Portugal's 19) but almost the same amount of shots on target (4 to Portugal's 5). In the match against Spain, Greece's possession percentage was 42%, but they were almost as threatening (11 shots for Spain to 9 for the Greeks.) They found the mark as many times as their opponents (twice each). During Greece's worst game, the defeat by Russia, the Russians had greater possession (53%) and more shots (18-12, with 9 and 4 respectively on target.)

Against holders France, Greece had 44% possession of the ball. While they had less shots (11-5), they had more shots on target (5-4). In the semi-final with the Czech Republic, Greece had 49% possession. The teams had the same amount of shots on target (5-5) despite the fact that the Czechs had more shots overall (16-9). During the final, Portugal had 58% possession, many more shots (17-4) and had 5 efforts on target, to the winners' one. Greece's effectiveness in front of goal was matched by their efficiency in defence: they did not concede any goals in their knockout games.

They had 8 shots per match on average, with 4 of those on target. As the tournament progressed, however, Greece became more focused. They averaged 10 shots in the group stage, with 3 shots on target. In the three knockout games they had an average of 6 shots per match, with 4 shots on target. Greece finished the tournament with 67% accuracy in passing. They won the trophy with 260 completed passes per game. Portugal had 417 completed passes per match, France 467, Czech Republic 356, and Holland 411. The performance of the Greeks seems to have matched exactly Otto Rehhagel's philosophy of 'controlled offensive'. 4 out of 7 goals were scored in the second half. Of the remaining 3 goals, 2 were scored in the first half and 1 during extra time.

Greece, a team which found itself on the defensive most of the time, ranked second to last in fouls committed in the tournament (17), right above France (17.75). Portugal (20.17), Holland (21) and the Czech Republic (19.2) committed more fouls. The Greek players accrued four more yellow cards than the Portuguese (18-14). Greece led the tournament in defensive tackles (293 to Portugal's 183). Nikopolidis, their goalkeeper, was in second place behind the Latvian Golinko, for most saves (21-26). Three Greek players made the most tackles (Zagorakis 59, Katsouranis 36, Seitaridis 35). Midfielder Karagounis ranked second for amount of fouls won (19) behind Deco (29).

In September 2008, Birmingham Business School and Aberystwyth University published a joint study by Fiona Carmichael and Dennis Thomas. The two mathematicians' teams sifted through the statistical data generated by the 16 teams during the 2004 Euros for their paper on 'Efficiency in Knockout Tournaments'. The paper compares team performances at Euro 2004 using average and frontier production functions to examine the relative efficiency of each team.

The authors drew up efficiency indices by comparing the defensive and offensive behaviour of the teams, taking into account the ratio of successful attempts versus overall attempts and other metrics indicating the ability of the teams to convert their match play into a positive goal differential. The evidence suggests that while the eventual tournament winners were not obviously superior in terms of a range of individual performance criteria, they were one of the most efficient teams in converting overall match play into results. Not only does their conclusion vindicate mathematically Rehhagel's philosophy of 'controlled offensive', the authors also considered him to be the best manager in the tournament. The more salient parts of the text follow below:

An examination of Greece's tournament profile shows that they were only the 7th ranked team entering Euro 2004 in terms of pre-qualifying performance, and joint 14th in pre-tournament betting odds. Their group stage seeding made them the 5th ranked team in terms of difficulty of group stage opponents, and their progression through the knockout stages displayed the 2nd toughest schedule at the quarter-final stage and the most difficult schedules (in terms of cumulative opposing team strengths) at the semi final and final stages compared with other teams. In terms of the total match points achieved out of a possible maximum in their tournament matches, Greece ranked 2nd to the Czech Republic.

Overall, Greece's match play performance data appear generally unexceptional. From an attacking point of view, they recorded low averages with respect to Shots and Shots on Target, while defensively Greece recorded high averages for Tackles Made and the Tackles Made/Tackles Suffered ratio (184.28), while being relatively fouled against. Given that Greece recorded the joint lowest Goals Conceded average, and a 'middle of the range' Goals Scored average together with a relatively high Goals Scored/Shots ratio (14.89%), the team's overall performance statistics would seem to suggest that their tournament winning success was based on a limited but organised and effective defensive (although not necessarily aggressive) approach, and a relative efficiency in converting goalscoring opportunities.

As the losing finalists, Portugal's tournament play data display high Own Ball Possession Share, and the highest Shots and Corners averages but low averages with respect to Shots on Target and Goals Scored. While the team also had a low Goals Conceded average the team recorded the highest Tackles Suffered average and the lowest Tackles Made/Tackles Suffered ratio (57.19%), and overall the host nation's performance indicates a relatively ineffective attack combined with outfield fragility.

Unmeasured factors that are difficult to capture in this kind of statistical exercise, such as injuries and luck, also played a part.

'n Euro 2004 Greece's actual success is not reflected accurately by its goal difference which was the fourth best overall, although teams with better goal difference did generally do better in the tournament. Greece ranked more highly in terms of the defensive measures than either goal difference or the attacking measures suggesting, as already noted above, that Greece's defensive qualities were more influential in winning the tournament than their attacking skills.

While our initial data analysis indicates that Greece were worthy winners of Euro 2004 in terms of overall performance and quality of opponents faced, our estimated production function model generates predicted rankings which suggest that, on the basis of our model specification, Greece were only average in terms of the quality and quantity of their attacking play although they were above average in terms of their defensive play.

Given their resources and potential (reflected in their pre-tournament ranking) and the nature of the competition,

Greece's success came down to tactics, confirming the importance of good management combined with team morale and cohesion.

Tactical Notes and Comments

THE AUTHORS of the 2004 Euro UEFA technical report summarised what they believed to be the definitive qualities of the Greek team's style of play:

- Man-to-man marking mentality – some strict, some in the zone and for the duration of the attack.
- Outstanding teamwork – remarkable work ethic/ discipline, good organisation and clever use of substitutes.
- Highly competent defending in 1 v 1 situations – don't 'sell themselves'.
- Counter-attack with direct running with the ball or long passes to the front.
- Dangerous on set plays – corners, indirect free kicks and long throws.
- Press in their own half – hunt in packs, the whole team co-operates in recovering the ball.
- Good composure on the ball – brilliantly led by Zagorakis.
- Attack with 1-3-3-3, defend using 1-3-5-1 (battle for everything).

- Good use of long diagonals: open play and indirect free kicks.
- Control the game, even when not in possession, dominate in the air and pose difficult problems to the opponent.

Sir Bobby Robson, the Euro 2004 correspondent for the Portuguese sports paper *O Jogo*, had nothing but praise for Greece after the final: 'Portugal performed better when Rui Costa came on the field because, to be honest, Figo and Cristiano Ronaldo had been neutralised by Fyssas and Seitaridis who had absolute control of the wings. I wanted Seitaridis at Newcastle and I can honestly say today that we lost a great footballer. Scolari deserves congratulations for his work until the final but, in my opinion, Portugal should have played with two strikers, not one. Otto Rehhagel's Greece won the trophy fairly. They were the better and more efficient team in the final.'

David James, the England goalkeeper at Euro 2004, admired Greece for the decision to play a style of football that went against the grain at the time: 'There are different tendencies in football and depending on the period, almost everyone wants to employ the same style of play. Greece did not do that in 2004. Portugal won the trophy in a similar manner in 2016. They did not get there by winning by large margins. They won by small goal differentials, maintaining their balance. Sometimes, you have to go against the current, be different, in order to win. You do that either by scoring many goals, in order to always have more than the opposition, or by focusing on your defensive function. Greece did that in the best possible way. It is a great story.'

Alan Hansen, the BBC commentator during the tournament, wrote the following on the BBC website on the night of the final: 'People think that organising your defence is easy but it is not. What Greece did was to continuously make sure they did not defend very deep. There was an example of this during the final, when Giannakopoulos, after a foul won by Portugal, yells at his team-mates to come higher and move their defensive line. And he achieved it. We have to give Greece all the praise in the world for their style of play, for their physical condition and the way they defended. Dellas was a rock in defence, providing an example for everyone else. He kept his cool throughout the tournament and his defensive sense and positioning were excellent. This is a fantastic story for the Greeks and football.'

Jose Mourinho, who earlier that summer had won his first Champions League with Porto, wrote in the paper *O Jogo*: 'Football may be changing, with teams being the decisive factor, not units. I don't believe that Greece's tactics were negative, I noticed the exact opposite. Otto Rehhagel did a wonderful job adjusting his tactics to the level of his players. He did not have big names or players from the moon. They all played to win so their spirit was not different to that of my own Porto. When players with great egos realise that the team is more important than them the team becomes fantastic.'

Ivica Osim, one of football's wise men, had, by chance, spent two years at the helm of Panathinaikos FC around the time that the Greek national team had been preparing to take part in its first World Cup in 1994. As a member of the UEFA technical panel for Euro 2004, the Bosnian manager, who had reached the 1990 World Cup quarter-finals with Yugoslavia as assistant manager, wrote the following: 'When Greece went to the 1994 World Cup, the Greeks rejoiced simply because they were able to participate. Thanks to Otto Rehhagel, the Greek national team was transformed into a professional unit, which inspired all the smaller national teams to believe that they can succeed too.

'The Greeks managed to beat bigger teams thanks to good organisation, good technique, which they've always had, and discipline. The players obeyed Rehhagel, they no longer played to satisfy their ego, they showed team spirit and the ambition to achieve something together. What was important was that Rehhagel was a foreigner, without prior knowledge of how things worked in Greece. He was therefore able to come in and change things without pressure.'

Tactical Summary

Vasilis Sambrakos comments: I asked coach Athanasios Terzis, an acclaimed and experienced analyst of football tactics, to sum up his conclusions of the analyses he made for this book of the eight matches played by Rehhagel's team. I did not try to influence him by making available to him the players' interviews, the UEFA technical report or any other data used in this book:

'Otto Rehhagel's team debuted with a 5-1 defeat in Finland, but it was the 2-2 result against England at Old Trafford that was the first essential sample of his game philosophy and of the mentality he wanted to convey to the Greek footballers. The German coach employed the kind of logic and realism that distinguished him, as he was the first to admit several times. He took into account the characteristics of the players on whom he planned to depend, made sure to create a team that would exploit its strong points and diligently hide its weaknesses.

'It was a team that could win matches and bring success, not a team that would play entertaining football. This is the most important step in creating a successful team: properly evaluating the available human potential and building the game plan accordingly. Rehhagel realised that Greece could rely on a good defensive function that would ensure they would not concede goals while, offensively, he wanted to take advantage of the individual quality of some players and set pieces to score goals.

'He started by selecting Nikopolidis as his goalkeeper, who being in the best condition of his career, completely vindicated his coach's decision. He then chose Dellas as his centre-half. His aim was to take advantage of his experience of participating in a three-defender formation in Italy and his ability to read tactical situations. As a result he decided to give him a freer role, while at the same time he used one or two additional defenders for man-to-man marking, depending on the number of opposing strikers. In this way, he took advantage of Kapsis' ability in man-to-man marking, while securing numerical superiority at the back.

'In addition, he paid particular attention to reading the opponents' individual characteristics. The German coach would then pick defenders who matched the characteristics of the forwards. He did not hesitate, for example, to use Seitaridis as a central defender when he faced attackers with the characteristics of Henry and Baros. When he had to face forwards who dropped deep and played like attacking midfielders, such as Raul, he would select Katsouranis.

'In midfield, Rehhagel selected players such as Zagorakis, Katsouranis and Basinas, who are particularly adept defensively and had demonstrated the ability to win personal challenges. This choice, coupled with the tactical approach of applying individual marking in the players' area of responsibility, led to many personal duels in midfield, which suited the Greek players. The choice of these players, combined with Rehhagel's philosophy of not risking losing possession near Nikopolidis' area, led to an attacking plan based on long passes and the ability of the three players to claim second balls. Using Karagounis and especially Tsiartas centrally only took place when the occasion required the players to be more creative.

'To the left of midfield, Rehhagel used creative players such as Karagounis, Giannakopoulos and sometimes Tsiartas, who often converged towards the centre, giving Fyssas or Venetides the opportunity to move up. On the right, Charisteas played the role of an attacking midfielder. He, along with Vryzas, were the main targets for long-distance passes and any possible crosses into the opponent's area. The fact that Charisteas converged towards the area created room for Seitaridis, who was the most offensive of the full-backs and had an amazing tournament, both defensively and offensively. This was also proved by the fact that he was included in the Euro 2004 team of the tournament, along with Dellas and Zagorakis.

'In conclusion, Rehhagel's player selection was accompanied by the construction of a sensible and realistic game plan. The German coach was able to convince his footballers of his efficiency, to which end contributed the draw at Old Trafford. But the key point was the big away victory against Spain in qualification. Through successive wins in the next matches, Greece shaped the character that eventually led to winning the trophy and two more qualifications, the 2008 European Championship finals and the 2010 World Cup. This character was also preserved under Santos the next coach, as the Portuguese manager relied precisely on Rehhagel's logic and realism.'

ABOUT THE AUTHOR

Vasilis Sambrakos is an Athens-based journalist and analyst who covers international football. He has been one of the leading writers and broadcasters on Greek and international football for many years, with close  first-hand access to all the key individuals in the game. In addition to broadcasting, Vasilis is a publishing consultant at gazzetta.gr. (a leading sports portal in Greece) and has written numerous books.